D1046151

This book is dedicated to John, my husband of 24 years and to the churches and individuals who have supported me so faithfully for over 50 years.

# Who Am I

by Madonna Burget Spratt with Eleanor Daniel

Copyright © 2012 by Madonna Burget Spratt with Eleanor
Daniel

*Who Am I*
by Madonna Burget Spratt with Eleanor Daniel

Printed in the United States of America

ISBN 9781622300693

All rights reserved solely by the author. The author guarantees all contents are original and do not infringe upon the legal rights of any other person or work. No part of this book may be reproduced in any form without the permission of the author. The views expressed in this book are not necessarily those of the publisher.

Unless otherwise indicated, Bible quotations taken from the NEW AMERICAN STANDARD BIBLE®, Copyright © 1960, 1962, 1963, 1968, 1971, 1972, 1973, 1975, 1977, 1995 by The Lockman Foundation. Used by permission.

www.xulonpress.com

# WHO AM I?
## by
## Janice and Faye Rostvit

(1) God of power and might,
You who made the sun to shine so bright,
And who made the moon to rule the night
I look to Thee,
From the Mountain's height,
Seeing snow that glistens pure and white,
And an eagle taking off in flight,
I look to Thee.

Chorus:

Who am I?  Who am I?  Who am I?
Who am I that You should be mindful of me?

(2)  Such a lovely place,
Is this world that You have hung in space,
Oh, that everyone would see Your face,
Almighty God.
Can You find a trace,
Of Your love within the human race,
How we fail You, yet You still have grace.
Almighty God.

(3)  When Christ Jesus came,
He was never seeking worldly fame,
But in love He glorified Your name,
And all for me.
He was not to blame,
Yet they crucified Him just the same,
There He suffered agony and shame,
And all for me.

# Foreword

Many of my friends and supporters have insisted that I should write a memoir about my years as a missionary nurse. I have hesitated to do it—it isn't easy to write about oneself. I do it now because I pray it will encourage all who read it to understand that if God is allowed to have His way in your life; He can use you in wholly unexpected ways as He has used this farm girl from Indiana.

# Prologue

# Here I Am, Send Me

I was born December 15, 1933, to Dale and Mary Burget in Prairie Township, Tipton County, Indiana, the third and middle child. My brother Gerald and sister Marianna were 9½ and 8½ years older than I, and Don and Marilyn were younger. Since my older brother and sister were so much older than I, I didn't really know them that well.

We lived on a farm owned by my Papa Wheatley, though Daddy did the farming. Papa was a rural mail carrier. We lived in a small community. I had a good life growing up, never lacking anything, although we were not allowed things we didn't really need.

Since I was tall for my age, Mom convinced the school authorities to allow me to start school at Prairie Township School when I was five. I enjoyed school and was in a class where a lot of us made very good grades. I enjoyed sports and played softball and basketball.

My first memory of church was when I was in elementary school. Don, Marilyn and I went to Normanda Christian Church for Sunday school and worship with Papa Wheatley. We left home promptly at 9:15 A.M. to be there in time for Sunday school at 9:30 A.M. My favorite Sunday school teachers were Ikie McIntire and Wilma Jean Dawson, two people who really studied and knew the Bible. I will ever be grateful to them for how they taught me to love God's Word. Until I started high school, we had a part-time minister, Rev. Miller, who preached only every other Sunday.

I grew up in the midst of laughter and teasing. My dad was a big tease—I think it was passed on to me. I remember one of those incidents clearly. Daddy had a younger brother, Oral, who was very excitable. Men in the community loved to play jokes on each other. One evening two men called Daddy, telling him that they were bringing Uncle Oral over to pretend to steal our chickens. They said Daddy should be ready for him. Daddy got a gun and we kids gathered up rocks and went to a shed with a tin roof where we hid. When the chickens starting squawking, Daddy started shooting in the air and we threw rocks on the tin roof. Thinking he would be shot, poor Uncle Oral ran to a nearby ditch and laid flat.

*Madonna at two years of age*

In July 1947, I attended a Christian service camp for the first time. It was the first year for the new Hanging Rock Christian Assembly near West Lebanon, Indiana. I understood about salvation and had been encouraged to give my life to Christ, but it wasn't until that week at camp that I knew I couldn't resist any longer. I gave my life to Christ and was baptized in the river at the camp. When I returned home, Normanda Christian Church had a new minister—the first full-time minister in the history of the church. Roger and Peggy Westmoreland had a big influence on my life and helped me to grow in Christ.

Peggy was my Sunday school teacher. She was an excellent teacher. Roger and Peggy started a youth group that began to grow, and Roger really encouraged me to "stand tall," not only in the faith, but also physically. I was the tallest in my freshman class in high school and tended to slump. Roger cured me of that by thumping me between

10

the shoulder blades when he saw me slump and by telling me to be proud of the height God had given me.

I really looked forward to going to Hanging Rock during the summer of 1948, not realizing that this week would change my life and give me direction for how I could serve the Lord.  Laverne Morse, who was only nineteen years old, and Matthew Ikeda, a Japanese preacher, influenced me to make the decision to be a missionary.  I was so impressed at the dedication of Laverne and his family to share Christ in spite of adversity.  His father, J. Russell Morse, had been in prison for the cause of Christ.  The preaching of Matthew Ikeda touched my heart, and the last night of camp I dedicated my life to full-time Christian service.  It was then that I knew that God was calling me to be a missionary nurse. With encouragement from Roger and Peggy and people like Ikie McIntire and Wilma Jean Dawson at Normanda and spending three more weeks of camp at Hanging Rock, I never turned back from that decision.  As I thought of being a missionary, I could see that being a nurse would give me an opportunity to serve in a healing ministry.

I worked hard in high school. By my senior year, I needed only biology plus 1/10 of a credit to graduate.  So during my senior year, I worked in the cafeteria as well as in the principal's office.

I enjoyed acting and was in the senior play when I was a junior, but chose not to be in the play my senior year.  A classmate and I did a skit between acts of the play.  I was to start singing a song and he was to interrupt me by coming from the back of the room yelling, "Peanuts for sale." But he waited until I had nearly finished the song, smiling at me and deliberately waiting.  It is perhaps ironic that he and I received the American Legion Award when we graduated!

I graduated from Prairie High School in May 1951 and started nurses' training at Ball Memorial Hospital School of Nursing in September of that year. I will ever be grateful for the University Christian Church and people like Eno and Beryl Nation and Lance Van Tassell for their encouragement and teaching during the three years I lived in Muncie. Lance was my Sunday school teacher, and any Sunday that I was free to go to church, the Nations treated me to Sunday dinner. I was active in the youth group at the church as well.

In my class at Ball Memorial, few girls were strong Christians. Even though I was still young in my Christian faith, I was able to be an example for Him. No one was more surprised than I when I was elected president of our class for our second year.

Betty Lee Isenburg and I loved to play practical jokes on our classmates. It came to the point that whether we played the jokes or not, we were accused. Every year an alumni dance was held at the country club. Betty Lee and I didn't go the first two years. We knew that most of the girls would come home having drunk alcoholic beverages. Knowing that they would head quickly to the bathroom, we locked the doors of the toilets—we crawled out underneath the doors after we locked them. The girls got back to the dorm and raced to the toilets, but couldn't get in. It didn't take them long to figure out that Betty Lee and I had done it!

Each summer when I had my vacation from nurses' training, I went to Hanging Rock as a dorm mother or nurse. One summer there was a group there from Atlanta Christian College, and they nearly persuaded me to attend college there. But the influence for Johnson Bible College by Roger and Peggy had been greater, so with their encouragement I made the decision to attend JBC. I went to J.B.C. for their graduation services in May 1955, and that visit further influenced my decision. Roger and Peggy left Normanda after

12

my senior year of high school, but Lanis Kineman, also a
Johnson Bible College graduate, followed Roger as minister.

I worked at the Tipton Hospital between completion of
nurses' training and enrollment in Bible college. I was unable to attend church much at my home church because I
was often on call for surgery. I roomed with my cousins,
Fern and Gordy Wheatley, and attended church most Sundays at West Street Christian Church in Tipton.

Finally, I arrived at Johnson. I will never forget my first
interview with Dean Floyd Clark
at Johnson Bible College. All of
us were awed by this tall stern
man. When I went into his office, he said to me, "Young lady,
you have already been to college,
so we will expect above average grades from you." I wanted
to say, "But, didn't you see my
transcript? I didn't always make

JBC, 1956

above average grades in nursing school." But I didn't dare
say a word, and I surprised myself by making above average
grades all four years at Johnson. As I sat in his office that
day, little did I dream that thirty-one years later he would be
the cupid to bring John and me together.

Because I was a registered nurse, I became the school
nurse and continued in that position for my entire four years.
During the first two years, I lived on the second floor of the
dormitory. I lost count of how many times a day I ran up
and down the stairs from my room to the nurse's room on
the first floor. I was overweight when I started college, but
running up and down the stairs helped me to lose weight in
a hurry.

My four years at J.B.C. were a blessing in every way. Not only did I learn more of the Bible and how to study it, I learned the importance of faith, prayer and work. I also learned that those who go to Bible college are far from perfect. That lesson in itself proved to be helpful in adjusting to life on the mission field.

As I look back on those days, I can see how God was preparing me to be a missionary. During my first year in college, I was involved with the Africa for Christ mission group. I was also active in the jail and mountain mission groups. The work with jail missions gave me experience in personal witnessing and the work with mountain missions gave me experience in house-to-house calling. And I taught children at the Vine Street Christian Church, an African-American congregation in Knoxville.

It was through the Africa for Christ mission group and correspondence with Max Ward Randall that I learned I would be better prepared for the mission field if I had midwifery training. That was excellent advice: my second week at Mashoko there was a maternity emergency when Dr. Pruett was away that I could not have handled if I had not been trained as a midwife.

The summer after my freshman year was my last to go

*Vine Street Christian Church, Knoxville, TN, 1957*

to Hanging Rock for awhile. For five weeks of the summer of 1956, I was camp nurse and stayed on for a sixth week to be Dean of Women for a high school week. Also during that summer, I worked at Tipton County Memorial

Hospital and, for two weeks, in a doctor's office to relieve my older sister, who was on vacation.

Al "Sonny" Hamilton, who had graduated from J.B.C. in 1956, went to Phoenix, Arizona, to begin a church among African-Americans in the south of the city.  Sonny had been a part of the Africa for Christ mission group, later to become Ambassadors for Christ to accommodate those interested in going to other countries.   Al asked for some of us to go to Phoenix for the summer of 1957.  He also mentioned the need for a bus to pick up children to take to Sunday school. Larry Johnson, a freshman at J.B.C., told us of an old bus his dad had and was willing to fix it up for us.  The bus was painted blue, and my sister painted Ambassadors for Christ on the side.

So in the summer of 1957, Larry, Annette Coppess, and I drove from Indiana to Phoenix in the bus.   We drove to Iowa and picked up Dwight Abbott.  To save on lodging costs the seats were stacked so we could put a mattress in the back where Larry and Dwight could sleep at night and Annette and I in the daytime.  We also took furniture for Gene and Mary Helen Sandefur who were to join us later.

What a fun trip that was!  I still remember the astonished look on the face of a service station attendant as I pulled in to get gas.  It was 4:00 A.M., and he saw only Annette and me since and Larry and Dwight were sleeping.  In 1957, it wasn't the usual thing to see two young women driving a school bus.  We arrived safely in Phoenix, and what a blessing the bus proved to be.

Annette and I shared an apartment with a friend of mine whom I had known growing up.  Both Annette and I worked at night at Good Samaritan Hospital and slept all morning and part of the afternoon, after which we went calling with the others.  We had a big Sunday school that was held in a school building.  Thanks to the help of the area ministers, we were able to take some of the children to a week of camp at Camp Christian in Prescott, Arizona.

Annette and I shared our income with the Sandefurs so they could work full time in the ministry.  So I went back to J.B.C. with no money to pay for my junior year of school. I got a job for two evenings a week at Baptist Hospital in Knoxville in order to pay my tuition.  However, when I went to the office to pay my bill, I was informed that it had been paid by someone who wished to remain anonymous.  I was overwhelmed with thanks, one of the many times when God has provided for my needs, reminding me of the promise that He knows our needs before we ask Him.

Later, quite by accident, I found out that my co-workers, Al and Annette Hamilton and Gene and Mary Helen Sandefur, had paid the tuition.  (Annette had stayed in Phoenix to marry Al.)  Later Al and Annette went to South Africa as missionaries, and I was with Annette when their first son was born in Kimberly.  Unfortunately, he died as an infant with cystic fibrosis.  Gene and Mary Helen were my second forwarding agents, serving in that capacity for about twenty years.

In the summer of 1958, I again returned to help in the work in Phoenix. This time I rode with Jim and Helen Curtiss who served with us that summer.  We had two weeks of Christian service camp that summer—one at Camp Christian and one at First Church of Christ Camp in Mayer, Arizona. I will never forget the narrow, curved road to that beautiful camp site in Mayer.  I drove Jim's car and he drove the school bus—no easy job.  I'll also never forget the cold icy showers at the camp!

During my junior year, I first heard about the hospital that was to be built at Mashoko Mission in what was then Southern Rhodesia (now Zimbabwe) in Africa.  When I first made

16

the decision to serve the Lord as a missionary nurse, I had thought of India as a place of service. But now, after corresponding with Max Ward Randall, I sensed that God was calling me to Africa. I felt that with a new hospital being built in Rhodesia, I could best use my talents as a nurse and midwife there.

It was both a happy and sad day when I graduated from J.B.C. in May 1959. I was happy because I was nearer my goal of being a missionary nurse, but sad as I said goodbye to so many dear, close friends.

During my senior year, I began inquiring about where I could study midwifery. I found only two programs at that time. One was at a Catholic school in New Mexico, and the other was a joint program in New York City and Johns Hopkins in Baltimore—four months in each place. I applied to the New York-Baltimore program, but as I was waiting to be accepted, God used dear friends to point me to a third school which would prepare me even better for the mission field.

Dick and Sarah Robison had learned from a friend of the Frontier School of Midwifery in Hyden, Kentucky. I wrote for information and made application, but learned that it would be May 1960 before I could start. My home congregation had already pledged monthly support for me and was prepared to pay for my midwifery training. I asked for their advice, and they told me to make the decision. After much prayer, I felt that the experience I would get at Hyden would better prepare me for the mission field. In the meantime, I had been accepted at the other school, but withdrew my application.

Leaders at the school at Hyden suggested that I arrive early to work in the hospital. I decided I would receive some good experience, which I did. I began work in September

1959.  I learned to take x-rays; to do hemoglobin's, a blood exam for anemia; and to type and cross match blood for transfusions.  I also became acquainted with roundworms at Hyden—a new experience.

Hygiene in many of the homes in the hills of Kentucky left much to be desired.  Children with thin limbs and big bellies were admitted to the hospital.  I'll always remember the medicine Multifuge that we gave. The result would be twenty to fifty squiggly white worms when the children went to the bathroom.

I will never forget being on duty one evening when one of the other nurses went to change a dirty diaper.  All of a sudden, I heard her scream, "Madonna, please come."  She sounded frightened.  I went to the ward and burst out laughing, much to her dismay.  It was her first experience changing a dirty diaper full of worms.  By that time I was used to it.  That prepared me for my ministry in Honduras years later when one lady passed 152 worms after having been treated for roundworms.  Patients always counted the worms.  Ugh!!

Several of the nurses celebrated Thanksgiving at the home of Mary Breckinridge, the founder of the Frontier Nursing Service.  Just before Thanksgiving, we had heard that there had been a cancellation for the midwifery class starting in December 1959. Both another nurse and I very much wanted that vacancy, but rather than ask for it, we decided to pray and see how the Lord worked.  On Thanksgiving Day, I was informed that the place was mine.  I was very happy, for that meant I could be on the mission field in 1960.

I am deeply grateful for the training at Frontier.  Our teacher, Dr. Beasley, had been on the mission field.  He taught us many things: we were allowed to do episiotomies and tubal ligations; suture abdominal incisions; do complicated deliveries such as twins and breech deliveries; and do manual removal of placentas. We also did home deliveries, sometimes even going by horseback, carrying our equipment in saddlebags.

The contrasts were significant among the people who lived in that area of southeastern Kentucky. Many lived up creek beds. One house would be spotless while next door the house would be filthy dirty. One day on a post-partum home visit, I finished my exam of the patient. As I waited for my instructor to come from a visit further up in the mountains, I swept out the house. The dust flew. It didn't look like the house had been swept for days.

The Bible studies we seven midwifery students had each week were a real blessing. One motto in the Christian Church has been, "Christians only, but not the only Christians." I found this to be so true. All seven of us had either already been on the mission field or planned to be. My fellow students were Mae Mast from the Christian Reformed Church who had served in Nigeria; Loraine Lundeen of the Evangelical Free Church who had been in the Belgian Congo; Ruth May who had served with the Grenfell Mission in Labrador; Nancy Tappan of the Baptist Church who planned to go to Colombia in South America; Hilda Hansen of the Church of God who planned to serve in Mexico; and Leona Carlson who planned to work in Portuguese East Africa with the Free Methodist Church. I learned much from Mae and Lorraine and continue to be in contact with Lorraine, Mae, Nancy and Leona.

*At Frontier Nursing School in 1960*

19

Mae and Lorraine continued to serve in the Congo and Nigeria for some time and are now retired. Leona never made it to Portuguese East Africa because she suffered a back injury while she was in language school in Portugal and the mission board felt it best she not go. She taught nursing at Roberts Weslyan College in North Chili, New York. She married Robert Hayes, and together they served for a short time in Lusaka, Zambia, where Bob worked on developing a high protein food for malnourished children. Nancy served for many years in Villavicencio, Colombia, where she had an orphanage, and her Colombian co-workers still run a school. Hilda served for a time on the Mexican border, and Ruth returned to her work for the Grenfield mission.

I completed my midwifery training in May 1960, and visited a few churches before leaving for Southern Rhodesia in August. Between visits to churches my sister helped me to pack a drum that would be taken to Kentucky to Lester and Carmie Cooper to be shipped with their belongings. They planned to go to Southern Rhodesia by ship in September.

The time for my departure to Southern Rhodesia came closer, but my permanent resident papers had not yet arrived. I called the Consulate of Southern Rhodesia in Washington to learn that the papers had been sent to Hyden, Kentucky. During the time at Hyden, most of us had attended the small Baptist Church, where for a time, I had taught a Sunday school class. One of the members of the church was the postmaster. I called him to see if the papers were still there. He remembered having seen them, but he thought they had been sent back to Washington. He said he would check and if they were still there, he would send them to me in Indiana. If he didn't call back, that meant that I would receive the papers. He didn't call. The papers came on the Friday before I was to leave on Monday!

I was now ready to be a missionary nurse!

# Chapter 1

## Missionary Life Begins

## A Trip to a New Land

On Monday morning, August 1, 1960, my dad, mom, and Marilyn traveled to the airport in Indianapolis where I would begin my journey to Southern Rhodesia. Daddy had not expected the traffic to be so heavy in Indianapolis, so we arrived at the airport barely in time for me to get my flight to New York City. I said a quick goodbye to Mom and Daddy. Then Marilyn and I ran to the gate. I was the last passenger on, and the doors were closed as soon as I arrived.

In New York, I changed planes for London. I had a day in London, so I did some sightseeing before I boarded the plane bound for Salisbury, Southern Rhodesia. Not knowing Southern Rhodesia well, I had mistakenly thought that Bulawayo was closer to Mashoko than Salisbury was, so I had made reservations there. But because of some conflict in the Bulawayo area, I had been advised by Dr. Dennis Pruett to get off the plane in Salisbury.

The plane landed in Salisbury at 2:00 P.M. I quickly went through immigration and customs, but when I exited, I didn't see anyone who seemed to be looking for me. Soon the airport emptied and I was left alone. I had a telephone number in Fort Victoria and phoned there, but there was no answer. So I waited and prayed and hoped that someone would eventually come.

About 4:00 P.M., people started coming into the airport again. Soon I recognized Dr. Pruett and Pauline Bell, a nurse at the Mashoko Hospital, looking at the board that displayed arrival times.  I walked over, tapped Dr. Pruett on the back, and said, "Are you looking for someone?"  They had expected me to arrive around 5:00 P.M. and were dismayed to know that I had been waiting about two-and-a-half hours.  I had never met either Dr. Pruett or Pauline before, but I had seen their pictures and was very happy to see them.

We spent that first night, August 3, in Salisbury (now Harare) and the next night in Fort Victoria (now Masvingo), where there was a house for Lucy Pruett and her sons to stay when the boys were studying there.  On August 5, we arrived at Mashoko.  At last I would start my life as a missionary nurse.

## Settling In At Mashoko

When I arrived at Mashoko, I shared a home with Betty Iddings and Pauline Bell, both nurses.  Betty was from Ohio and Pauline from Capetown, South Africa.  Also living at the mission was Dr. Dennis Pruett, his wife, Lucy, and their four children, and Berry Kennedy and his wife, Amy, and their five children.  John and Marjorie Pemberton and their family were on furlough when I arrived.

We had no electricity or running water, so I had to learn how to manage a kerosene refrigerator and lamps called Tilly lamps.  We had a zinc tub to serve as a bathtub, and we carried water for bathing.  Pauline and Betty were both very short.  But I found out quickly that the tub that was big enough for them would not hold me and the water for a bath.  So I had to buy a bigger tub.  We had an outdoor toilet.  My bedroom was at the back of the house nearest the three-seater outdoor toilet.

One day I heard someone running from the toilet to my room. Betty came in out of breath. She had gone out to the bathroom and discovered bats inside the toilet. She moved out of there in a hurry! I don't remember what we did to get rid of the bats.

When I arrived, the big 130-bed hospital was under construction, so our medical work was done at the old government Matsai Clinic about two miles from the mission. This clinic had six large thatched roof buildings and a smaller one for an exam room. One large building was a delivery room and post-partum ward; one was a pediatric ward; another was a ward for female patients. Yet another was a ward for male patients; one was the treatment room; another was a supply room. There were also thirty to forty smaller huts where the patients lived while they were receiving their treatment. It was not safe to send medicine home with them, so from one to four times a day they would go to the treatment hut to get their medicine.

Nearer the mission was another building used for surgery and post-surgery wards. There was a generator there so we could have lights when we operated.

We put in long days—starting work at 7:00-7:30 A.M. and working until noon when we went home for lunch. Then we went back to work until we finished seeing patients. Sometimes it was dark when we examined urine specimens by the light of the Tilley lamps to see which patients had bilharzia, a parasitic disease that caused them to have blood in their urine. We would get home between 6:00 and 7:00 P.M. and then often had to sterilize things for surgery in the pressure cooker type sterilizers. Some days we did surgery, but not many in the beginning because the people were afraid of surgery.

On Sunday, we worshiped in one of the classrooms of the primary school with one of the missionaries preaching. There was also a Bible college with just a few students. One year I taught church history to only one student and later taught Greek to one student.

Soon after I arrived, Lester and Carmie Cooper and their two children, Edward and Patsy, arrived for Lester to begin his ministry as the principal of the teacher training school where Carmie also taught. At first she stayed in Fort Victoria with the children, but later the children had their own school at Mashoko.

The Kennedy family built a home soon after I arrived. They had been living in the Pemberton's home, but the Pembertons were due back from their furlough.

We missionaries had wonderful fellowship. We had a potluck dinner on Sunday and played games and sang a lot. Every time there was a birthday we had a party—always trying to make it a surprise, which wasn't always easy, but it was fun to try.

I enjoyed visiting the village churches. Most of the time those who went drove, but I also enjoyed walking. One day I was walking back to the mission when a small child saw me and ran off, crying. I guess he had never seen anyone with a white face and I really frightened him.

## Real Medical Work

One of my early unforgettable experiences occurred soon after I arrived. Dr. Pruett had gone to Salisbury to work on the movie, *The Mashoko Story*. I don't remember where Pauline was, but only Betty and I were at the clinic. A lady was in labor in the delivery room. I had checked her and had gone back to the exam room to see patients. It was soon after that when Betty came running to tell me that the woman had delivered the baby and was hemorrhaging and the placenta would not come out. This was the first of many times that I was thankful I had been advised to study to be a midwife. I had to remove the placenta with my hand, a procedure we had not been taught in nurses' training. I could still remember the lecture from Dr. Beasley on the manual removal of a placenta. He taught, "Once you get your hand on the placenta, don't pull on it, but work it loose with the tips of your fingers. And don't take your hand out until you have the placenta in your hand." I followed these instructions, and what a wonderful feeling to have the placenta in my hand and to feel the uterus start to contract. Immediately, the bleeding slowed down.

I also learned how strong the Black Rhodesian village women were. The next morning, in spite of losing a lot of blood, this new mother went to the river to

wash clothes. In the States, a woman would have been given anesthesia for this procedure, but I did it without giving her anything for pain.

It was an interesting experience to do the hut rounds with Dr. Pruett. Each day we visited the patients in the huts who were too sick to go to the treatment room. It wasn't uncommon to see rats roasting over the open fire or to see ants cooking in a pot. I still remember one day when Dr. Pruett and I saw a pot of ants all cooked and ready to eat.

Dr. Pruett said: "I'll eat some if you will"

I replied, "I'll eat some if you will."

We neither one were game to try one, but the children of the missionaries ate them and loved the taste.

Betty Iddings was the head nurse at the hospital. When I arrived, I assumed that she would be there for a long time. It was a shock to learn that she was ill and would be leaving, not to return for some time. When she left, Dr. Pruett informed me that I was to be the matron, or director of nurses, when the new hospital opened. Not only that, but I would be responsible for starting the nursing school. This was once again when I was aware of God's timing. I knew without a doubt that He had a hand in my having been chosen to fill the vacancy of the midwifery class. He knew I was needed at Mashoko before December 1960. I had to ask His help to give me the strength and wisdom for this big responsibility.

The first year at Mashoko passed quickly. The daily routine was busy enough, but soon we also had to order beds, equipment, linens and other materials for the new hospital which was scheduled to open in September 1961. At noon every day we looked at the progress of the construction when we went home for our noon meal. Dr. Pruett insisted that we wear the white pith helmets to protect us from the sun. (These were white hard hats like hunters might wear.)

Dr. Pruett was the only doctor at the mission. He taught the nurses how to examine patients and take care of emergencies so we could take turns being on call at night, permitting him to get more sleep. His teaching has helped me through the years when I have had to "play doctor" in India and Honduras.

Each week we had to take chloraquine and daraprim tablets to prevent us from getting malaria. We also slept under mosquito nets. It was hot sleeping under these nets. When I found out that Dr. Pruett wasn't using them, I also quit.

The time when Dr. Pruett had malaria is etched in my memory. He had the falciperam type that could go into cerebral malaria. He had a high fever and kept talking about seeing snow outside. Snow in hot Africa! We sent for a doctor who worked in a government hospital some distance away to come to see him. Fortunately, with the treatment he was soon better, but for a couple of days, we did a lot of praying for him to get well quickly.

## Day-By-Day Away From Work

Dr. and Mrs. Pruett, Denny and Lucy, as we knew them, made frequent trips to Salisbury to work on two movies *The Mashoko Story* and *A Hospital Is Born*. Besides my nursing duties, I was also the official babysitter for the Pruett children David, Darel, Danny, and Denise. Sometimes Denny and Lucy took Denise with them since she was not yet in school, but if given the choice to go or stay, she would often choose to stay with Aunt Madonna. I was also the babysitter for the Kennedy children, but not as often. One time Berry and Amy took a week of vacation and I stayed with their children. Their youngest, Joy, was only about two years old at the time, and when they came back, she cried as I left.

At our weekly Sunday dinners we talked about things we had done before arriving at Mashoko. Lester and Carmie Cooper were from Kentucky. One day I told them about some of my experiences in Kentucky when I was doing my midwifery training. After a while, Lester, who had a dry wit, said, "Shut up; you are making me homesick." We all burst out laughing.

In 1961, more missionaries arrived to work at the hospital. Sylvia Menhinick came from Capetown, South Africa, to be the hospital secretary; Mary Bliffen, an R.N. and a graduate

27

of Kentucky Christian College, came to work with Pauline and me; and Gladys Jongeling came from Oregon to be the medical technologist. The little house for single missionaries became so crowded that for a time before the hospital opened, Mary Bliffen and I used the labor room for our bedroom. Soon the Kennedys moved to Bulawayo to serve there and we single women moved to their home where there were four bedrooms.

One day I will never forget was the day the wiring was finished in the hospital and in our homes. One evening the big generator was started and the lights of the hospital and our homes were turned on. We drove a distance from the mission and then turned around and went back toward the mission where we could see the lights from the hill. Yea! No more Tilly lamps!

# Chapter 2

# The New Hospital Opens

## A Grand Occasion

Tensions were high as everyone rushed around in August 1961 to get the hospital ready for the dedication. We had a big drug room and a linen room. I remember that Denny and I got into a big argument about where to put the extra sheets. He maintained that they should be put in the drug room and I said they belonged in the linen room. Lucy finally had to settle us down. Even missionaries are human!

The dedication of the first Christian churches/churches of Christ hospital on a mission field occurred at Mashoko on August 27, 1961. The day was beautiful. Four thousand Black Rhodesians were present plus those from neighboring missions and friends from Fort Victoria who had helped with the construction of the hospital. Immediately before the dedication, we had hosted a church conference, so missionaries from Dadaya, Bulawayo and the Zambezi Valley were at the dedication. Many of the Black people had never seen such a modern looking building.

Dedication day occurred during my weekend on duty, so I had to check on the clinic patients. I also supervised getting the hospital clean and ready for the dedication services and for the open house to be held afterwards.

Chief Chamburikira, who was recovering from a stroke, was transported from the clinic to be the first patient admitted to the hospital. We thought it fitting that he be the first patient admitted. I used the Pemberton's station wagon to

*Medicine for a woman, Zambezi Valley, Southern Rhodesia*

take the Chief from the clinic to the hospital, and he was admitted after Dr. Garfield Todd cut the ribbon to officially open the doors. (Dr. Todd had been at one time a missionary with the New Zealand Churches of Christ and also for a time the Prime Minister of Southern Rhodesia.)  Much to our embarrassment, the Chief needed a bedpan soon after his admission, but we had failed to get one to the hospital.  Someone had to run to the clinic to get one for him.  Oh well, you can't do everything perfectly!

On September 1, we moved all of the patients from the Matsai Clinic to the new hospital.  It was wonderful to have everything in one building at last.  The new hospital also brought some changes in the cost to the patients.  They had to pay more than they had at the Matsai Clinic—it took some explaining from Dr. Pruett, but they agreed.

The big hospital was divided into wards on one side. These were the pediatric, women's medical and surgical, and labor and delivery and post- partum wards.  In the center of the hospital was the outpatient department which consisted of the exam and treatment rooms at the back.  The laundry room and sterilizing room were on one side toward the front with the kitchen on the other side.  Further on were the major and minor surgeries, the laboratory and linen room while toward the front were the drug room and three offices.  On the other side were the male and tuberculosis wards.  Mary Bliffen was in charge of the male and tuberculosis wards, and Pauline Bell was in charge of the female, pediatric and maternity wards.  I was the matron, or nursing superintendent, and in charge of surgery and outpatient departments. All three nurses helped see patients in the outpatient department, and Mary Bliffen also gave anesthesia to the patients during surgery.

# Starting the Nursing School

My major responsibility was to open the nursing school. We had many applicants for the school, but could take only a limited number. We interviewed the applicants who seemed most promising. Though the school had a three-year curriculum, it wasn't until 1962 that the government gave formal approval for the program. This meant that the first class had to stay for four years. As a result, in the final year, we were down to six students. Most had dropped out because of failing grades or, in the case of some of the girls, because they were pregnant.

Pre-marital pregnancy was a major problem in African culture. Most couples had intercourse before marriage to make sure the girls could get pregnant. Even though we tried to keep males and females separated, they found ways to sneak out of the dorms.

It was a challenge to teach nursing in English when most of the students had studied English for only six years in primary school. As a result, I read some really strange answers on some of the test papers. Here are some of them:

*Teaching nursing students to give injections*

1. You must wash and iron the patients.
2. An enema is given to empty the bowl.
3. A hot water bottle is used for cold-blooded patients.
4. A hot water bottle is used for premitive kids.
5. Be sure to remove all crumps and crisis from the bed.
6. The containers (of milk) must have tight lids and kept closed every now and then.

7. Bottles should be labeled and cocked.
8. If the patients cannot swallow the tablets, crash for him.
9. When pouring the medicine be careful to soil the label.
10. Plaster of Paris is used to collect deformity.
11. Sand bags are used to give support to a limp.
12. I tell the patient to lie on his right side and fold his left leg.
13. I call the tray to the bedside.
14. I tell the patient to open his mouth and rise his tongue.
15. To make the night comfortable for the patient listen to what he tells you.
16. I must work on him graciously throughout the night to avoid some discom-
fortabilities.

The government program for training rural nurses was a three-year curriculum. Graduates were called medical assistants when they were finished. They had to take an exam at the end of the first year and again at the end of the third year. The exam was both written and practical. I worked hard on the lessons and spent hours with the students teaching them to set up trays for catherization, change dressings, remove sutures, etc. I was more nervous than the students when they took their first-year exam. The night before the exam, I had them over to the nurses' home for tea and pie. The students from other mission hospitals couldn't believe they had been in our home. Many of the missionary groups had no social interaction with the Africans.

Our graduation rate from our first class was not good. Only one man and one woman passed the final test. Two men failed it, and two of the women were pregnant and had to leave before the exam. I learned a lot teaching this group, and the graduation rate improved. But I was happy to turn the nursing school over to Donna Kreegar when she arrived in 1965!

# Chapter 3

# Baby Bundles
# and
# Maternity Experiences

When we first moved into the hospital, women did not come to give birth to their babies. They had felt comfortable in the clinic, but they did not like going to the hospital. When I had been at the Frontier Nursing Service in Kentucky, we had given the women a large bundle of baby clothing if they would pay their bill before delivery. I thought that if we gave the women a small bundle of baby clothes, perhaps they would come to the hospital to have their babies. I mentioned this in my newsletter, and women from many congregations took this on as a project. A bundle contained three diapers, a blanket, a little shirt, gown or pajamas, bib, booties or hat. It wasn't much, but it did bring the women to the hospital.

Many of the women came from some distance and stayed in the ward before the birth of their babies. Finally we had to build a place where they could stay until time for them to give birth.

*One of the many babies delivered by Madonna*

I really enjoyed delivering babies. Now I wish I had kept a record of how many I delivered, especially how many twins.

After one successful Caesarean Section, we did many more. I assisted Dr. Pruett in the surgeries and really enjoyed that. He often allowed me to close the wound. He taught me so much that in my later years, I could "play doctor" based on what he had taught me.

I had two different horses at Mashoko. Sometimes I would ride down to the hospital on the horse and tease those whom we called "the ladies in waiting," telling them that if they rode my horse, they would have their babies sooner. This always brought a lot of laughs. I rode my horse near the tuberculosis ward and gave the children rides which they enjoyed.

One of my most unusual deliveries came in 1962 when the Pruetts were on furlough. Dr. Richard Lee from Carbondale, Illinois, had come to serve while the Pruetts were away. One Saturday morning I was called over to the delivery room and delivered a tiny little boy who was breech to a lady whom we discovered had twins. The baby weighed only 2 lbs. 10 oz. We didn't have an incubator, so he lived only a few hours. Then the lady stopped having labor pains. We didn't know what to do, but after Dr. Lee and I read some of the textbooks, we decided to tie off the cord with a suture, put the lady on medicine for infection and wait to see what would happen. We kept a close watch on the fetal heart rate, and finally on Thursday evening, I was called to the hospital because the lady was once again in labor. I arrived just in time to deliver a little girl weighing 3 lbs. 3 oz. I named her Chitkatyambudzi which means "Surprise." She lived, and when I returned to Mashoko in 1981, her mother brought her to the hospital for me to see. Not many midwives get to deliver twins five-and-a-half days apart!

When Dr. Lee came into the delivery room right after the delivery, I was putting some pressure on the woman's abdomen to help get the placenta out. She pushed my

*A common sight in Southern Rhodesia*

hand away, sat up, stuck her finger down her throat, gagged and out popped the placenta. Dick and I laughed and laughed. She had taught us a new way to remove the placenta!

In August 1962, Ziden and Helen Nutt and their daughter, Karolyn, came to Mashoko from Chidamoyo Mission for Dr. Pruett to be able to deliver Helen's baby which was due in September. August 16 was a day to remember. Helen and Ziden were living in a camper near the nurses' home. Ziden had gone to Salisbury for a meeting, and Denny and Lucy had also gone there to work on one of the movies about the hospital. Helen came to our house to tell us that her membranes had ruptured and she had started having labor pain. But the pains weren't coming too close together. We hurried to the hospital to the radio telephone to call Dr. Pruett to ask him to return. Even though it was some distance, we thought he had time to get there since her labor pains were so far apart. But soon after we called, Helen told us that the pains were coming closer together. We took her to the hospital, and it wasn't long until I delivered a healthy baby boy who weighed just over five pounds.

When Dr. Pruett got to Enkledorn, he called us again. We told him that Helen had a small, but healthy boy and that he could return to Salisbury. The Pruetts decided to have breakfast before returning, so when Ziden came through on his way to Mashoko, he saw them casually eating breakfast. He wondered why they weren't hurrying to help his wife. Denny congratulated him on the birth of his son—and Ziden made record time getting to Mashoko to see the baby!

To this day, the Nutts and I have formed a close bond as a result of that delivery.

In 1961, Berry and Amy Kennedy were expecting their sixth baby. They had three sons and two daughters. Berry was sure that Number 6 would be a girl to even things out. Dr. Pruett delivered the baby, and I assisted him. Amy and I kept telling him that it would be a boy. Finally he said, "Burget, if it is a boy, it is yours." Dr. Pruett did deliver a boy, and Jeff was told for years that he really belonged to his Aunt Madonna because his dad had given him to me before he was born. Jeff later attended and graduated from Johnson Bible College, though his father had graduated from Kentucky Christian College. Berry told me that I had corrupted his son since he went to Johnson. My reply was, "It is only right that my son should go to my Bible college." When I finally married, Jeff's wife Karen sang at our wedding. Jeff told people at Johnson that he was happy that I was finally getting married so he could be legitimate!

# Chapter 4

# The Big Tumor
# and
# Other Interesting Cases

An unforgettable patient was a lady who had such a large stomach that she looked as if she were pregnant with a giant baby. But she wasn't pregnant; instead she had a huge tumor in her abdomen. An x-ray showed no evidence of cancer, so Dr. Pruett decided to operate to remove the tumor. Dr. Lee assisted, and I was the scrub nurse. When her abdomen was opened, we found a big adenoma on her intestines. It took some time to get it out, and I had to hold the tumor up. We later weighed it—nineteen pounds! It filled a big dishpan. It was real work to hold that big mass up as they cut. My arms were really tired by the time the tumor was removed.

Before this event, people were most reluctant to have surgery, but they came from miles away to see the big tumor and then to see the woman alive and well. After that, a lot of people came to have tumors removed. We eventually had to burn the giant tumor—after a few days, the smell was too much!

In 1962, Milliam, a little girl who was about seven years old, was attacked by a crocodile when she was bathing in a river. It was a miracle that she had been rescued, but the rescue was not before the crocodile had torn pieces of skin from her back and buttocks. When she arrived at the hospital, she was in terrible condition. Dr. Pruett cleaned the wounds and later had to do skin grafts so she could heal completely.

When I returned to Mashoko in 1981, one day I was doing the pre-natal clinic. It wasn't unusual for me to examine as many as a hundred pregnant women in a day. This Tuesday I examined a young lady who was nearly as tall as I was. After I finished, she said very quietly, "Sister Burget?" I said, yes, I was Sister Burget to which she replied: "I am Milliam." Of course, I had to look to see if the scars from the crocodile bite were still there. They were. She was expecting her first baby and soon after delivered a healthy baby.

One year when Dr. Pruett was away, Dr. Gloria Cobb was serving an internship at the hospital. One day a lady was brought in who had been bitten in the upper thigh by a hippopotamus. Let me tell you, she had a nasty gash! But we cleansed the wound, put in sutures, gave her antibiotics—and the wound healed.

The nurses usually saw the out-patients. Then if we had a major problem, we sent the person to Dr. Pruett or, later, to one of the other doctors. One day a man came in with abdominal pain. He had been drinking the night before, so I thought it was, at least in part, the result of too much homemade beer. But just in case, I sent him to the ward for Dr. Pruett to see. Dr. Pruett called me on the phone and asked if I had listened to the man's heart. I had not, and was Dr. Pruett disappointed. It turned out that all of the man's organs were opposite the normal position—his heart was on the right, his appendix on the left, his liver on the left, etc. Dr. Pruett was hoping he could tease me about not noticing his heart was on the right side. It turned out he had a bowel obstruction that required surgery, and Dr. Pruett removed a large portion of his gangrenous bowel.

One of the major problems was that of babies who came in after having been treated by the local witchdoctor. The witchdoctor would give them a medicine that must have

*Another tiny baby*

been like a narcotic. We called it "Intoxication with African Muti." Muti was the Shona word for medicine. The babies were doped and very dehydrated. We were able to save the lives of some of them by using fluids, but many came to us too late.

Poisonous snakes were common in Rhodesia. We received snakebite victims mostly because the local people put a tourniquet on the bite, but didn't release it for a short time. By the time they got to the hospital, the limb could be gangrenous and infected. One time Dr. Pruett told the family that he needed to amputate its little boy's leg, but the family refused. Instead he cleaned away all of the dead skin, treated the boy with antibiotics and later did some skin grafting, and the leg was saved. That was one time when Dr. Pruett was happy the family had refused the amputation.

One of the saddest cases was a little boy who had been bitten by a rabid dog. He came in too late to get the vaccine. It was pathetic to see how he wanted water, but could not swallow. It was a blessing when he died and the suffering ended.

Mukanga was one of the local witchdoctors. He often told people where they should go for treatment instead of treating them himself. One time his wife came to the hospital to have surgery. After the surgery, he came to visit her and he was drunk. I told him that he had to leave. I had no idea who he was. Little did I know that for a few days the hospital staff watched me to see if anything happened to me. They were certain he would cast a spell on me or cause me to be sick since I had chased him out of the hospital. Finally they told me of their concern. I assured them that he had no power over me since God protected me.  Later, many of his sons became Christians, some even becoming teachers in the mission schools.

We regularly saw pain and suffering compounded by ignorance.  It was a blessing to be able to shed the light of God's grace into a dark place.

# Chapter 5

# Life with Co-Workers

The missionaries who served at Mashoko had a close bond, the result of being out in the middle of nowhere. We enjoyed potluck meals and were really one big family. Some workers departed over the years to serve in other areas, but new co-workers became part of the family.

The Kennedys left in 1961 to go to Bulawayo to work, but the Pembertons returned from furlough. Then Dr. Jerry and Marietta Smith and their three children came to serve with us. Jerry was a dental surgeon, but after he and I did a couple of C-Sections, he later moved to Salisbury and studied medicine. Dr. Jon Durr with his wife Ginny and their daughter, Elizabeth, served for two years.

I was particularly happy to welcome Cyril and Mary Simkinns who came from Johnson Bible College to teach the ministers. He had been one of my professors at Johnson, and finally I had someone else from J.B.C.!

Don and Emma Stoll came for Don to work as the pharmacist. Jon Durr delivered their daughter, Jane, the only girl to be delivered to missionaries at the hospital. She joined her older brothers, Barry and Tim. Tom and Norma Thurman taught in the teacher training school. Later Lester and Marjorie Van Dyke came with their children, Larry, Steve, Jocelyn and Greg.

At one time seven of us lived in the nurses' home: nurses Sara Stere, Donna Kreegar, Mary Bliffen, and I; Gladys Jongeling, the medical technologist; Marilyn Steinmetz, a teacher; and Marcia Kay Thomson and Sylvia Menhinick, secretaries.  Later Sara Hewitt, another nurse, came, and Betty Iddings returned.

We had some funny experiences in our house.  One time a cobra got into our bathroom.  No one wanted to get near it, naturally, but one of the girls had a gun and thought she could shoot it. The only problem was that another of the girls was in the way.  We solved the problem by getting Bullet, the Pemberton's Alsatian dog, a good snake killer, and he took care of the cobra for us.

Early one morning the phone rang. I was on call and should have answered it, but my room was the farthest from the phone, so Sylvia, who was nearer, got up to answer.  She slipped on the floor and fell.  Everyone in the house woke up.  The call was from the hospital.  To this day I don't remember the problem.  Whatever it was, I was able to give instructions over the phone and didn't have to go to the hospital.

Since everyone was up, they were taking turns going to the bathroom.  My turn came after Mary Bliffen. I didn't have my glasses on, but it looked like Mary had had a bowel movement and had not flushed the toilet—but then I realized that what was there was moving.  There was a rat in the stool!  I really didn't want to sit down, so I went out and said, "Bliffen, you are sick."  That got everyone's attention and I told them to look in the toilet.  I said, "I think Bliffen is passing rats."  We finally succeeded in flushing it down the stool.

Dr. Dick Lee was ready to believe nearly anything after having removed a nineteen-pound tumor. I will never know how I talked to him without laughing, but the next day I called him into the drug room and said, "Dick, I am really worried about Mary Bliffen."  He asked me why, and I said, "Well, I know people pass different kinds of worms, but have you ever heard of anyone passing rats? Last night after Mary went to the bathroom there was a rat in the toilet."

Dick said, "What are we going to do?"

It was then that I started laughing and told him what had happened. But until I told him otherwise, I had him convinced that Mary really had passed rats!

One time when Sara Hewitt was with us we had beets or beetroot for a meal, and Sara really pigged out. The next day she was really worried, thinking she had blood in her stool. She gave Gladys Jongeling a stool specimen and Gladys brought back the diagnosis. She had the "dreaded beetroot disease." We all had a good laugh over that.

Since we lived so far away from the city, we had our own entertainment. Visitors never knew what might happen when they came. One time we went to Don and Emma Stoll's house when her parents were visiting. Don had not come home yet, so we waited in the dark to throw stones on the roof of the house. We had contours for drainage, and I was hiding in one of those when one of Don and Emma's houseboys came out to relieve himself. He got pretty close to me—too close for comfort. I could hardly keep from laughing. Don wasn't very happy when he found out that his houseboy hadn't used the bathroom.

One of our favorite pranks was to throw firecrackers near the homes. One night Lester Cooper called our house. I answered the phone. Lester said, "Madonna, are you all at home?" I assured him that we were. He had heard what he thought were gunshots, but decided to check to make sure we weren't setting off firecrackers. It turned out that Lester and some of the other male missionaries caught an African poacher.

We loved birthdays and always had parties to celebrate. We tried to make every birthday party a surprise. We always knew we would have a party, but never knew when. The day of Denny Pruett's fortieth birthday everyone kept quiet all day. No one wished him a happy birthday. In the evening I took a big cardboard box, painted it white with shoe polish and then decorated it with icing and put in forty regular sized candles. At 10:00 P.M., all of the missionaries, dressed in pajamas and bathrobes, went to the Pruett's house with all forty big candles lit. Lucy said she thought the Ku Klux Klan was there. We did have a real cake and some cold drinks to celebrate—and then played basketball.

During her internship with us, Dr. Gloria Cobb had a birthday. To surprise her, I called her to the hospital, supposedly to check on a labor patient. But I had placed a piece of paper with the words "Happy birthday, Gloria" on the patient's abdomen. When Gloria pulled the sheet down to check the patient, she got her surprise! The patient enjoyed participating in the surprise.

I think it was in 1964 that we got a "Mrs. Chase" doll—a life-sized doll used to teach students how to bathe patients, give enemas and do catherizations. We had fun dressing her up in clothes, putting her in the pickup and driving around the mission. Crispen Mutukwa, the head orderly, got a good laugh out of it, but some of the house girls were frightened of her and didn't want to be near her.

Obviously, life was never dull at Mashoko. It would take pages to tell all the things we did to have fun.

# Chapter 6

# Making Disciples

The greatest blessing of our ministry at Mashoko was to see people come to Christ and to be baptized. Our Savior Jesus had a ministry of teaching, preaching and healing. Through the hospital ministry many people gave their lives to Christ and were baptized. But it wasn't just patients who became Christians, but also many staff members and nursing students.

It was a time of great joy when Crispen Mutukwa, the head orderly, gave his life to Christ and was baptized. The devil is never happy when people give their lives to Christ, and in 1966, after I returned to Mashoko from furlough, we were most disappointed to learn that Crispen had been drinking. It was difficult, but we called him in to talk to him, reminding him of his responsibility as the head orderly and as a Christian. I am happy to say that during the rest of my time at Mashoko, he stayed strong in his Christian walk.

The village churches grew. One reason was because when patients came to Christ, we directed them to the nearest village church where they could be a part of the congregation. Marietta Smith and I worked with the Christian Endeavor group. We met on Saturday evening with students from both the teacher training school and nursing school attending.

One year I had a choir made up of some of the nursing students. I got some Fred Waring youth choir books to use. The students had wonderful voices and harmony came naturally to them. I regret that I lost the tape of their songs.

I enjoyed visiting the village churches. Many times I went with one of the missionary children, such as Edward Cooper, Sherman Pemberton, or David and Darel Pruett, who enjoyed preaching. The people always appreciated it when we visited.

One Sunday a Bible college student and I walked to a church located near the mission. But when we arrived, we found that we were too late for the service. We decided to go on to another church. It was a long distance. I don't know how many miles I walked that day, but I didn't think we would ever get back to the mission station. After we got back, all I wanted to do was soak in a hot tub of water. (By that time we had running water in our homes and could enjoy a regular bathtub.)

Most of the time in the early days, village churches met under a tree. Or if there was a school, the church used one of the classrooms to meet. They sang—the Zimbabwean people had beautiful harmony—prayed, observed the Lord's Supper and took an offering. Most of the time, the wine was grape Koolaid served from one cup. Then there would be a message. Sometimes an African-American preached; sometimes the preacher would be a teacher from the Christian school. Sometimes we had benches, but at other times we just sat on the ground.

# Chapter 7

# The Mission Expands to Hippo Valley

In 1963, the mission was given opportunity to work with some sugar companies of the Hippo Valley Estates in Chiredzi to establish a hospital and schools. This expansion meant that Mary Bliffen would move to Chiredzi to work, which in turn meant that we would be short of nurses at Mashoko. Dr. Pruett asked me to take a short two-and-a-half month furlough to recruit more nurses. I visited my few supporting churches in Indiana and Tennessee and some of the Bible colleges.

I will never forget how nervous I was when I spoke to the students at Lincoln Christian College. I had never been up before so many to speak. I was telling them about my work with the nursing students and teaching them to give shots and administer medication. I made the statement: "Believe me, that takes patience, patience and more patience." Everyone started laughing. It took a while for me to figure out why. I was thinking of PATIENCE, ENDURANCE, and they were thinking of PATIENTS, PEOPLE. That broke the ice and I continued without being so nervous. The good thing that came out of that visit was that I was able to recruit Donna Kreegar to go to Mashoko.

Just before this furlough Sara Stere from Altoona, Pennsylvania, came to Mashoko to serve. She had been a captain in the Air Force; her nickname was Captain.

I returned to Mashoko in December 1963, and Mary moved to Chiredzi in January 1964. It was very busy until Donna came because Sara and I also had to relieve Mary at Chiredzi. We worked eighteen days with three days off.

I had two unforgettable weekends when I relieved Mary at Hippo Valley. The first was a weekend when Dr. Pruett was gone, though a British doctor and the Van Dykes were at Chiredzi.

One evening an Italian lady came in to have her baby. The doctor decided she needed a C-section. But he had never before done one on his own. Marjorie Van Dyke was a nurse, but had not been active in nursing and had not worked as a scrub nurse in surgery for years. She had never given anesthesia, so we decided I would have to give the open drop ether anesthesia and she would be the scrub nurse. Meanwhile Steve Van Dyke, Marjorie's son, was very sick with a high fever. No one could figure out what was wrong with him, so he was in a room near the surgery.

The doctor started the surgery—and the first thing he did was to cut into the bladder by accident. Instead of clamping it off and delivering the baby, he decided to repair it. I was concerned for the baby since we were giving the mother ether. Marjorie and I did a lot of praying that night. Finally the baby was delivered, and all at once I had three jobs—getting the baby to breathe, giving the ether while trying to decide if I was giving enough or too much; and operating the suction machine with one foot. And we could hear Steve calling, "Mom, Madonna, help me!!" What a night!!

We finally finished the surgery, and both the mother and baby were fine. But Steve was still very sick. We finally called Dr. Pruett and asked him to come, and we ended up getting a plane to fly to Salisbury with Steve. It turned out that he had a severe staphloccic septicemia and we got him to Salisbury just in time. By the time that weekend was over, everyone was exhausted.

The next event was not an emergency for me, but it was for a woman's husband. A man from Fort Victoria brought

48

his wife to the hospital. They were visiting friends for the weekend when she went into labor. She had not had a baby for thirteen years and wanted to go back to Fort Victoria to deliver. Her husband did not like that idea at all. Dr. Pruett was due to arrive in Chiredzi later in the day. I checked her and told her that she didn't have time to get back to Fort Victoria. I assured her and her husband that everything was fine, but that if Dr. Pruett didn't get there in time, I was a qualified midwife and could deliver the baby. Her husband was very relieved that he didn't have to take her to Fort Victoria. I delivered a healthy baby girl just as we heard Dr. Pruett's plane arrive. The family was very grateful and later gave me a beautiful bouquet of flowers and a big box of chocolates to thank me.

# Chapter 8

# Auto Accident and Other Tales of the Road

The single women looked forward to weekends off work. We often drove to Fort Victoria, about a hundred miles away, for a weekend of swimming and relaxation. One Friday evening, Sylvia Menhinick and I borrowed Jerry and Marietta's Smith's Volkswagen station wagon and headed off.

When we knew that another missionary was away from the station, we were very careful to stay well on the left side of the road as we drove, but that day we didn't think anyone else was gone. So I wasn't being careful to stay to the left side. We had traveled about ten miles from the mission when we started around a sharp curve—and there were Edward and Carmie Cooper in their Landrover. I swerved to get further to the left, but we had a head-on collision. I don't even remember the actual impact, so I must have blacked out. The next thing I remembered was seeing Edward looking in the car window and me saying, "Hi Ebby."

He later said that was music to his ears because his mother had told him, "Ebby, you have killed them both."

Few think clearly at a time like this. Sylvia apparently had a concussion and kept saying, "Madonna, where am I?"

We managed to get her out of the car and found a place for her to lie at the side of the road. Then when I looked down, I realized that I had something wrong with my left leg—it was crooked and to try to move it was excruciatingly painful.

Edward borrowed a bicycle and headed to the mission. He might have taken the Landrover, but in the excitement, it wouldn't start. But, unfortunately, a young African fellow got on his bicycle and reached the mission before Edward. He had seen me bleeding—I had a laceration on my head. He told Dr. Pruett that Miss

*A road into one of the missions*

Menhinick and Sister Burget were dead. Denny got into his car to get to us and, in his haste, didn't take along anything for pain, even though Sara Stere was yelling at him to stop to get some pain medication. When he arrived at the scene of the accident, he tried to move me, but I screamed that I could not take the pain. It turned out that my left knee was dislocated. Finally someone at the mission brought morphine to Dr. Pruett and he gave it to me intravenously. I was moved into Don Stoll's station wagon and taken back to the mission.

Dr. Jerry Smith sutured the laceration on my head. While he was doing that, the policemen came to investigate the accident. I quickly told him it was my fault because I was not on my side of the road. Jerry told me to shut up—the road was so narrow there was not a wrong or right side. After Jerry sutured me up, Dr. Pruett got my knee back in place. Sylvia and I shared the room set aside in the hospital for missionaries. We were spoiled royally as the different families took turns sending our meals to us. I taught Greek to Enock Jiri from my hospital bed and in a week was back teaching the nursing students. Believe me, after that I was very careful to drive well on the left side of the road when I drove to Fort Victoria!

During the time I was in bed recuperating, the exam results for the first-year nursing students came.  I wrote this in a letter to my parents on February 21, 1965:

> We received the examination results for the first-year students last week.  I was so happy.  All of them passed the Nursing and Hygiene.  That is what I teach.  And all but three passed Anatomy and Physiology.  They can repeat that in July, so maybe we will have 100% passes.  They pushed me out on the front verandah of the hospital on the cart and I called all of the students there and gave them the results.  You should have seen the girls.  They all were sure they had failed and they came walking from the dormitory like they were going to a funeral.  The boys were so mad at them.  They were all dying to hear the results and I wouldn't tell them until they all arrived.  As I read the names, they all clapped their hands and shouted.  You should have seen them.  Then they all nearly shook my arm off.

When we left Mashoko to go to Fort Victoria, we always hoped there would be no river flooded.  After I returned from furlough, I was stopped however.  I wrote in a letter to my parents at the Fuve River onJanuary 9, 1997:

> After 6½ years in Rhodesia, I finally got stopped by one of the rivers in flood.  With me were Greg Van Dyke and Smitty, Sara Stere's dog.  We had thought we are going to Fort Victoria tonight and then on to Salisbury tomorrow so that we would be in Salisbury in plenty of time to meet Sara and the Dr. Jerry Smith family on Wednesday.  I don't know how long we will have to sit here--maybe all night—to wait for the river

to go down.  Greg and I waded across just a little while ago and it was almost up to my knees.  My car is so low if I tried to cross now, it would come in the doors, so we will just have to wait.  We finally did get across the river and did meet the Smiths and Sara on time.

Such were the perils of driving in Rhodesia.

# Chapter 9

# Furlough

My furlough in 1963 had been very short, but now with more nurses committed to work in Africa, I took a longer furlough from August 1965 to April 1966.  I bought a round-the-world ticket and flew to New York via England.  I was able to buy a Volkswagen Bug in the States.  After visiting my supporting churches in Indiana, I drove west and visited many of the women's groups that had sent baby clothes.

I remember an experience of reverse culture shock in Hugoton, Kansas.   I was visiting the forwarding agents for Dr. Gayle Kenoyer.  These hosts owned a motel and provided a room for me.  I got ready for a bath, but I couldn't get the water to turn on.  I tried and tried, but nothing happened. I was embarrassed, but I dressed and went to ask for help. I had not experienced taps that are pulled to turn on wa-ter—and that was all I needed to do!  Even now, John and I sometimes have trouble trying to turn on showers.  Oh, these modern conveniences!!!

What a time I had driving on the freeways in the Lost Angeles and San Francisco areas!  My dad had told me that I could get arrested for driving too slowly.  Most of the time I had good directions, but I would not want to drive those freeways too often.  I had car trouble, so I had to creep to Oregon.  Fortunately, I arrived with no problems and Gladys Jongeling's parents and Al and Wilda Leeseman from the Milwaukie Christian Church helped me get the car fixed.

I goofed on my schedule.  I spoke in Corona, California, on Monday night and had to be in Clinton, Oklahoma, by Wednesday night.  I drove all the way from Corona to

Albuquerque, New Mexico, on Tuesday, found a motel and asked them to give me a call early in the morning. I arrived in Clinton on time to speak at First Christian Church where my J.B.C. classmates, Bob and Glenita Fulton Moorhead, ministered.

When my furlough was over, I continued my round-the-world trip. I flew to San Francisco where George Alder and his wife met me. I spent the night with them, and the next day they took me to the ship that would take me to Los Angeles, Bora Bora, Tahiti, the Cook Islands and Auckland, New Zealand.

I met a lot of interesting people on the ship. One lady from near Chicago, decided that she wanted to see my slides of Rhodesia. She arranged for the purser to allow me to show them in the ship's theater where a Jewish doctor ran the slide projector. Several people came to see the slides. Later some contributed to help us get an incubator for Mashoko. A couple from near Seattle, the lady who arranged for me to show the slides, and a man from Detroit, Michigan, contributed to the ministry for several years.

Isabel Knapp was to meet me in Auckland. She and her husband Ray had been missionaries at Dadaya Mission with the New Zealand churches of Christ before Ray had died in Rhodesia. Isabel had continued her work at Dadaya, but was on furlough. She had arranged that her son Brian drive us around in New Zealand to visit churches where I would share with them about the ministry at Mashoko and she would share about the Dadaya Mission.

Unfortunately, the night before I arrived, Brian had an appendicitis attack that required emergency surgery. Isabel was afraid to drive, so guess who drove the little Vauxall from Auckland down to the South Island! After having been in the States for over six months driving on the right side of the road, I now had to drive on the left side again. Fortunately, we made the trip with no problems.

It was a blessing to visit the congregations in New Zealand, and I made many new friends. I learned that New Zealand is a beautiful country with beautiful seashores, green pasture lands with sheep grazing, snowcapped mountains and many lakes. We visited Rorutanga, seeing the hot springs and the boiling mud. We also flew to Queenstown where we took a ski lift up a mountain. Even though we had heavy coats to wear, by the time we got back down, our feet were so numb with cold that we could hardly stand. We took a boat trip down a lake near Queenstown to visit a sheep farm and had tea at the home of one of the farmers.

I shared with several different congregations to thank them, for it had been the New Zealand missionaries who had started the work at Mashoko. They were able to see how the Lord was continuing what they started.

I returned to Auckland and flew to Australia. The flight took me to Sydney, Melbourne, and Perth, then to the Mauritian Islands and finally to Johannesburg. By the time I arrived in Johannesburg, my feet and legs were really swollen. Al and Annette Hamilton met me at Johannesburg, and I enjoyed visiting with them before I returned to Mashoko.

By the time I returned to Mashoko, Lester and Marjorie Van Dyke had arrived for Lester to serve as the hospital administrator. Dr. Jon and Ginny Durr were there as well. With Sara Stere, Donna Kreegar, Sara Hewitt, and I, the work load was not as heavy as it had been before furlough.

One of the many blessings after I returned was the baptism of a very old African woman. Our African evangelist in the hospital, Augustine Makuku, was doing an excellent work teaching the patients about Christ, and it was through his efforts that this lady came forward to be baptized. We knew, although we had not yet told her, that she was dying with cancer so it was thrilling for us to know that she could look forward to a home in heaven.

In my newsletter of November 1966, I wrote the following:

> We were happy about three weeks ago when Gordon Gwinji, the son of Mrs. Gwinji, our African nursing orderly in charge of the female ward, came forward during one of our morning worship services to give his life to Christ and was baptized immediately after the service. Gordon is working in the hospital in our record department and also doing all of our X-rays.

# Chapter 10

# On to Chidamoyo

Ziden and Helen Nutt were in the process of building a hospital at Chidamoyo. Betty Iddings, who had been serving there, was returning to the States, so I felt led to move to Chidamoyo in January 1967.

The first patients were admitted to the hospital on March 5, 1967. The women's group at the mission made the hospital gowns.

During my first year at Chidamoyo, no doctor lived there. However, Dr. Westwater, a government doctor, said she would cover for me. In fact, she told me that if I needed to do a Caesarean Section, she would assist me! Fortunately, that never happened.

I started three well-baby clinics in March. One was at the hospital, one at a school five miles away and the third at a school ten miles from the mission. The government provided the vaccines for smallpox, polio, tetanus, diphtheria, whooping cough and tuberculosis. I also weighed the babies and taught the mothers how to prevent some of the diseases the children often contracted. At the end of each clinic, I also gave a Scripture lesson.

By April we were very busy in the hospital, treating almost a hundred patients a day in the outpatient department. But only thirteen patients were in the hospital. I had a good African male orderly who helped me.

One of my first interesting cases at Chidamoyo was a lady who came in after having been bitten and beaten by her husband's younger wife. She had part of the lower lobe of her ear bitten so severely that it was just hanging. I tried to sew it back on, but I never saw her again to learn if it stayed in place.

I found myself doing skin grafts, mostly on patients who had been burned. I wanted to send one little girl to Karoi, but her father refused. Jerry Smith was present to give her anesthesia, and I did the graft. I had learned from Dr. Pruett to do what are called "pinch grafts" which were done by inserting a needle just under the skin, cutting off a small portion of good skin, putting it in a salt water solution, and then grafting it into the burn area. It worked quite well, and the little girl did fine.

Maternity work kept me busy. One weekend I had a difficult breech (bottom first) delivery, and by the time I finished, both the patient and I were exhausted. But the mother and baby were fine. Later that weekend, two young girls came, both expecting their first babies. I was back and forth from my house to the hospital checking on them all afternoon and evening. One of them delivered at 11:30 P.M., but we finally sent the other one to Karoi in case she needed a C-Section. Every bed in the maternity ward was full; we even had to put two women in the labor ward.

One of the most exciting days at Chidamoyo was when a man came to report that there was a leopard near his village. It had been killing goats, and some dogs had chased it up a tree. He wanted the missionaries to come to his village and kill it. We all went—the Nutts, the Ammermans, the Kelleys, and I. We had to walk a distance. When we arrived at the place where the leopard was supposed to have been, it was gone. We waited and listened. Soon we could hear the dogs barking again. Off we went to find the leopard. We went down a dry river bed, up again, across a corn field, and then down the same river bed again when those who were ahead stopped and pointed. High up in the fork of a tall tree was the leopard with several dogs who were barking at the foot of the tree. All three of the men—Ziden, Bruce, and Chuck—took aim. Ziden shot first because he had the most powerful gun. The first shot killed the leopard. We hurried to the carcass to keep the dogs from eating it. What an exciting adventure!

*Lepard killed near Chidmoyo*

It was a blessing to serve with Ziden and Helen and their three children, Karolyn, Lynda, and Tom. One time Lynda had a bad case of diarrhea, and how we prayed as I used the old method of giving her subcutaneous liquids to rehydrate her. She was one sick little girl, but she recovered. I am sure it was more the result of our prayers than my treatment.

In September, Ola Marian from Kentucky arrived to teach the missionary children. She shared a house with me. She taught Amy Ammerman and Tom Nutt for kindergarten as well as teaching the older children. Each day she started Gay Ammerman and Karolyn Nutt in their studies, then began teaching the younger children who arrived at school a bit later.

Chuck and Carol Kelley had arrived to work with the schools and evangelism. Now we had three families and two single women on the mission.

The five women missionaries went calling each Sunday in the hospital on the maternity and female wards. Usually ten of the African women went with us. We had ten baptisms, and three of them were patients from the hospital.

The women's group continued to grow. Usually more than thirty attended the meetings. The missionary women who knew how to sew helped the nationals make dresses. It took all five of the missionary women to keep seams and darts pinned, etc. Sewing was never my thing, but I helped all I could.

I enjoyed going calling with the women. We visited mothers with new babies, and they always gave us sadza, the cornmeal mixture, with some kind of relish—greens, chicken or beans or sometimes boiled peanuts. I loved the sadza. One time when we went calling, we passed a home where a beer party was being held. We sang as loudly as we could as we passed by to try to drown out the drums.

The new hospital was dedicated on January 20, 1968. More than one hundred were present including missionaries and visitors from Karoi and Salisbury.

Dr. Dale and Sue Alice Erickson arrived in 1968 for him to be the doctor at the hospital. I don't know who clapped the loudest—me or my head orderly. Sue Alice was a nurse, so she worked in the hospital too.

With the new missionaries, Housing was a bit short, so Ola and I moved out of our house to allow the Ericksons to live there. Ziden and Helen moved their small camper to near the house where my houseboy used to sleep. Ola slept in the camper and I slept in the little house. We fixed our breakfast and supper together and ate in the camper. Ola had her noon meal with the Ammermans, and I ate with the Nutts.

During the week, Dale was in Salisbury getting some experience in tropical medicine, so I still had to run the hospital during the week.

Soon after the hospital dedication seven people were baptized in the hospital baptistery. The first two were the head orderly and his wife, who was one of the nurses. We showed filmstrips in the hospital chapel on Wednesday night and had a worship service there on Sunday morning.

*Dedication of the hospital at Chidamoyo, 1968*

I mentioned that when I first moved to Chidamoyo, Dr. Westwater, the provincial medical doctor, told me I could do a C-Section and she would assist. Well, I did one, and what an experience!! It was on a lady who was dying with tuberculosis meningitis. She was nine months pregnant and the baby was alive, so I told the family they had to decide whether they wanted me to try to save the baby by doing a C-Section. As I waited in my little room that night, I didn't know how to pray.

The family came early in the morning to tell me that they wanted me to try to save the baby. Dr. Erickson was in Salisbury, and we didn't yet have electricity in the hospital. Sue Alice and a Rhodesian nurse helped me. I know that

*Madonna delivered this child by C-Section*

God had to guide us every step of the surgery. When we told the woman we were going to try to save her baby, she really calmed down. I had to use a local anesthesia because the woman was too sick to use ether. Once again I was thankful for Dr. Beasley of the F.N.S. who did C-Sections using local anesthesia. With God's help, we delivered a healthy baby boy. The woman actually seemed to be a bit better after the surgery and lived for thirty-six hours. But finally the meningitis went to her brain. She pulled out her I.V.'s and died. We kept Benjamin in the hospital for two years until his aunt could take him.

The same day Benji's mother died, I arrived home to receive a lot of mail. One piece was a registered letter from Larry Johnson, the minister of my home church. I had written to him earlier about my need for a pickup truck to replace the car I had been driving. My car wasn't running well, if at all, and I needed a truck to be able to get to all of my well-baby clinics and to carry the women when we went calling at a distant village. I thought the truck could also serve as an ambulance for the hospital.

When I opened the letter, the first thing I noticed was a check for $2,300. Then I hurriedly read the letter. He had read my letter to the Keystone Class of the church. The class had taken a loan of the amount of the check to send me so that I could purchase the truck immediately. They would be responsible for raising the money to pay off the loan. What faith for a small class to take on this responsibility! Tears of happiness streamed down my face.

After sanctions were imposed, it was not easy just to go out and buy a vehicle in Rhodesia, but I sent word to Chiredzi where many of the missionaries had purchased Peugeot cars to see if there would be a pickup truck available. Fortunately there was, and on March 15, the truck was purchased. Every Tuesday it was used to go to a well-baby clinic. Most Sundays it was full of women who were going calling.

We continued to have regular baptisms either through the hospital ministry or the well-baby clinics. I took our hospital evangelist with me to the well-baby clinics, and he taught while my team and I vaccinated and weighed babies. After one of the clinics, a woman invited us to have a worship service in her village. Following the service, she and her son gave their lives to Christ and were baptized.

In June, the regular hospital evangelist arrived. Sam Togarepi had graduated from the Bible college in Fort Victoria the year before. He was busy all day teaching the patients about Christ and telling them how they could have salvation through Christ. We regularly had two or three baptisms a week. On Sunday, instead of

*Women's Conference, 1968*

65

teaching Sunday School at the mission, we took the pickup to visit villages where people who had been baptized were living. By September, Sam had baptized almost ninety people.

One Sunday I went to one of the new churches at Chanet-sa. Sam, along with ten Christian women from near the mission, went with me. At the service two women gave their lives to Christ. We took them to a pool not far from the village for their baptism. It was thirty miles to the village, so we didn't get home until 5:30 P.M.

One day in August, I was awakened by the sound of women talking outside my window. I wondered what was going on. It was 5:30 A.M., and Mr. Nyasha, who ran the bookstore and was an elder in the church, said a girl had been assassinated. They wanted me to go get her. I hurriedly dressed and went outside to get more details. The girl was not dead, but had been stabbed in the side by her uncle. She was a Christian, a member of the church at Gwaze. Her two sisters had come for help. All of us got in the truck and went to get her to bring her to the hospital. On the way we were stopped by the chief's policeman who was all excited because he couldn't arrest the man since he had lost the key to his handcuffs!!

Meanwhile, the girl had been moved away from the village where she had been stabbed. Later we learned that the man had tried to stab her mother and the girl had defended her. We also learned that she had run away and that it was after she had run a distance that she had discovered she was hurt. Several men carried her up the hill to the truck, and I took her to the hospital. It was a Wednesday, the day Dr. Erickson always flew to Binga. As soon as I examined her and saw the wound was serious and required surgery, I went to tell him so he would not go to Binga. Then I took her sister to catch the bus so she could report the incident to the police and tell her brother. I then went back to the hospital to set up for surgery. The wound was small, but it had gone through one part of her intestines. Fortunately, she was a young healthy girl and soon recovered. Her mother had just been discharged from the hospital on Monday of that same week and had given her life to Christ and was baptized on the Sunday before she was discharged. She had told Sam that she feared that she would not get to attend a church service because she thought she was going to be killed, but she was thankful she was prepared for death.

Carol Kelley gave birth to a daughter, her third child, at Chidamoyo in September. Dr. Erickson delivered this first baby born to a missionary at the hospital. She was a big baby, weighing 8 pounds and 11 ounces, and she had blond hair. I told Chuck and Carol that she should be mine. Her name was Cheryl. I stayed with Carol for a couple of nights because Chuck had to go to Salisbury. After the Nutts left for the States, I always had Sunday dinner with the Kelleys.

The hospital stayed busy. We were seeing a hundred patients a day in the outpatient department and had over fifty in the wards. Dr. Erickson did a C-Section on a lady who had had six pregnancies with only one baby surviving. He did the C-section before she went into labor, and this time she had a healthy boy who weighed 6 lbs. 6 oz. When she came back from surgery, her brother and sister and all the patients in the ward were singing because they were so happy for her.

One of our favorite patients was Egnes who was in the hospital for about two months with a broken leg. She was a good grandmother to Benji, the boy I had delivered by C-Section. While she was in the hospital, she gave her life to Christ and was baptized. After she went home, she fell again and was back in the hospital for three more weeks. This time, however, she had only a sprain. When we took her home, Sam, the hospital evangelist, went with me, along with several of the Christian women. We had a service with her and her husband and several others of the village and promised to return the next Sunday to have worship services.

Egnes' husband told me it was only a short walk to their village from the mission and that the road that we drove was the long way. I decided to walk there for the worship service. An African co-worker went with me. I wore my pedometer so I would know how far it was. We had walked two-and-a-half miles when my companion said: "Look, there is the path."

The path he showed me was up the side of a very tall mountain. I didn't think I would ever make it, but I kept going, when I finally made it, I could look out across from where we had come and see the tops of the buildings of the mission. One hour and twenty minutes after we had left the mission, we arrived at Egnes' village. It was 5¾ miles.

One hour after we arrived, the service started with thirteen present. After the service, two young ladies and two boys gave their lives to Christ. We started for home soon after the service because I was supposed to take my companion to Chanetsa in the afternoon, and it was already noon. About six of the young girls and boys from the village walked with us, not just to the top of that big mountain, but down it. Therefore, they would have to climb it again to get home. I doubt if I would have done that.

Soon after they turned back, it started to rain. At first the rain was very light and felt good since it was hot, but soon it started coming down harder and harder. Both my companion and I were soaked. We found a small shelter where we could stay for a while. We started on. When we arrived back at the mission, it was almost 2:00 P.M. Chuck Kelley had gone to Chanetsa and Carol fixed me something to eat. It goes without saying that I was tired. But, in spite of it, I had enjoyed my walk very much. The next day I drove to the village to bring back the four who had given their lives to Christ so they could be baptized.

At Christmas in 1968, I took a vacation to Johannesburg to spend time with Al and Annette Hamilton and their four children. I really enjoyed my time with them. I had fun taking their two oldest Christmas shopping for their family.

In my January 1969 newsletter I noted that we had admitted a total of 1,075 patients to the hospital in 1968, and that we had seen a total of 4,161 patients in the outpatient department. Through the hospital ministry two new village churches were established and a total of 250 people had given their lives to Christ.

March 1969 was a busy month at the hospital with a lot of malaria patients. We averaged seeing twenty new patients each day and saw 694 people in the outpatient department. Many people came with fevers of 104 and 105, and one day a boy walked in with a fever of 106. I was always amazed at the endurance of these people. Most of them were well in three days, which is the number of days it takes to treat malaria, but many of them got pneumonia or something else when their resistance was low.

In March, we also completed a new building called the "Mutumbe Hut." This was a building where women who were expecting babies could stay. We often called them our "ladies in waiting." They wore hospital gowns and had their food from the hospital, but stayed in the building until they went into labor.

A church was established at Musabakaruma n 1969 through the hospital ministry. The attendance at the church grew quickly, and on most Sundays eighty to a hundred people attended the services. A total of fifty people were baptized. It was a long drive there—thirty-nine miles—but since it was a new congregation, we felt someone should visit each week. Dr. Erickson, Chuck Kelley and Bruce Ammerman took turns going. Sometimes I drove over and took one of the church elders or our hospital evangelist.

In my May 1969 newsletter I wrote the following about our Easter meeting that year:

> We enjoyed our Easter meeting so much. I had company for the weekend. Gladys Jongeling and Rosemary Swarms came to visit from Bulawayo. The meeting started on Friday, but on Thursday night about 12:30 A.M., I was awakened by the sound of singing when the lorry from Sinoia arrived carrying Christians from the Sinoia area. I had been up late waiting for Gladys and Rosemary to come, so I hadn't been in bed too long. I got up and went up to the church where they had stopped and directed them down to the school where they would sleep. The first service was on Friday afternoon. On Friday night we had a message from one of our African ministers. Then we had special numbers in song from many of our village church groups and from different groups that lived at the mission. On Saturday morning there were sessions for the women, men and children. The same program was followed on Sunday morning. Karolyn Ammerman had the session for the women on Saturday, and I had the session on Sunday morning. Saturday afternoon and Saturday night we had several messages from the African ministers. Early Sunday morning we were awakened by the sound of singing. We had set our alarm clocks so we could get up in time for the sunrise service which was to be held on the hill above the hospital, but we didn't need the alarm clock. The women had been up all night

singing, and near the time for the sunrise service they had come singing from the school to the church building. We all went up the hill for the service there and Bruce Ammerman gave the message. The last service of the meeting was on Sunday night. We had close to four hundred for the meeting as all of our village churches were represented.

We had been having sewing classes at our women's meetings, but in May, I started teaching them to bake. First I taught them to make scones (biscuits) and cornbread. They baked it over an open fire in their sauce pans and then put hot coals in the lid turned upside down to cook the top. I enjoyed teaching cooking much MORE than sewing.

I continued to go to the village churches with Sam, the hospital evangelist. One Sunday morning we went to the area of Mujinga to have worship services. Bruce Ammerman had gone to this village to begin the village church. When we arrived at the village of Laxon, a man who had become a Christian in February 1968 through the hospital work, had just completed the services. He was getting ready to go to the village of Chief Mujinga for services. We took him and some of the others from his village to the services at the chief's village.

Chief Mujinga was a very old man and was chief in name only. His son did most of the actual duties of the chief. Both of them had been patients in the hospital so we knew them. As soon as we arrived, we were greeted and taken to a thatch shelter where the services were to be held. When the services started, about twenty people were there, but more and more kept coming until by the time the services were over, about fifty were present. At the invitation, twenty-three went forward to give their lives to Christ, the brother of Laxon leading the group. Because there were more than I could take in the truck, we divided them into two groups for their baptisms. We first took the ones from Chief Mujinga's village to a river about a mile-and-a-half from his village. We met the others later, changed the load, and then took them back to Laxon's village where they were baptized in a river near his home. We then went to his house where we were served sadza, pumpkin greens and cooked pumpkin. It had been a wonderful day.

We had some excitement at the hospital on May 23, 1969, when triplets were born. It was the first time I had seen triplets born and the first for Chidamoyo Hospital. The Rhodesian nurse had delivered two of the babies when she realized there was one more, so she called me. I was there when she delivered the third. There were two girls and a boy, and they all did well.

Chidamoyo—a place of never-ending ministry!

# Chapter 11

# Final Months at Chidamoyo

Back in 1968, an evangelistic team from the States had visited Chidamoyo.  One of the members of the team was Sharon Stewart  who was planning to go on to India to visit the Kulpahar Kids' Home run by Dolly Chitwood and Leah Moshier.  Sharon had a great interest in Kulpahar because her father, Kenneth, at that time the president of Pacific Christian College where Leah and Dolly had gone to school. They and the Stewarts were close friends.

Sharon kept saying that she wished Dolly and Leah could get some help because they had their hands full with the school and orphanage in Kulpahar.  I wasn't even aware that I had asked a lot of questions about the work, though Ola Marian told me later that I had.  Not long after Sharon left, I would awaken in the night and Kulpahar would come to my mind.  Even though I was very happy in my ministry at Chidamoyo, I felt that God was calling me to India.

I wrote to Leah and Dolly to tell them that I felt called by God to help them.  They weren't especially encouraging at first, telling me that I would have to learn the language and that I would not have the freedom to share God's Word as we did in Rhodesia.  That didn't discourage me, and we continued to correspond.  They suggested that I visit there before I made a final decision.  I asked Sara Stere to go with me.  I knew that if she saw something that she felt should keep me from going, she would tell me.  So Sara and I made our plans to sail to India from Beira.

Meanwhile, we  enjoyed having people who came to help at the mission. In June 1969, we welcomed Dwain and Marilyn Illman.  They had both attended Lincoln Christian College where Dwain had graduated in 1965. Marilyn had then gone on to receive a degree in elementary education. Dwain had gone to medical school in Chicago and Marilyn had taught while he was in school.

They had met Dr. Erickson when he had spoken at Lincoln, and this influenced Dwain to go to medical school. The Illmans came to Chidamoyo for three months to see if this was where they might serve later. Dwain stayed busy in the hospital, and Marilyn served as secretary to Dr. Erickson and me and helped with records. One week she went with me to a well- baby clinic and helped by giving the oral polio vaccine to the children and charting the dates on the records. This was a big help when I had seventy-five children to vaccinate. She enjoyed that one trip so much that she continued to go with me. She learned three Shona words and phrases that helped her in giving the polio vaccine: shama, "open you mouth"; budisai rurimi, "stick out your tongue;" and medza, "swallow." She had all of the mothers and children convinced that she could speak Shona very well.

I learned that a missionary has to be a "jack of all trades." I wrote to my parents in August about being a mechanic. I had gone to one of our new areas for church on Sunday morning and needed to be back at the mission for the wedding for Sam Togarepi. We were about five miles from the mission when the car stopped running. It had been jerking like there was dirt in the petrol line before it stopped altogether. I got out and started cleaning the filter to get the dirt out, but it still wouldn't start. I finally had one of the men with me blow into the petrol tank. When he did, the petrol finally came out the hose. It was then that we discovered the hose had a hole in it. Fortunately, the hose was long enough we could tear it off at the hole, fasten it and go on. I arrived home just about thirty minutes before the wedding ceremony.

In August 1969, Benji, the little boy I had delivered by C-Section, had gone home where his aunt who would rear him. We missed him, but knew that he needed to be with his family.

I continued to teach the women how to cook new dishes. One week it was hush puppies. Since seventeen women had attended the previous meeting, I took enough ingredients for twenty-four women—plenty, I though. But twenty-nine were present this time. I ran out of cooking oil; some of the women had to wait until someone else was finished with the oil before they could cook. The smell was very appealing with all the hush puppies cooking. One little boy could hardly wait to get a taste. His mother was one of the group who had to wait to cook. I had mixed one batch, and someone else was cooking them. As soon as she got one done, she gave it to me to give to the little boy. He ate it in a hurry and cried for more.

One day at Chidamoyo is especially memorable. A car, truck or any vehicle driving on the bush roads could take only so much wear and tear. One Sunday afternoon I was returning to Chidamoyo with my truck loaded with ten people. That wasn't so many except that most of them had all of their sleeping things because they had been at a meeting at Chanetsa. That morning I had left Zebedee Togarepi, the brother of our hospital evangelist, at Chivakanenyama for the service. I was almost back to Chivakanenyama when I heard a terrible noise at the back of the truck. I stopped and got out to look. One of the men, who also had a car, found that the trouble was in the springs on the right side. I asked him if he thought we could go on. He said we could if I drove slowly, so I proceeded onward.

We picked up Zebedee and had gone about three miles when I heard another noise even louder than the first. I knew that this time we were stopped permanently. Here we were, twenty-five miles from Chidamoyo, no bus scheduled to come along and probably no other car to travel this way. I knew that one of the missionaries would eventually come looking for us, but I had given them no time to expect me and I was pretty sure they wouldn't come early since we were often late after these meetings. I had been at the meeting the night before and hadn't arrived home until about 10:30 P.M. Chuck Kelley had already started out looking for us and had made an unnecessary trip, so I knew he wouldn't look too early.

We started walking—ten adults and two children who rode on someone's back. It was quite an interesting walk. Of course, as we met people, they asked, "Wakaitase (What has happened)?" Our answer was, "Motorcari rakafa," "The car is dead."

We arrived at a village that was having a big beer party. One man, so drunk that he could hardly walk, came rushing out to shake my hand and to tell me how happy he was that I had reached his village. We hurried on, needless to say.

We continued walking, taking a couple of shortcuts. I was getting tired, and since I didn't have on walking shoes, my feet were getting very sore. I finally decided I could not go beyond Chigede village, which was still eleven miles from the mission. We stopped at one village and everyone who had pockets filled then with monkey nuts (peanuts) that we were given. I didn't have any pockets, but the man ahead of me kept filling my hands. Before we arrived at Chigede where there were Christians living, it got dark and I was really stumbling along. I don't know when I had been so happy to arrive at anyplace as I was to arrive at the village.

As soon as we arrived, those greeting us brought out chairs and put them around the fire. Sweet potatoes were produced very quickly, which we ate, and then sadza and greens were brought to us. Then they roasted corn for us. We were given a royal welcome. As it grew later, they built up the fire and brought a mat for me so I could lie down. They insisted that I have sheets as well, and I soon went to sleep. When

I awoke, I found that someone had also covered me with a blanket.

Just before we all were deciding to sleep, we saw a car coming from the direction of the mission. There were two ways to get to Chidamoyo from where we had been. I had forgotten to tell anyone that I had taken Zebedee to Chivaka-menyama, so the car paused at the seven-mile marker and followed the other road. Chuck Kelley and Bruce Ammerman arrived at Chanesta to find that we had left there. When the people heard that we hadn't arrived at the mission, they all became very worried. The leader of the church there came by bus to the mission the next day to find out if we had arrived safely. Bruce and Chuck went on around, soon found my pickup and about 11:00 P.M., found us all at Chigede. I was tired, but had rested and eaten well, thanks to our Christian friends.

In October, Dr. Gloria Cobb and I went on holiday. We first went to Zambia where we had quite a time crossing the border because the immigration official on the Zambian side was drunk. But he finally stamped our papers. We were to visit Leroy and Gayle Randall in Lusaka the first night, but drove and drove without finding their place. We went to the police station, and they allowed us to phone Gayle. Leroy had been gone for a week having services, but he had just arrived home. He came on his motorcycle and led us to their home. On Sunday morning we went with them to church at Matero. There people met in a home, and the room was very crowded. On Sunday afternoon, Gloria and I drove to Kitwe to visit Bill and Jackie Brant, where we stayed until Thursday when we we went to Ndola to spend a night with Dean and Judy Davis. All of us had supper at the home of Charlie and Betty Delaney. Dean and I were up late talking about memories from Johnson Bible College. On the return trip to Rhodesia, we spent another night with the Randalls. We spent a week at Kariba Dam before returning home.

Judy Pickett and Pat Kennedy arrived at the mission in October. Judy, who had been a classmate at Johnson Bible College, was to be the hospital secretary. Pat was a medical technologist who would run the laboratory. Both were immediately busy. Not only did Pat work in the lab, but she also gave anesthesia since the Ericksons were returning to the States the first part of January.

Just before I left Chidamoyo and Rhodesia, Dave and Susie Campbell arrived to do the maintenance work previously done by Chuck and Carol Kelley who had returned to the States. I had been doing two of the women's meetings that Carol Kelley had led, but Susie took over one of these and Pat the other.

Just as I was ready to leave, we welcomed Bill and Jeannie Nice to the mission. Bill was a doctor and had done an internship at Chidamoyo; Jeannie was a nurse. I hated not having much time with them. I had hoped Dale and Sue Alice would be there to help them, but they left early and I had my reservations, requiring that I leave too. I gave them a quick tour of the hospital. Bill gave me a hard time for leaving them so quickly.

My last day was January 9. On last my evening, all of the missionaries came with cake and ice cream to say farewell to me and to welcome the Nices. It was a sad, yet happy occasion for me.

The next morning I was awakened when the hospital staff stood outside my window and sang in Shone, "God be with you 'til we meet again." The tears streamed down my face, for I didn't think I would ever see them again in this world. The next day I left to meet Sara Stere. The Nutts would take us to Beira where we would board the ship—and I would begin the next chapter in my life.

# Chapter 12

# New Ministry in India

Sara Stere and I sailed from Africa on a British ship carrying both cargo and passengers. We first sailed to Dares Salam, Tanzania, where we had only stayed a short time. From there we went to Mombasa, Kenya, where we spent a day.

Many of those who boarded the ship in Mombasa were Indians who had been chased from Uganda by Idi Amin. Most of them were deck passengers. It was sad to see the tears of one Indian young man as we left Mombasa. He had lived all his life in Uganda before being exiled.

The next stop was the Seychelles, a beautiful little island where we spent a day. The beach's white sand and the so-clear water were beautiful. From there we traveled to Karachi, Pakastan, where we rode a camel and took a tour of the city. The next stop was Bombay where we went to the intermission organization and had a letter from Leah Moshier.

We spent the night hosted by a man who worked with the intermission group. His wife and children were not there, but he hosted us and a young couple who was serving in the Peace Corps. They had been working in the Punjab in North India and told us of their delight to be able to sleep in a room free of rats.

We flew from Bombay to Gwalior where Leah met us. We had a flat tire on the way to Kulpahar, delaying our arrival there until 11:00 P.M. We had a midnight supper and slept until 9:00 A.M. the next morning. We saw the babies and young children living at the Kids' Home. They were so cute.

Many of them weren't feeling too well. Some had mumps; others had chickenpox.

The next day I visited the school. The children put several malas (leis of flowers) on me, sang a welcome song in English and performed a skit. Children from both the orphanage and the village were enrolled in the school.

Leah and Dolly had their hands full running the orphanage and school and maintaining the buildings. They had a small dispensary, and an elderly Indian doctor came once a week to see sick children and some of the village people.

I had been praying since 1968 about serving in India. I had always loved children, but I think one incident on my visit was what convinced me that this was where the Lord wanted me to serve. One day Leah asked me if I would like to go to the clinic to see the local Indian midwife deliver a baby. Of course, I did. The midwife was delivering a baby to a young girl who was having her first one. It was a difficult delivery, but I think that if I had had the necessary equipment, we might have saved the baby. But there was nothing to use to suck the mucous from the baby's mouth and nose, and the baby died. How I wished for my vacuum extractor and a catheter or a bulb syringe to help the baby live. I could see right then how I could be used in this little dispensary.

When Sara and I returned to New Delhi, Sara said to me, "You are going to have to return to Kulpahar, aren't you?"

I said that I would to which she replied, "And, I can't say anything to stop you."

After we left India, Sara and I visited Athens, Greece; Zurich, Switzerland; and missionaries in Germany, finally to arriving in the States. Sara went to her home in Pennsylvania and I to Indiana.

My home church provided me with a house next to the church building, and I lived there while I waited for my visa to enter India. Many said I would never get a visa to work there, but I knew that if the Lord wanted me in India, He would take care of providing the necessary papers.

I wrote the following in a newsletter in May 1970:

> I have presented the work of Rhodesia and India at 19 different churches and groups. At some of these churches I have showed slides and also talked to Sunday school groups. I have traveled about 4,400 miles and have written about 120 letters. I have also had time to rest and have enjoyed my house at Normanda. One night I fixed tacos for the choir at Normanda. Most of my time has been spent here in Indiana, but I have also been in Kentucky, Ohio and New York. In May, most of my time will be spent in East Tennessee with a trip to West Virginia and then to Oklahoma. I also will be doing four Daily Vacation Bible Schools and eight weeks of Christian Service Camp.

One of the highlights of my furlough was a visit to Johnson Bible College in May. It was a thrill to drive through the gates to the college and see the familiar buildings where I had studied for four years. I treasured the memories from when I was a student and was thankful for the example of the professors under whom I studied and of fellow students. It was at J.B.C. that I had learned that the one who prays must have faith. I was thankful for the opportunity to speak in chapel and to show slides of the work in Rhodesia and India. I also had opportunity to teach in the missions classes. It was the week of graduation and I enjoyed the special activities—the awards banquet, the music festival, the Erosthe program and the commencement with a most inspiring message. And after having been gone for eleven years, I was asked by Professor Rowland if I would like to singThe Battle

Hymn of the Republic with the choir at the commencement program. I sang, and it was a thrill to be a part of the J.B.C. choir one more time!

I sent my visa application for India on June 1. After the visa office received it, I had a letter requesting a letter from Kulpahar to verify that I was needed to run the dispensary and also to provide the documentary evidence that I had the ability to do so. I wrote to get the letters I needed, and I asked for prayer that my visa would be granted. I finally had all the papers submitted to the visa office by September.

In the meantime, I was asked to accept a position at Johnson Bible College as missions teacher for the first semester of the school year beginning in August 1970. I accepted the position and looked forward to my ministry at J.B.C. That required me to cancel some speaking dates and to rearrange for dates for other churches. During that semester, I traveled from J.B.C. to Indiana on most weekends to speak.

By the time I finished eight weeks of Christian service camps I was tired, though I had enjoyed my time with the young people. The offerings I received were designated to apply to the cost of a Jeep I hoped to buy when I arrived in India.

It was then time to start my ministry at J.B.C. as a teacher of missions. I also taught a health class to twenty-three students. One of my students was Billie Clark, the wife of Dean Floyd Clark.

My visa application was received in India in October. On October 24, Leah wrote that a man from the Hamirpur District office had taken the application to her and Dolly. He had gone to Kulpahar about Dolly's trip to the States, but he then pulled out my visa application and asked them if they knew a Miss Burget. Leah wrote out a two-page supplement to the report, and he indicated that his report to New Delhi would be favorable to my receiving the visa.  While Leah talked to him, Dolly went to another room and spent the time in prayer.

Even though I didn't have the visa in hand, I began to pack the drums I planned to send to India.  Actually, my older sister was doing the packing; she does a much better job that I do!

Our prayers were answered, and I received the visa.  Dolly Chitwood wrote:

> I nearly jumped for joy when the cable came from Leah saying your visa had been granted!  It surely is an answer to prayer!  I feel like a great burden has been lifted in view of the help I know you will be in the work here.  Leah and I are getting no younger, and I've been concerned about what the future held in store for our "kids" if the government wouldn't let anyone in to keep things going.  Now, we can hang on for a good while longer with you there to lend a hand too.  Praise the Lord!

Leah wrote:

> Praise the Lord!  And how sincerely thankful and grateful I am.  Just this afternoon the word came from the Home Department here saying they have di-rected the Consulate General of India in New York to grant your Visa.  I can't relate on paper how thrilled I am; how thankful—how tearfully happy!  I opened the letter in Mr. Lal's office and I think he nearly cried too.  (Mr. Lal was the head teacher at the school at Kulpahar.)

Since Dolly had been in the States for a short furlough, I traveled to India with her.  I flew to Los Angeles on January

23. Dolly and I spent two nights in Hong Kong and arrived in India on January 27. Because of fog at the New Delhi airport, we first had to go to Karachi, Pakistan. We were supposed to be in New Delhi at 4:30 A.M., but we didn't arrive until 8:30 P.M. Leah had a lot of business in New Delhi, so we were there for three days before we flew to Gwalior and then drove the 150 miles to Kulpahar.

*Arrival at Kulpahar*

Dolly and I had quite a welcome. When we arrived, some of the girls decorated us with flower leis, malas in Hindi. Some of the girls who spoke English sang a song in English. After Sunday school at 4:00 P.M., some of the boys came to sing and decorated us with more malas. We had an official welcome on Tuesday morning at the school with the children performing several skits.

A new chapter in my life had begun.

# Chapter 13

# India:  The First Year

## Life at Kulpahar

Dolly had started teaching me Hindi before we left New Delhi.  After I reached Kulpahar, I continued to study with a retired teacher from a language school in North India.  Leah and Dolly provided him with a room and cooking facilities so that he could teach Monday through Friday.  I had lessons for four hours on Tuesday, Wednesday and Friday and two hours on Thursday.  I spent every evening during the week studying and even studied some during the day.

In the midst of my study, I began to get the dispensary ready for use.  It had been closed just before Christmas when the woman who worked there had been let go because of her poor attitude and performance.  I found that she didn't know the meaning of the word clean.

With help from some of the girls, we cleaned all of the cupboards and drawers and covered all of the shelves with plastic to keep them cleaner.  I threw out medicine that had been there for over ten years and antibiotics that had expired.  Prem Sheila, a lady who started working for me, sorted through patient records.  We hired builders to add a couple of doors, brick in another door, add two sinks, pipe water to the building, whitewash inside and out, and paint the woodwork.  The goal was to begin seeing village patients in two weeks.  Leah also wanted to have an official opening, inviting the village officials to participate since they had written a letter requesting a visa be granted to me.

In the meantime, I had over a hundred children to keep well. Some of the little ones, especially, seemed to have something wrong with them, such as sore eyes, sores on their feet, etc. Soon after I arrived, I gave one hundred smallpox vaccinations. Health officials gave the vaccination every two years because of the high incidence of smallpox in the country. I also gave them oral polio vaccine and the diphtheria, whooping cough and tetanus vaccine. Needless to say, I kept busy with language study, getting the dispensary ready and tending to the care of the children.

Since we were in a very orthodox Hindu area, we didn't eat beef. We ate mostly goat meat. Live goats were brought twice a week so the cook could choose a good one. He bought the goats live because it was very easy to get bad meat if it was bought at the meat market. The goat was roasted like steaks or ground and used it for meatloaf or meat balls. It didn't taste much different than beef. Occasionally a man selling fish came by. We also ate a lot of canned meats from the States, and we especially enjoyed ham.

The cook fed us well. He was a Muslim who had cooked for Leah and Dolly for many years. His son assisted him. I loved to cook, but if I did when he was there, he thought I didn't like his food. I tried to do my cooking on his day off so I wouldn't hurt his feelings.

In the cool evenings we often sat by the fire. One of us would read a book while the other two crocheted. But it soon got too hot to do that.

One night in early April we had some excitement when a wild cat fell through the chimney into the living room. We didn't hear it fall, but when Leah went into the room, she saw the foot prints from the soot. The cat had taken refuge in one of the bathrooms so we shut all of the other doors. The watchman was able to chase it out of the house.

Crows were abundant.  One day when I went to check a sick child at the girls' hostel, I saw one two-year-old girl standing outside eating a chipati, a whole wheat Indian bread, when a crow swooped down and tried to snatch it out of her hand.  She came running and crying toward me. Leah had told me that crows did this, but it was the first time I had seen it happen.

The swimming pool behind our house was one of my favorite places where each day at 6:00 P.M., I went for a swim. The exercise helped me to lose the weight I had gained. Many of the girls could swim and enjoyed it too.  The pool was also used for baptisms.

Services were conducted each evening the week before Resurrection Sunday.  Leah and Dolly had purchased a very good filmstrip on the crucifixion and resurrection, and Mr. Lal had put the narration on tape in Hindi with Leah playing the organ in the background.  Several special numbers from the children and adult Christians were presented each evening. A Communion service was held Thursday night, and Friday morning special services were conducted.  Ralph Harter, a missionary from Kanpur, came to present the message.

A sunrise service was held on Sunday morning at 5:00 A.M. with the final filmstrip shown. At the close of the services on Sunday morning, some of the girls sang a song about Christ in the garden.  Worship services were at 9:00 A.M. with Ralph once again bringing the message.  We were thrilled when seven children stepped forward at the close of the service to make their confession of faith.  They were baptized on Wednesday afternoon after prayer meeting.  We sat on the floor on long rugs for services.  As I write this after having two knees replaced, I know I could never do that again.

The official opening of the clinic was held in May. Only men were invited to attend because to have women and children would have made too big a crowd. Leah tried to point out to me all of the merchants and

*Learning Hindi from a pundit*

political leaders of the village. They seemed impressed with the improvements that had been made to the clinic. Leah organized the program and arranged refreshments while I got the clinic ready. Soon after the opening, I began to have many more village patients. That, along with doing the examinations of the children, kept me busy, but I continued to work hard on my Hindi.

In June, several weddings occurred. I wrote to my mother and dad in June.

> We had a wedding here yesterday and one about 25 miles from here the week before and we have another one in less than three weeks. The one last week was one of the boys that Leah and Dolly have raised. Their mother is alive and works here, but Leah and Dolly have paid for all of his education. He is a teacher and married a teacher who had been teaching here for four years and they will both continue to teach in the school here. Yesterday, the wedding was one of the girls raised by Leah and Dolly and she married the

brother-in-law of our electrician.  The next wedding will also be for one of the girls raised here.  She is marrying a Christian boy from Kanpur.  She has never seen him.  His father came to make the arrangements.  He said he trusted his father to pick out a girl he would love.  His father was certainly a sweet man.  She has seen her future husband's photo and that is all.  But, that is the custom here in India.

The Church wedding yesterday was at 5 P.M. and was much similar to weddings in the states.  Then they have a tea party and they have the wedding cake and other Indian "sweets".  Later in the evening around 8 P.M. they have the wedding supper which was rice and meat curry and hot peppers and a crisp bread called poppadum.

I taught some of the older girls some songs in English.  It took a lot of time and patience to help them to pronounce the words correctly, but they loved to learn, and I enjoyed teaching them.

## Medical Ministry

I checked all of the children in the orphanage every week, taking them hostel by hostel.  I took the baby room for the little ones who couldn't walk, the girls who were from two to seven years of age, and the older girls.  Then I took the younger boys and finally the older boys.

Most of the children had excessive wax in their ears.  I think it took me six months to get it all cleaned out.  Dr. Singh, a lovely lady Indian doctor from Chattapur, came every two weeks to check the children, but she didn't have an otoscope that would allow her to really see inside their

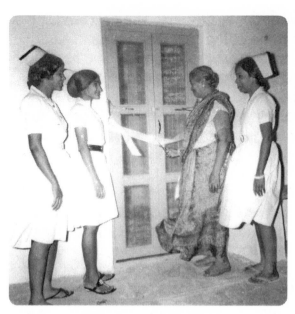
*Dedication of despensary*

ears. Later when I saw so many ear problems after I opened the clinic, people called me the ear specialist. It was amazing the things I removed from ears—flies, maggots, ticks, cockroaches, and a combination of a leaf and salt that was as hard as a rock. The last took some time to get out. The worst was a two-year-old who had had an ear infection for a long time—and I took out twenty-one maggots. Yuk!!

Having children around can keep a nurse busy. One time a little boy was cut on his head when a girl threw a stone at him. I think she was trying to get tamarinds from a tree. Fortunately, I had just received sutures, so I could suture him up. I decided that as punishment for her, I would make her watch me suture him. I had two children crying, but I hope that helped her to know that she shouldn't throw stones any more.

On another day three of the three- or four-year-olds put something in their noses. Two of them put in seeds from the tamarind tree. One little boy was so good as I took the seed out that I gave him a piece of candy. Unfortunately, he thought that was a good way to get candy: he did the same thing the next day. Needless to say, I no longer gave him a piece of candy.

My first maternity case occurred in May. I had to send the woman to the hospital in Chattarpur because there was an arm presentation that required a C- Section. She was transported in the mission bus. The next morning when I went to check on her, she was sleeping, but she had delivered a healthy baby boy. The grandmother was beaming with happiness.

I had ordered a Jeep ambulance that I planned to use to conduct mobile clinics. It seemed to take forever to get it, but finally the body work was begun in Lucknow in June. I looked forward to having it for patient transport and to go to the rural clinics. Finally by September, it was ready.

In June, I gave over two hundred typhoid and cholera vaccinations in three weeks. For cholera I had to give a shot and then wait two to three weeks to give a second injection. Many Indian peopled died every year from cholera; we prayed that it wouldn't affect the children at the orphanage.

In July, I began to have more village patients. It seemed to take some time for them to trust me to take care of them. Women also finally began to come for delivery. But during my first year at Kulpahar, I delivered only eleven babies.

In August, the medical equipment I had ordered from the States finally arrived. I had to pay 100% customs on the equipment! But since they were things I couldn't find in India, it was worth it though.

One week was accident week. One of the girls fell when she was playing and

*Kulpahar Christian Dispensary*

lacerating a knee that required suturing. Not ten minutes later, another girl fell from one of the pieces of play equipment and had an even larger laceration on her forehead. The very next morning a three-year-old fell while climbing on one of the beds and had a laceration on her forehead. However, this one took only two stitches. I was thankful that I could do the suturing instead of having

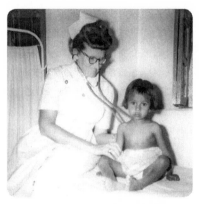

*Madonna examining one of the Kulpahar Kids*

to take the children to the hospital located about forty miles away.

When the Jeep ambulance came in September, I started mobile clinics in some of the villages. The first one was at Larpur. I reported in detail a day in my November 1971 newsletter:

> Three times a month now on Tuesday morning, I get up a bit earlier in order to get started for one of the mobile dispensaries. I would like to share with you as I go to the village of Larpur, about five miles from here. On this trip, Prem Sheila was unable to go with us as her little girl was sick with hepatitis. So, about 7:45 A.M. on September 21, Sheila, my nurse; Vena, one of our college girls who was home on vacation from school and who had been helping in the dispensary; Valarie, one of our office girls; Mr. Paul, our evangelist; Vijay, my driver; and I started out. Even though the village is only about five miles away, it took us over 15 minutes to get there because of so many cows and goats on the road. At night the cows and goats are taken to the villages and the next morning the people herd them out to the fields.

92

Before going to Larpur, Mr. Paul, our evangelist, had talked to the head of the village and had arranged for a place where we could park the Jeep.  We drove into the gates leading to the home of one of the poorer families, but the home was partially behind a wall and this helps to keep so many onlookers from coming.  The woman hurried to sweep the ground around where the Jeep was parked and we put up our folding tables outside the Jeep.  On one was the record player where Vijay would play records in Hindi of sermons and songs and one table for me where I could put the things needed for examining patients.  One little boy who wasn't really sick came, but he allowed me to listen to his heart and then I let him listen and you should have seen his big smile when he heard his own heart thumping.

Soon the people started coming to be examined.  We had several people with scabies, a very common skin disease in India.  There was a woman who was anemic, another very common problem in India as most of the Hindu people will not eat eggs or meat because of their religious beliefs.  There was the complaint of one or two of abdominal pains, which could mean they have one of the many parasitic diseases that are so common in India. After I examined the patients and wrote the medicines they should have on their cards,

*Mobile dispensary*

93

Sheila, Vena and Valarie counted out the pills or measured the liquid medicines and made out the bill for the medicine. We do charge for the cost of the medicines and the usual bill ranges from $.50 to $1.00.

After we were finished seeing the patients that were there, one man wanted to discuss a medical problem with me. When he was finished, several other men had gathered—not to be treated, but just to look—so I took the opportunity to tell them about the inoculations that I could give their children to keep them from getting diphtheria, tetanus and whooping cough. By this time it was evident that we were not going to have any more patients, so we put the examining equipment and the tables in the Jeep and went to the center of the village. We had told the head of the village council that we would make a house call to see one of the women at his home.

Vijay parked the Jeep and stayed with it while Sheila, Valaria, Vena, Mr. Paul and I walked through the narrow streets to the home where we were to visit. We went only a short distance when the street curved to the right and then back to the left again and then we saw that there was a long street going back much farther that one would think just passing through the village. There is such a contrast in the homes. You would see a small squat looking homemade of mud with a straw roof and not whitewashed, then you would see a large brick home with a flat cement roof, whitewashed and perhaps decorated in some way. The home that we visited was at the very end of the village. It was one of the largest homes in the village. We were sent up to a verandah, through a room and into an open courtyard. Then we were shown into a room and soon a young woman came in. Her chief complaint was dizziness and on doing a hemoglobin,

94

we found she was anemic.  She was a sister-in-law to the man on the village council.  She was a young woman of 27 years and had been a widow for 13 years.  According to Hindu custom, she is not allowed to marry again.  Her husband had died soon after their marriage.  She had had no children.  After we examined her and started back to the Jeep, an elderly woman came to ask me to look at her eyes.  She had a bad conjunctivitis, but also had cataracts.  I told her I would give her medicine for the conjunctivitis, but she would have to go to a hospital for an operation for the cataracts.

When we arrived back at the Jeep, quite a crowd had gathered and so Sheila gave a lesson, using flash cards on what mothers should feed their babies in the first year of their life.  After this there were three or four more patients and one man who had heard us tell about the inoculations, brought his little girl to have her first diphtheria, tetanus and whooping cough inoculation.  By this time we had finished seeing all those who wanted treatment and so we headed back to the mission.

Pray for us as we go to each of these villages that as Mr. Paul does personal witnessing, as Vijay plays the messages on the record player and as we try to show them the love of Christ as we treat them, they will see how much joy that they can have in Christ if they would only give themselves to Him.

My maternity work continued to be slow, but in November, I had two deliveries.  They came at about the same time. Since I had only one room for patients to stay, one of them stayed in the delivery room.  One of the women came from a village some distance away at the advice of someone else from her village who had come earlier to deliver her baby. The woman had been in labor for two days and continued in labor for about twelve hours before I delivered a nice baby boy at 10:00 P.M.  The father had gone home for the night, but was he ever happy to learn that he had a healthy son when he returned to the clinic.  Just before they went home, I showed the mother how to give the baby a bath and gave her a small amount of baby clothes.  She had nothing but one cloth with which to wrap the baby before she received the clothes.

# Life with When Co-Workers Were Away

In September, Leah left for furlough.  While she was away, the remaining members of the mission team assumed her responsibilities.  I discontinued my Hindi lessons to take on the extra responsibility with the children, handling some of the discipline in her absence.  I sometimes had to give a put put or spanking or mete out other punishment.  I checked the baby room more often.  And I planned the meals for Dolly and me.

Dolly kept more than busy with the school, working hard to make the Kulpahar Christian School far superior to most of the primary schools in India.  About half of the children in the school were from the village, some from Hindu and Muslim families.  One evening we had a visit from the village chief of police.  One of his first comments was that he had heard about the good school we had.  Many of the fairly well-to-do people in the village sent their children to the school, as did many of the government officers.

Each morning before instruction began, each class had morning prayers.  Even some of the Hindu children memorized the Lord's Prayer and often asked to be the one to lead in prayer.  The Bible classes were not compulsory, but most of the Hindu and Muslim children attended.  The school was another of the ways we witnessed for Christ.  Every teacher was a Christian, faithful in worship attendance.

In October, three more children gave their lives to Christ and were baptized.  Many of these children were from Hindu or Muslim families, but this time one was from a Christian family who lived next door to the mission.

We continued to take in more children.  Many of them were malnourished when they came, but with good food, they soon looked much better.

## Happy Birthday, Merry Christmas, Happy New Year

When Leah returned from the States, Pat Brown, the forwarding agent for her and Dolly, came with her.  She was there for my first birthday in India.  We received royal treatment when we had a birthday.  The kids at Kulpahar loved it when one of the "aunties" had a birthday.  In India, when a person has a birthday, it is the custom to give out candy to those who come to wish a happy birthday.  Leah arranged for a woman in the village to make candy for all of the children, mission employees, and the families who lived at the mission.

The night before, I mentioned to Pat that they might start coming to sing to me by 6:00 A.M.  She didn't think they would come that early, but the first group arrived at 6:15 A.M. when we heard the sound of a harmonica playing Happy Birthday.  Soon that was joined with the voices of the older boys and Mr. and Mrs. Lal and their two children. I hurried and put on my bathrobe and went out to the back porch to get a tray of some of the sweets to take to them. They sang several verses of the song, starting with "Happy birthday to you," then "Many blessings to you;" "Happy long life to you;" "Good morning to you;" and finally "Many flowers to you." With that final verse they put several marigold flower garlands on me. The boys put three or four garlands on me, placed two on my wrists, and gave me a bouquet of flowers. Then one of the boys set off a firecracker. About thirty minutes later the girls came and all of the baby room kids who were a year old or more. I was given more garlands. Then two more groups of boys came with more garlands. Finally the oldest girls came. Birthday gifts came along with the garlands.

After my birthday we were busy getting ready for Christmas. Each child received a new outfit of clothes and other gifts. They came hostel by hostel to the house to sit down and enjoy the big lighted Christmas tree and to receive their gifts and listen to the reading of the birth of Jesus recorded in the Bible. Then we had a big Christmas dinner that everyone enjoyed.

We had a New Year's gift with the arrival a baby girl at 1:10 A.M. on New Year's Day. Leah came bursting into my room, turned the light on, and said, " Happy New Year!" She scared me half to death. She wanted me to look at the new four-day-old baby who weighed only 4 lbs. 12 oz. The mother had died and the father was in Bombay so the grandparents brought her from Hamirpur about seventy miles from the mission. She had a club foot which we would take care of later. Then about 6:00 A.M., I got called for a delivery patient, but she wasn't full term and the pains stopped, so she went home.

On January 4, I delivered twins at the dispensary—one at 11:15 P.M. and the other at 11:30 P.M. The first was a boy, and then his sister came. I had been seeing the mother and had told her that I thought she had twins, so it wasn't a surprise. This was her eleventh pregnancy, and she now had eight living children.  She was a relative of one of the employees at the mission.

Six more children gave their lives to Christ and were baptized the first Sunday after New Year's.  I missed the baptismal service because a patient had come, not having passed urine for four days. I had to catheterize her and removed two quarts of urine.  I thought she also had a brain tumor, but the family refused to take her to a hospital.

Quite a first year it had been.  But I was now very much a part of the Home and the ministry was ready to expand.

# Chapter 14

# The Second Year and Beyond

## Day-by-Day Life

Life at Kulpahar was routine at times, surprising at other times, but always interesting. With so many children in the Home, I always found something to do! For example, I taught the girls to play volleyball as part of the physical training class at the school. I was happy when Leah brought a volleyball back from the States. The ones at the Kids' Home were so hard that it felt like your hand was going to break when you hit it.

One Sunday in February was a day of both joy and sorrow. I was called out of the worship services when Dr. and Mrs. Devol from Chhatarpur brought the body of little Savita who had died in the hospital the night before. She was the baby, weighing only 4 lbs. 12 oz., who had been brought to us on January 1. She had seemed to be doing better until two days before her death. However, the joy came at the close of the worship service when three of the children went forward to give their lives to Christ and Mrs. Jolly Herbert, one of the teachers at the school, became a part of our congregation.

I continued my Hindi lessons in 1972, but for only eight hours a week plus study for two hours a day. I sometimes was able to spend more time on language study if I wasn't too busy in the dispensary. At the end of the year, I traveled to Dehra Dun to take my First Year Hindi examination—a progress test and an oral examination which was the examination that is usually taken after five or six months of study.

But my studies had been "hit and miss." However, I passed the exam—I was first in the class of two!

I started studying Hindi again in July 1973, with my original pundit. I had classes with him from 6:00 to 7:00 A.M. and in the afternoon from 5:00 to 6:00 P.M. I tried to study in the afternoon. By the end of the year, my Hindi had improved enough that I started teaching a Bible school class of third graders—three boys and three girls—outside on the grass each Sunday.

Because I was so busy in the clinic, I eventually had to give up formal Hindi study, but teaching helped me to do better with the language. I also started a youth choir to teach them songs in English. I taught them songs that I had used for the nursing school choir in Rhodesia. It was more difficult teaching the children in India since they didn't know English as my students in Rhodesia had, but we hoped to prepare songs to sing for church.

I often took walks with the children. I wrote this in my October, 1972 newsletter.

> This evening when I was taking some of the girls for a walk, this verse of Psalms 19:1 came to mind. "The heavens declare the Glory of God; and the firmament showeth His handiwork." Our children here have something that I think few children have in America—that is a love for God's creation. They have this because they don't have television, movies, parties and all the other activities that American children have. As we walked along the road to our local railway station, the children were delighted when they saw a hyena run off in the distance and then they had another treat when they saw a fox run off in another direction after pausing to look at us several times. The next exciting thing was when they heard the squeal of a wild pig that was tied upside down by the

legs on a pole and we followed the men carrying the pig to the railway station where it was put into one of the box cars. On the way home, we took some of the paths across the pastures and for a rest climbed up a rocky hill and watched the sun set. It was a beautiful sunset as the sun went behind a cloud in a glory of redness. High in the sky were other clouds that looked like wisps of cotton. The children didn't enjoy the walk and the beauty any more than I did—and it was all God's creation. As we came into the gates of the mission compound, the girls over and over said: "Thank you Auntie." I should have been thanking them. How thankful and blessed I am that God sent me here.

Early in 1973, the government began to cut off the electricity leaving us with power for only six hours a day. During that April, temperatures commonly reached 108 degrees. We didn't usually have that kind of heat until May. I was so thankful for the Willing Workers Class of Normanda Christian Church that headed up a drive to raise money to buy a generator. We were fortunate to be able to find one; everyone was buying one because of the electricity cuts and the heat.

The generator arrived the day before Resurrection Day. This allowed us to show filmstrips for the meetings before Resurrection Day. It also allowed us to keep the baby room cool twenty-four hours a day. It came just in time: in May the temperatures reached 118 degrees.

We rejoiced when the young people made the decision to give their lives to Christ and to be baptized. One young man, a teacher in the Christian school, and the husband of one of our girls, also a teacher, declared their faith in Christ and were baptized. This decision motivated another young man to examine his life and to question what he was doing for the Lord. Two of the young men began working with some of the younger children to form a youth choir.

The family continued to increase. In October 1973, eight children, five of them babies under a month old, arrived. Two girls and a boy, brother and sisters eight, eleven, and thirteen years old, arrived first. Their Christian father was trying to care for them after their mother had left, but he could not manage any longer. They were very thin when they came, but two of them gained 1½ pounds in two weeks.

Four babies, three girls and a boy arrived next. The first little girl was brought in the morning followed by the twins who were only two days old. At midnight another little girl arrived. She weighed only 3 lb. 8 oz. We sent her to the Christian hospital in Jhansi. Later another little girl joined us. Her birth date had been October 9, the same as Leah's. With all of the extra little ones, those who worked in the baby room were extra busy. Some of the nurses, one of the older women, and I took turns feeding the tiniest one every three hours during the night until she went to Jhansi.

1975 started out as a sad time for me. My dad died instantly on February 11, when a thousand-pound bale of hay fell from a loader and hit him. I was thankful that he didn't have to suffer. But because the mail was so slow and we had no phone, it was over two weeks after his death before I learned of it. I was so thankful for the many cards and letters and for many gifts for the medical work in his memory. We used those for digging the well at the spot on the compound where we hoped to build a hospital.

Engagements were always happy occasions. And we were especially happy for the engagement ceremony for Goodwin Herbert and Sheila Anthony on March 19, 1975. This meant that I needed to build a house where they could live after their marriage.

The staff housing—two rooms for single male staff with storerooms and bathrooms and a house for a married couple—was finished on July 27, just in time for Goodwin and Sheila to move in after their wedding.

Back in August of 1973, the ladies of the Cicero (IN) Christian Church had sent fourteen boxes of food and clothing. By the end of 1973, only four of the boxes had come.  It was disheartening, to say the least, to think of the work of packing, collecting and mailing that many boxes for them never to reached us.  I was surprised when in December 1975, two years later, the rest of the boxes came.  One slide that I used on furlough that people loved was of one of the little boys wearing a pair of Osh-Gosh-Bi-Gosh overalls which had been in one of the parcels.  Not an Indiana farmer, but an Indian one!

# An Expanding Medical Work

### Babies, Babies, and More Babies
On January 4, 1972, I delivered the first twins ever to be delivered at the Kulpahar Christian Dispensary.  The mother brought them back when they were a month old.  She had been anemic before the delivery, but her hemoglobin was back to normal at the end of the month. The boy had gained 8 oz. to reach 8 lbs.  that month and the girl had grown from 5 lbs. 2 oz. to 6 lbs. 14 oz.  The mother had dressed the babies so nicely in the baby clothes we had given her. It looked as though she hadn't used them before.  A trip to the dispensary must have been special.  Though some in her village had told her before the babies were born that she

would never live through the delivery of twins, both she and the babies were doing well.

Most people in the part of India where I served were small. One woman was so short that her head came just barely above my waist. I helped her give birth to her second baby, a little girl weighing only 4 lbs. 10 oz. This was her second difficult delivery. Dr. Potham at the Chhatarpur Mission Hospital had delivered her first baby with forceps. I had to use my vacuum extractor to help her with this delivery, but even though the baby was tiny, both mother and baby did well.

It seemed that hardly a day went by without a delivery or a new maternity case coming for examination. The latter, of course, would come later for the birth. In October 1973, twelve deliveries occurred with fourteen more in November.

The most exciting of these deliveries was on November 13. I was called just past midnight for this case. When I went to the clinic, I saw the husband of a woman whom I had examined about three days before. He immediately gave me a letter to read. That day they had gone to the Christian hospital in Chhatarpur, as I had advised. I was sure she had twins and I wanted advice from the doctor whether I should try to manage the delivery or whether she should go to Chhatarpur. I had also wanted them to do an x-ray to verify the twins, for I really suspected she might have triplets. But the doctor there said she was sure she had twins and that an X-ray wasn't necessary. She had advised them to return to Chhatarpur for the delivery.

Soon after they arrived home from the hospital, labor pains started and they came to the clinic. But labor was too far along to try to make the fifty-five miles to Chhatarpur. At 1:35 A.M., I delivered the first baby, a girl. As soon as I delivered the baby, I said quietly to the nurse, "Aniti Dean, I think it is possible that there are two more babies." I wasn't absolutely certain so I didn't want to alarm the mother or her mother-in-law who was with her. At 1:50 A.M., I delivered another girl. After the delivery of this baby, I told the nurse to see if she could tell if there was another baby while I clamped the cord of the one just

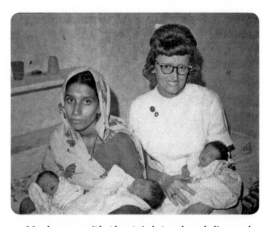

*Madonna with the triplets she delivered*

born. The mother-in-law said, "It is only a big placenta." But, Aniti said. "I think there is one more." And there was a third one, a boy who came feet first at 1:57 A.M. This was the first time I had delivered triplets, and as far as anyone in Kulpahar could remember, it was the first time that any woman in the village had given birth to triplets. The babies were all good size, weighing 4 lbs. and 8 oz., 5 lbs., and 5 lbs. and 9 oz. Needless to say, the father of the babies could hardly believe his ears when he was told he was the father of three new babies.

Unfortunately, about three days after delivery, the smallest little girl, the second to be born, started vomiting and stopped having bowel movements. I suspected an intestinal obstruction of some kind. I tried to persuade the father to take her to Chhatarpur for an x-ray, but he refused. Leah also went to the clinic to talk to him and to the mother. The mother would have been willing, but the father kept saying, "If it is God's will for the baby to die, then what can I do?" If it had been the son, he would have allowed him to be taken. They were in the dispensary for a week, and I did all I knew to do, but the baby did not look good when they took her home. We learned that she died at home about three days later.

As one can imagine, this delivery was the talk of the village for a few days. One of the employees who lived on the mission heard the news in the village when he went to do some shopping. We learned later that the two living babies were doing well. Needless to say, it was my most exciting delivery.

One week three deliveries occurred in one day. Since the nurses were midwives, they delivered some of the babies. We had learned from one patient that one of the village Indian doctors referred to our dispensary as the "Women's Hospital of Kulpahar." He referred female patients to us, including several who came for delivery.

One night a young girl came to the dispensary. She looked young—not more than sixteen—and I was sure she must have been expecting her first baby. But this was her second. Sheila delivered a baby girl about 3:00 A.M. Later as I talked to our Muslim cook, he told me that in India, especially in rural areas, if a girl doesn't marry very young, she will get a bad name, that people think there is something wrong with her. Some had as many as seven children by the time they were twenty-six years old. This was not the case with the Christian girls, however.

By July 9, 1974, we had already delivered seven babies that month. And in August, we had a total of seventeen deliveries, a new record. One day I had six post-partum patients. They filled all of the rooms and women were in three rooms of the dispensary. A total of 188 babies were born in the dispensary in 1974, compared to only 66 in 1973.

In December 1974, two-and-a-half sets of twins were born. The first were identical girls born prematurely, weighing only about three pounds each. Even so, they were doing well when they went home. The second woman delivered only one baby in the dispensary. The first one was born at home around 4:00 A.M. She then traveled five miles by ox cart and delivered the second one in the clinic about 10:00 A.M. The final births were twin boys. This mother came by ox cart for eight miles, then by horse drawn tonga for another seven miles to get to the dispensary.

Most of the people who came to the dispensary had no idea of their own birth date. I became increasingly convinced that I should give a birth certificate for each baby born in the dispensary. At least those born in the dispensary would know their birth date.

### And Other Medical Cases

I saw my first case of leprosy in November 1971. This lady was of one of the lower caste. Mr. Paul had seen her husband who said that his wife was sick, but hadn't been helped at any place she had been. Her leprosy was so typical that one look told me what disease she had. One finger had been amputated, and two others were now affected. She also had one toe affected and had open wounds on both of her feet. She had been treated for almost three years without anything providing help. Unfortunately, I didn't have any appropriate medicine, but she promised to come back the next day. She came every Thursday morning to get a weekly supply of medicine. At first she had to have a dressing applied on the open wounds. With treatment, the open wounds improved in a short time. I charged her only about seventy cents for the vitamins and medicine and gave her the dressings free, hoping she would encourage others to come.

It was never dull at the dispensary. One day Prem Sheila's son swallowed a fish bone when he was eating his supper. His mother said she had seen it in his throat. It took me awhile to find it; I wasn't looking deep enough. I finally found it sticking out below his left tonsil. Seeing it was one thing—getting it out was another! Every time I put the tongue depressor on his tongue to try to reach it with a forceps, he vomited. Finally, with a small tongue depressor that fit on to a long otoscope light, I was able to get the forceps in and bring out the fish bone. What a relief it was to me, his mother, and most of all, him!

The days at the clinic were always busy, it seemed. May 1972 was a record month when I saw 114 patients from the village. The most I had seen in any month before that was 89. I also delivered three babies that month and had two other maternity cases that I had sent to the hospital because of complications. Fortunately, the children stayed well! By October, the number of village patients had reached 174, more than double the number the previous October.

With the heat of May and June, many of the children had prickly heat and developed boils and abscesses. Some of them were miserable. With the rains came mosquitoes— and that meant malaria. The children slept under nets, and I gave them anti-malarial tablets. But some still got malaria.

My March 1973 newsletter described one busy day in the dispensary and the variety of patients I continued to see.

> The first thing on that busy day was to examine the rest of the baby room children—fifteen in all. Most of these were from one year to three years. Many of them who used to cry when I put the tongue depressor in their mouth to look in their throat now open their mouths quite willingly and don't cry at all. Soon after I finished examining the children, village patients started coming and they didn't stop coming until after noon. The first one was a young man who had an abscess on his leg that had to be drained. The next patients were the twins that I delivered in January. They were both having some diarrhea, but not bad and they had both gained weight. Next were two

women who had come with the parents of the twins
with some minor complaints.  Before I finished examining them, a woman who had a severe headache
and fever came from a village about five miles from
Kulpahar.  I felt sure she had malaria so gave her
something for pain and fever and started the treatment for malaria and by the time she was ready to
leave, she felt some relief.  I went to the house to see
Leah about something and while I was there one of
our workers came to say his father had been gored by
an ox and could he have time off to go and bring him
to the dispensary.  By this time it was getting near
noon, so Leah and I quickly ate our dinner and then
I went down and put five sutures in the laceration
of the arm of our field worker's father.  Before I had
even started on him, another patient came from a village some distance from the mission.  She had been
having stomach trouble for five years, but she didn't
want to pay for the medicine unless I would give her
a guarantee that it would make her well.  This is a
very common request from people—that they pay for
the medicine only if it makes them well.  The only
problem with that is that they never return to pay for
the medicine and you never know if it is because the
medicine didn't work or if they just didn't want to pay.
I had a big stack of patient records of people who had
never come to pay.  If we really felt the people were
too poor to pay, we don't insist on the money.  But
many of them will say they are poor even when they
may have more than enough money with them to pay
the bill.  One Sunday morning Sheila and I spent over
half an hour explaining to an old man that we just
couldn't afford to give free tuberculosis treatment to
his son as we received no help from the government
and the treatment was too expensive.  He just kept
insisting that we give him more medicine.  Finally, I
went out and reminded him of the many times when

his son was in the hospital in Chhatarpur that we gave free transportation to members of the family and also took clothes and food for them. I told him that he could get free treatment in a government tuberculosis hospital. After all this talking, he pulled out a Rupee 100 bill which was what he owed for medicine. He had the money all the time, but he wanted to see if we could feel sorry for him and not charge him. Rupees 100right now is about $12.73. Even though some don't want to pay others have said we should charge more than we do.

Malnourishment was common in India. Leah had read that 100,000 children died monthly as a result of malnutrition. I was seeing only a hundred or so patients a month in my little dispensary, but in two months I saw two children who were severely malnourished. One little girl was one-and-a-half years old and weighed only nine pounds. Not too long after I had seen her, a very malnourished five-year-old boy came. He weighed only 13 lbs. 10 oz. The parents were giving him from one to two cups of cow's milk each day and not much else. We persuaded them to buy powdered milk and showed them how to mix it. The little boy swallowed half a cup without taking a breath. He was supposed to have had typhoid for a month, but the only treatment he had received was from a local doctor who had given him some kind of ashes. (Yes, ashes!) Ashes were used on wounds, on newborn babies' cords and for other things as well.

Much of the malnutrition was the result of poverty and the scarcity of food, but some of it was also because of ignorance on the part of parents about what they should feed their children. Part of it was because most of the Hindu people do not eat meat or eggs.

Some of the home remedies commonly used were as bad as or worse than the witchdoctors' treatment in Rhodesia. I once saw a little baby with an ear infection that had been treated with oil mixed with black pepper. Ugh!!

I was continually amazed at what I found in the ears of children and adults both from the village and the orphanage. One week when I was examining four- to eight-year-old girls, I noticed something in one little girl's ear. It was pushed way back in the ear canal. When I finally got it out, I discovered two wads of paper. After the struggle of getting it out, you can imagine my chagrin when the very next little girl had a tamarind seed in her ear. Fortunately, the seed was near the outside, and I had no trouble removing it. The week before at the mobile dispensary at Larpur, I had seen three children with ear problems. The first little boy had an infection in his ear, the second had two flies along with infection, and the third had four flies in one ear and one fly, one grain of wheat and two small stones in the other ear. It took me nearly half an hour to remove the various objects. Then, as if I hadn't seen enough ear problems for the day, as we were leaving the village, a man came running behind the Jeep to say that he wanted me to look in his ear. I inwardly groaned as I told the driver to stop the car. Again I found a bad infection. I finally decided that the reason I saw so many ear problems was because I was the only one nearer than the hospital in Chhatapur to have an otoscope.

Late in 1973, a man came to the clinic with a severe case of lepromatous leprosy, the type that causes big nodules on the body. The nodules were mostly on his face and ears. The first time he came, he had his head wrapped to hide his condition. It was wonderful to see him come in February without his head wrapped. The nodules were gone and he looked back to normal, though he would continue to have to take treatment for at least a total of two years. He had been told he had "bad blood" and that there was no cure for his disease.  Two months after he started treatment he brought his nephew who had tuberculoid leprosy, the type where the person has white spots without any feeling.  If the person is touched with a needle, he or she feels nothing.  By early 1974, five people were coming for treatment for leprosy.  How thankful I was for Dr. Louise Westwater, the doctor in Rhodesia, who had taught me to diagnose leprosy.

March of 1974 was a month of stress.  Beginning March 15, several of the babies at the Home started having very bad diarrhea and vomiting.  By March 29, three of them had gone to be with the Lord.  Two died in the hospital, and one died at Kulpahar.  We were never able to get a diagnosis, but I am sure it was atoxic bacillary dysentery.  We were thankful when it was over and the babies were healthy again.

In September 1974, another new record was set when we saw 249 patients.  In 1974, the total patient count was 1714, compared to 1203 the year before.  Since Goodwin Herbert by that time was present to do laboratory tests, many people who had not come to us before began to come when they knew we had additional help to diagnose their diseases.  Some doctors also sent patients only for laboratory tests.

### Mobile Dispensaries
One mobile dispensary was held in Kulpahar at the village council grounds.  One day Pat Brown, who was visiting with us, went with me.  We hadn't been there long when one of the wealthier men of the city asked me to go to his home to visit his sick mother.  This family was of the Brahmin caste.  Brahmins do not allow women to go out in public, so I made home calls on some of them.  I had gone to his home a couple of months earlier to see his aunt.  I was happy to see that both his aunt and mother were doing well.  While I was there, I also examined a little girl who had tonsillitis.  When

we had finished, they served us tea and cookies and some Indian savories.

After tea, we went back to the grounds and waited. No more patients came, so we decided to go home. But just as we were leaving, another lady came. We used the ambulance as a place to examine her. When I finished seeing her, three boys in the family came, all of them with ear infections.

Every two years a dentist and his son, an optician, came from Jhansi, about a hundred miles away, to check the teeth and eyes of all the children except for the very smallest ones. They had to bring all of their equipment with them. They worked for two days. The dentist taught me how to easily pull the children's baby teeth. At first, the children were afraid, but when they found out that it didn't hurt much, they would tell me if they had a baby tooth loose.

## Expanding The Facilities

We began early in my tenure at Kulpahar to improve the clinic by putting in new ceilings. With the remaining funds we started adding a laboratory. Goodwin Herbert would soon finish his advanced training as a medical technologist in New Delhi. When he finished, he would return to Kulpahar to serve. The laboratory was necessary or his work.

The continued growth of the medical work required additional facilities. As the Lord provided funds, I started two building projects. One was to add three more rooms for post-partum patients at the dispensary. The other was to build housing for the single nurses. I noted in my news-letters that even before my requests for funds for these projects could have reached my supporters, they had responded.

With that experience and my later reading about the life of George Mueller, I never again asked for funds. I knew that God knew my needs and would provide—and He did.

The three rooms for post-partum patients were finally finished, but we had to put patients in the rooms before the electricity and ceilings were finished, though there were screens on the windows. When we had three deliveries on one

Sunday, we would have been at a loss for a place to put the patients without the added facilities.

After completing the laboratory and the three rooms for post-partum patients, I continued construction on a building for four single female staff. I received enough gifts at the end of 1973 to put the roof on the building. I was also able to help with the cost of building a wall around the compound where one day I hoped to build a hospital, to share in the expenses of keeping the generator running, and to buy laboratory equipment for Goodwin's use when he came.

Work continued on digging a well at the site where I hoped to build the hospital. On April 26, 1975, water started coming in after digging down to seventeen feet. From then on the workers had to empty the well so they could continue to dig to forty-five or fifty feet in order to assure a really good water supply. A police official told me that to find water in the area was "luck." I told him that it was an answer to prayer. A medical salesman said, "It is a miracle." I think he was right. With a good water supply, I hoped to start building an outpatient department in July. This would be the first stage of the hospital.

Even though some of the laborers went on strike for more money, work continued on the well with some of the older boys who were on vacation from school joining with the workers not on strike.  It was hard work to use chisels to break the stone as they got deeper.

Work on the well was suspended for a time because there was so much water that the three-inch diesel pump could not keep the well emptied. The workers had dug down thirty-eight feet; when the well filled up, there was 31½ feet of water.

It seemed that I was constantly having something built. In May 1975, I had the builders start on a building that would be used for male staff members or for a married couple.

July 21, 1975, the day ground was broke for the foundation of the outpatient department, was a special day.  Mr. MacLawrence Lal, the headmaster of the school and preacher at the church, read Scripture and led in prayer, and my mother, who was visiting at the time, turned the first spade of dirt for the Kulpahar Christian Hospital.  The following day, the laborers started digging the foundation, and on August 4, they started laying the stones.  The foundation was completed on September 18.  The outpatient building was 84½ feet long by 45 feet wide.  There was a verandah in the front and the back and a corridor down the center of the building.  The building would house  a laboratory, X-ray and darkroom for developing film, two bathrooms and a room for each of the following functions—giving injections, dispensing medicines, waiting room, and reception room—and two examination rooms.

Construction continued on the outpatient department, but it was not completed before I left for my first furlough in March of 1976.  Before I left, the builders did get the roof on and finished the outside painting.  But the plastering, floors and ceilings would have to wait to be finished when I returned in March 1977.

# A Growing Medical Staff

Goodwin Herbert finished his training in New Delhi to join us to work in the lab. Goodwin had come to Kulpahar as a young boy. His mother, two sisters, and a younger brother came after his father had died. Goodwin and his older brother, Jolly, came a year later. After doing a B. Sc. in Agra, Goodwin went to Barielly for a year of training as a laboratory technician. While he was at there, he was given the opportunity to do advanced lab training in the All India Institute in New Delhi. He was supposed to be there for only two years, but the curriculum was changed at end of his second year, requiring him to stay one more year to receive any credit for the two years he had already completed. But by doing this, he was graduated from this course with a B.Sc. with honors. He was first in his class, one of three to finish the course. Goodwin was a fine Christian young man and a willing worker. When Dolly found out that she would be one teacher short for the school year when he was returning, Goodwin willingly agreed to teach English to the high school boys in the afternoon.

Soon after Goodwin arrived, he began to do cultures that allowed us to know what organism we were contending with. He also gave sensitivity tests that indicated which antibiotics to use, if, in fact, they were needed. I didn't feel that I was working so much in the dark, so to speak, when I had the lab reports to help in the diagnoses of many illnesses.

By the end of 1975, the medical staff had increased to seven nurses, a driver, a medical technologist and his helper, a matron who looked after the single girls and a secretary.

# Praying for a Hospital—and a Doctor

By the end of 1972, I had begun to pray that God would guide me in a decision to build a hospital at Kulpahar. And I prayed that He would also provide a doctor. Two cases in particular illustrate the motivation for those prayers.

In November, an eight-year-old boy weighing only twenty pounds came to the dispensary. At first glance I thought he was a hydrocephalic. He was so thin that his head looked unusually large. When I examined him, I found a critically sick little boy. I soon found out why he was so sick: he had a typical tetanus spasm. The story was that twenty-five days earlier, he had typhoid. He was given "village" medicine, which meant some kind of herbs, and he supposedly got well. He was well for four days and then became sick again. He was given two injections from a local village doctor, but when he didn't get any better, he was brought to the dispensary.

I couldn't treat him for several reasons. First, I didn't have enough tetanus antitoxin on hand to treat him. Secondly, it looked as if he would soon need a tracheotomy, requiring a doctor to do that. He would need oxygen, which I didn't have, and he would need around-the-clock nursing care, and I didn't have enough nurses to keep someone on duty that long. I told the father that he needed to take the boy to the hospital at Chhatarpur as quickly as possible. I gave the boy a sedative to try to make the trip a bit more comfortable for him and didn't charge the father because he was so poor.

On another occasion, a Sunday morning, a lady was brought to the clinic by a man for whom she worked. She was moaning and groaning and holding her abdomen where she was having pain. She had experienced diarrhea and vomiting since the evening before and she was so dehydrated that her skin hung in folds and her eyes were sunken back into her head. As one of the nurses took her temperature, I tried to get a blood pressure. I tried once, then again, and finally asked the nurse to turn off the fan because I just couldn't hear. Finally with everything quiet, I realized that her blood pressure was so low that I couldn't get a reading. I then told her family that they should take her to the Chhatarpur Mission Hospital. I reminded them, as I had to remind so many, that I was not a doctor and that she should be under a doctor's care. But I was asked to do what I could because they didn't have money to go to the hospital and couldn't even pay for what I did.

The nurse wrote out a statement which said that the woman's condition was critical and that I was given permission to do what I could and would not be held responsible if anything happened to her. The father could not write, but he put his thumbprint on the paper and the son signed his name. As soon as they signed the papers, I started I.V. fluids. I felt fortunate to be able to find a vein for the fluids. I gave her pain medication and medicine for infection and told the son and father that they would have to take turns sitting and holding her arm so the I.V. wouldn't come out.

The nurse and I left her with the father and son and took turns checking on her every half hour to make sure the I.V. was dripping well and to change the I.V. bottles when necessary. We left a whistle with them and told them that if the bottle got low on fluids to blow the whistle and the watchman would call me. About two hours after we started the first I.V., I was able to get a blood pressure and just before she went home in the evening, it was up to 110/70. Before the last I.V. was finished, the woman was begging me to take the needle out of her arm, but I made her lie there until the I.V. was finished. The woman, who was carried into the clinic in the morning, got off the treatment table and tried to touch the nurse's feet as a gesture of thankfulness. She was told to thank God that she was doing better.

120

I continued to pray for a full-time doctor for the dispensary. Early one Saturday morning the night watchman came to tell me that a patient with a broken leg was at the gate. I couldn't even provide transportation because the ambulance had been sent to Jhansi with a sick child. I knew I couldn't set a broken leg, so I told the watchman to tell them to try to find transport.

I sent for a nurse to help me. The big gate had to be opened to let the girl to be brought inside the mission. It was obvious that she had a broken left femur. She also had a laceration on the lower part of her left leg and a long laceration at the side of her left eye. The unfortunate little girl had been in the middle of a couple of fighting cows, and their horns had caused the wounds. We splinted her leg and cleaned up and put dressings on the wounds. By that time those who had brought her had found a car to take her to Chhatarpur. Since I was not a doctor, I had no narcotics to give her for pain.

This little girl came from a village about five miles away. It seemed that everyone from this village had a major problem. About a month after the little girl patient had come to me, another patient arrived one afternoon from that same village. Usually I didn't see patients in the afternoon because that was when I did the routine exams on the children in the orphanage. When I went down to the dispensary, I didn't see anyone, but I could hear the sound of a woman crying and wailing, which meant that someone had died. I went out the gate and saw an ox cart. A man came to tell me that his baby had just died and that he also had a sick boy for me to see. He had given his six-month-old baby girl some herbal medicine, and she had died. It was too late for her, but I did see the little boy.

We had earlier offered to do a mobile dispensary in the man's village, but the village leaders had refused. Back in

1957, a work among the women of this village had been started by the missionaries then serving at Kulpahar. Edna Hunt, Helen Doyle, Leah, Dolly, and others had gone to the village to teach the women how to knit. As they knitted, the missionaries shared Christ with the women. But a tragedy in the village had ended the opportunity to witness there. A twenty-two-year-old man had died of pneumonia while his young wife was away. The Hindu priest convinced her that she should burn herself on her husband's funeral pyre, which she did. The holy man also convinced the women of the village that this double tragedy had occurred because they were listening to the teaching about Christ by the missionary women. From that time on, this village had been closed to Christian witness. This is probably why they refused to allow us to take the mobile dispensary there.

# More Than Medicine

When I started the mobile dispensaries, I went to three villages. Only the village of Larpur really needed my services. We went there not just to help with their health problems, but also to share Christ with the children who came to the dispensary. The teacher at the nearby school always arrived late, so usually many children gathered. One day, Prem Sheila used a tract to tell the children a Bible story. They were so eager to get the tracts that they pushed and shoved to get to them. We limited them to one tract each and told them that if they could tell us the story in the tract when we returned, we would give them another one.

Two weeks later when we went again, we found that most of the tracts had been torn up by their Braham teacher when they had taken them to school. Those that were not destroyed had been sold to people by one enterprising young man. At least the tracts got into the hands of someone interested enough to buy them.  Not one boy could tell any of the stories, so no new tracts were given out except to adults who wanted them.

Two weeks later, however, two boys told us the stories they had read.  One boy told us most of the parable of the Foolish Rich Man, and another told us the story of Jesus stilling the storm.  As a reward, we gave them a tract of the Life of Christ visualized books in Hindi and told them to keep it at home so it would not be torn up or sold.

## Serving with Colleagues

In 1972, Dolly was sick for some time with abdominal pain.  In late June, I went with her to Vellore Hospital in South India where she was admitted for X-rays and lab tests. After she was settled in the hospital, I spent a week visiting with Bill and Ethel Gulick at Christ Nagar Institute at Ennore, Madras.

Dolly left for the States for a year-long furlough in mid-1972.  This would be the first time she had been in the States for an entire year in ten years. She returned July 30, 1973.

There was a lot of coming and going from the mission in 1975. Dolly went to the States for thyroid surgery and came back feeling much better.  Leah then left on

*Mobile dispensary at Lanpur*

123

July 13 to complete her furlough.  She had to have surgery for a detached retina eleven days after she arrived in the States.

In addition to my work in the dispensary, I tried to relieve Leah of some of her many jobs by keeping the storerooms containing children's clothes straightened and by giving out clothes when needed.  Every year in October, we gave all of the children sweaters and shoes and socks.  (The rest of the year they wore thongs).  The girls received warm long pants to wear under their dresses, warm flannel nightgowns, and capes. The boys were given long pants and shirts in place of their pajamas—kurta (a loose cotton pants and shirt)—, wool scarves, and coats.  We also gave two wool blankets to each child because it got quite chilly at night.  Then in March, we collected all of these items and stored them with moth balls in big trunks until the next Winter.

## Visiting Other Works in India

As I mentioned, when I went with Dolly to South India in June 1972, I took the opportunity to visit other works in India.  One was the work of Bill and Ethel Gulick at Enmore near Chennai (then called Madras).  They had a very nice hostel for boys who lived there as they studied in junior high, high school and college.  The hostel also included two classrooms, one for each Ethel and Bill, and a chapel for daily devotions.  A vital part of Bill and Ethel's work was the Scripture studies they had with the boys.  Many of them came from Hindu homes, but each boy was required to have a Bible and a hymnbook.  They walked a mile to attend the Ennore Church of Christ.  Bill and Ethel were both fluent in Tamil.  In South India I felt like I was in a different country, for no one spoke Hindi.

One day while I was in South India, I went with Lois Rees to see one of the roadside leper clinics she and her husband David conducted in Andra Pradesh. A staff of ten to twelve men traveled in a Jeep to these clinics, holding three in a day. One clinic was held under trees to provide a shelter from the sun. I had never seen so many types of leprosy. I also saw some patients who were having reactions to dapsone, the medicine that cures leprosy. This was the first time I had seen any reactions to this medicine. Later David Rees took me to the site where the government had granted them land to build a hospital. Two buildings were nearly completed.

# A Holiday of Service

In May 1972, I took a two-week vacation to go to Sitapur to visit Bernel and Joan Getter. That was quite a trip beginning with trying to get my ticket in Jhansi. Since I belonged to the Trained Nurses Association of India, I was allowed a concession on a train ticket, but I found out that was only if I traveled third class.

Since I wasn't scheduled to leave Jhansi until later in the day, I took a boy I had with me to the Jhansi Christian Hospital for them to remove a small, infected wart on his face. The missionary nurse on duty asked me to eat lunch with her, so I went to her home and had lunch with her and Louise Russell, another missionary visiting from Kanpur. They told me how better to get my ticket, so I returned to the station where I bought my first class ticket . I learned that the way to get somewhere quickly was not to take a train— but to either drive or fly. From 2:45 P.M. when the train left Jhansi until 7:20 P.M. when I went to bed, the train had stopped six times. Some stops were for only two or three minutes, but the stop before I went to bed lasted for forty minutes. And it seemed that every time I woke up in the night, we were stopped. The next morning from 8 A.M. to 1:30 P.M., when I finally arrived in Raigarh, we had stopped ten times. When I mentioned to the Getters how often the train stopped, Joan said: "That train is an express. It doesn't stop much at all. You should be on the one that really stops often!!!" Was I ever happy I was on an express!!!

In spite of the long trip, I enjoyed myself. The scenery was beautiful, and it was Interesting as the vendors at each station came along calling out what they had to sell—tea, fruit, candies, various food items and books. And as usual in India, there were always some who, seeing a white woman, stopped and stared. In the station at Bilaspur, I saw one or two lepers begging, but with all the leprosy in India, it was surprising there were not more. I was glad to arrive in Raigarh after almost twenty-four hours on the train. I didn't have to wait long for Berne and Joan to arrive. Though we hadn't met before, we were able to recognize each other without difficulty. I was the only white woman in the waiting room; it was obvious who I was.

We made on our way to Burdadardh where we were to participate in a women's retreat. The scenery was beautiful. I saw some of the highest mountains that I had seen in India. The road curved up and down and reminded me of the scenery around Chidamoyo in Rhodesia. I really felt like I was back in Rhodesia again when the road became more of a path than a road and the villages that we passed through were more like the villages in Rhodesia that the ones around Kulpahar.

It had just begun to get dark when we arrived at Burdadardh. All the women and girls at the meeting were there to greet us. Several men and boys were there as well. They garlanded us with flowers and sang a song. Then we shook hands with everyone and gave their Christian greeting, "E-she Sahai" which means, "Jesus, the helper." Bernie had to return to Sitapur that night, so they gave us our supper soon after of rice and dahl (lentils) and a vegetable soon after we arrived. In this area the dahl is seasoned only with salt, so it didn't have as much taste as the dahl seasoned with chilis and other spices common at Kulpahar.

Before we ate supper, one of the boys helped Joan get our cots set up outside the house where we were to stay for the few days of the meeting. One of the Christian families had cleaned out their kitchen for us to use.

After the women had eaten their supper, we had our first short meeting. The wife of one of the ministers of the area gave a short devotional and Joan introduced me. I said a few words and we sang one or two songs. Then the minister's wife chose someone to cook the next day. (All the women had a turn in helping to cook.) Then it was time to go to bed. Some of the sixty women and girls had walked quite a distance to get to the meeting, so everyone was tired.

The next morning we were up about daybreak because the woman where we were staying was up early to do the sweeping. We carried our beds inside—we would rest inside out of the sun in the afternoon—and got ready for breakfast.

Several of the girls had ground rice into flour the night before so they could make rice bread for breakfast. The flour was mixed with water and rolled out to about the size of a tortilla and fried in just a bit of oil. It was quite tasty. We were also served tea that was sweetened with a brown sugar made from sugar cane. The people in this area put no milk in their tea. I tasted it, but it was too sweet for me. Joan had brought some Nescafe, so I had coffee. One day we had puffed rice and on another day channa (chick peas) for breakfast.

In preparation for the retreat each woman had been told how much rice and dahl to bring.  Or if she wanted, she could bring money in place of the rice and dahl.

The meeting started about 8:00 A.M.  Joan presented a flannel graph lesson on Christian growth to the entire group.  She gave the lesson in Hindi and the leader of the retreat translated into Kurukh since many of the women could not understand Hindi.  Using the book of James, I then taught a lesson on problems of life and how to solve them.  The retreat leader taught the other women.  I taught in Hindi with lots of help from Joan with vocabulary and sentence construction.  Since the girls could answer questions after the class period, I think they must have understood at least part of what I taught.

After the second class, we had our noon meal, once again rice and dahl.  One day we had some "jackfruit" with it.  Jackfruit is more a vegetable than a fruit, though I can't think of its equivalent to describe it.  But it is tasty.  On two days the girls climbed some trees and to get leaves to cook like greens.  They were tasty too.  The last day some of the men of the village gave us a treat by catching some fish in a nearby pond, and we had fish with spices.

As soon as lunch was over, we had a rest time.  The women and girls took this time to have a bath and to wash out saris.  Some of the women had only one or two saris, so they had to wash them each day.  After the rest period, I taught a health class to the whole group.  Joan again helped me with Hindi while the retreat leader translated into Kurukh.  Joan had brought along some flash cards to use for the health classes.  When the class was over, I held a dispensary from 4:00 to 7:00 P.M.  I saw only thirteen or fourteen patients each day, but I didn't have a nurse handy to help, requiring longer than usual to see one patient by the time I did the examination, maybe took a hemoglobin, gave an injection and counted out some tablets. I found out that a lot of the women and girls from this area were anemic.

When dispensary was over, it was time for the evening meal, again rice and dahl. Then one of the women led a short devotional and we had some songs and prayer—and it was time for bed again. I know Joan must have been pleased as she saw some of the women lead devotions for the first time. Some of them were not able to read from the Hindi Bible, but they knew the Scripture reference and would ask one of the girls to read and then would follow with their comments.

Our meeting at Burdadardh lasted from Sunday through Thursday. We followed the same schedule each day, closing the meeting after lunch on Thursday. Bernie came to take all of the bedding and some of the women to Murra Para where we were to have a preaching rally from Thursday night through Sunday noon.

Joan and I decided to walk with some of the women and girls to Murra Parra. It was a walk that again reminded me of some Sundays at Chidamoyo when I went calling with the Christian women. We walked the four or five miles to the village, making our way up and down hills and seeing small villages here and there. It was a warm day, so we were happy to finally reach our destination.

The meeting started about 6:30 P.M. with a sermon. After the message each evening, Bernie showed a movie—Zaccheus, the Prodigal Son, and The King of Kings on successive evenings. I was amazed at the crowds that gathered. It was difficult to count with so many, but the first night I am sure there were at least 500 with probably 800 the final night.

On Friday and Saturday morning, the meeting started at 6:30 A.M. with preaching. Then the men and women divided, and Bernie taught the men while Joan and I took turns teaching the women. After the separate classes, the women joined the men for announcements. The noon meal was eaten between 10:00 and 11:00 A.M.

On Friday after the meal, I made a call on a family in the village. Three people in the family were very sick and one little girl had died a few days before. All of them had malaria. Two had pneumonia and probably tuberculosis as well. I did what I could for them, and it was gratifying to see that they were better before I left. All of them should have been in a hospital.

Each of the two days starting at 2:00 P.M. and lasting until 7:00 P.M., I had a dispensary. I saw two bad cases of anemia—women with hemoglobins of only four grams. One woman had a typical case of pernicious anemia. I was able to give her two injections of Vitamin B12, but I left knowing that she needed more injections and also knowing that even though I recommended it, she would probably not go to a hospital. It was frustrating to leave knowing how much they needed help.

On Sunday morning we had a worship service with the Lord's Supper followed by Bernie's message. Classes followed and then the final meal. I went with Bernie and Joan to their home in Sitapur. It was good to be able to have a hot bath and to wash my hair.

On Monday morning we had eaten breakfast and I was helping Joan with laundry when we were interrupted with patients who started coming by 7:30 A.M. One of the Christian women who had been at the meeting at Burdadardh had told the people of her village that I would be with Bernie and Joan at Sitapur, so they had come early. Joan told me they had walked twelve miles. I started seeing patients at 9:00 A.M., taking a break for lunch and for tea at 4:00

P.M., and finished about 7:30 P.M. Joan sent two girls to help count out tablets and to translate for me, which really helped. Besides those who came from the surrounding villages, I also examined some of the hostel boys. The next morning I started at 8:00 A.M. and worked until 5:00 P.M. On Tuesday, I was able to examine all of the hostel girls, along with the other patients. The most pathetic case I saw was a little boy who was over a year old and weighed only 7½ pounds. At first glance, he also appeared to be blind, but he did respond to light. He had pneumonia and a severe case of Rickets. I mashed up a calcium tablet in water to give to him, and he took it down like the starved baby he was. We then tried some mashed banana and he ate some. Later Joan boiled an egg and mixed it with milk and he ate some of that too. It was obviously a case where the mother did not have sufficient milk and did not know she could feed the child other food.

On Tuesday night about 9:00 P.M., Joan, her son Timmy, and I left Sitapur to go to Bilaspur. We arrived there early Wednesday morning. On Thursday afternoon, Joan and Timmy and I left on the same train—I to go to Jhansi and Joan and Timmy to go to Mussorie to Woodstock School to be with the Getter girls for the summer months. I arrived in Jhansi about 9:30 the next morning where my driver was waiting for me. We picked up the boy whom I had left at the hospital, got some fruit and vegetables at the bazaar, and returned to Kulpahar. What a vacation!

## We Loved Visitors

One day during Pat Brown's stay, she, Leah, and I went to a meal with the family of the Maharajah of Sarila. It was a beautiful day for a drive; there even seemed to be fewer cattle and other traffic on the road. We started out in plenty of time so that if there was anything interesting for Pat to see, we could stop.  The first interesting thing was a group of men and women making bricks.

During the trip, we saw two elephants on the road.  Pat had said that she wanted to ride on an elephant; Leah said this was her chance.  Even though the elephant was small, it was still quite a climb to get on it.  For a person to get on an elephant, the animal must kneel down and the rider must climb up the back by stepping on one of the back feet.  I managed to get on, with some help from Pat, but she decided not to try.  As soon as I got on and the elephant stood up, he surprised Pat by swinging his trunk and hitting her with it.  I rode only a few steps, but long enough to know that riding on an elephant is more comfortable than riding on a camel.

After traveling on a very rough, dusty road, we arrived at the Maharajah's palace about 12:30 P.M.  He and his daughter-in-law greeted us, and we were seated in the large living room where we were served limeade and talked with them.  One by one the three children came in—two little girls and one boy.  They were a bit shy, but greeted us.  After talking for some time, we were called into the big dining room for a delicious meal of Indian food served by three Indian bearers (waiters).  After the meal, the Maharajah showed us pictures of his younger days when maharajahs had more power as well as pictures taken when he had been in London.  We were also shown some very old china plates that had an area beneath the plate where hot water could be placed to keep the food warm throughout the meal. Then we went outside and walked around the grounds and visited the women's quarters.  The women didn't live in the main palace, but in quarters adjacent to the palace.  In the early days, men were never allowed in the women's quarters, but that had changed somewhat in modern times.  After we walked, we went to the garden area for more conversation.

132

Later in the evening we had tea with more Indian food. It was a very enjoyable and informative day. I learned Indian history as we talked and discussed some of the days past in India.

In April of 1972, I welcomed my first visitor to Kulpahar. Pat Kenney, who had been serving at Chidamoyo Hospital in Rhodesia, visited on her way to the States. The children were delighted to have another Auntie Pat to visit and gave her a royal welcome. One little girl especially took to her. When I would go to the hostel, she would ask me to call Auntie Pat. One day some of the boys in the third grade or younger entertained her by telling her all the English phrases they had learned in school. They also recited for her Psalm 1, 23, and 100 in Hindi and sang some of the English songs I had taught them.

I was especially pleased when Jim Tingle, the minister of my home church, visited during the last part of January and the first of February 1974. He preached at our worship service on the Sunday he was present. At the end of the service three children came forward to give their lives to Christ.

We had a spiritual treat in March 1974 when we welcomed the Traveling College of Puget Sound Christian College in Seattle, Washington, led by Conley Silsby. I went with the driver to Kanpur to pick them up, but I had been give incorrect information and they didn't come the day I expected. I found a hotel and stayed overnight, but had no change of clothes. It was so hot that I washed my dress out, but then prayed they didn't call me in the night or I would have had to put on a wet dress. They arrived the next day, but it was the start of the Hindu holiday "Holy" when Hindus spray mud and colors on people. We prayed we would get to Kulpahar without being stopped and sprayed or having mud thrown on our vehicle. We arrived safely. The visitors led special services for four nights.

Conley and Carol Silsby told us that they wanted the members of the Traveling College to see what went on in running a children's home.  One morning I drafted five of the female members to help me collect the winter clothing.  Before the clothing was put away, each sweater was checked to see if buttons were missing and what needed to be mended or washed.  We checked the thirty-seven sweaters for the older girls and then went to the baby room to check sweaters, warm long pants, shirts, booties and hats.  One lady in the group said, "I have never seen so many clothes."

In October 1974, Gladys Jongeling, with whom I had served in Rhodesia, arrived.   She stopped in India on her way back to Rhodesia where she would continue her work at a medical technologist in the Mpilo Hospital in Bulawayo.  She had been in the States for two years and had just received her Master's degree in Medical Technology from the University of Oregon Medical School.  She was a great help to Goodwin, especially in hematology, her specialty and a weak area in his training.

Gladys described her visit by wring for my November 1974 newsletter.  She observed:

> An assault on all senses is immediately realized upon a first arrival in an Indian city.  There are a multitude of new sights, sounds, tastes and particularly scents to even a seasoned traveler.  Not unpleasant, but unusual to an American, yes, for that breed of culture is an insignificant presence in this vast land of blossoming population.
>
> Pleasant tree-bordered lanes lead the multitudes to innumerable destinations.  Single-laned tarmacadam arteries wind their ways out of the urban jungles to suburban habitations.  These pathways (well carpeted with pedestrians, cattle, water buffalos, wagons, bi-

cycles, buses autos, motorbikes, transport trucks, pigs or goats) were often also pleasantly lined by trees now grown to arching shade. Some thoughtful planners of generations back must have considered the current multitudes, the oppressive heat and the need for relief the shade gives. Attention to one's own presence is of necessity made with much loud beeping of horns; however this does not establish right of way, for what beast has yet attended traffic school? Such noise I am sure is for self reassurance that the battery of the vehicle is functional!

This former freeway driver survived the experience of back seat taxi driving and brought her jangled nerve endings to rest for a few weeks at Kulpahar Kids Home.

Although bush life is not unknown to me, I was sorely tempted to react at first by using such an expression as '"You're out of your guard"' or '"You need your head read"' to anyone who would elect to continue mission work under the conditions here. Not alone first day observations do I relate of this family within its haven of protective walls, but a considered reaction to what is being accomplished with and for these lives.

In no way is India simply a land of Hindus, Moslems. And a few Christians as geography texts might relate. More accurately this is a boiling mass of humanity in which a complicated cultural structure has evolved whereby society is served in all its places. Birth determines social position, but more importantly in a cash-and-carry world, birth determines occupation. Born of a sweeper family, a child will sweep. Born of a weaving family, a child will weave. Born of a professional family, a child may be privileged to enter a profession.

Why throw a spanner in the works and upset a workable system with something like Christianity?  A not impossible criticism of missions here.  But consider further.  These Kulpahar Kids are in a large part a result of the inherent faults of the established system:  products of unavoidable but unwanted pregnancies, illicit unions, inadequate parental provision for a number of reasons; none of these being fault that can be laid at the blame of the child.  These children have come here by way of distraught parents or relatives or concerned officials, continually with the plea, '"Help this child, I am unable to."

Here is the security of food, shelter, and clothing adequately provided.  In abundance is the love and discipline of a large family unit than can eliminate the fears of the abandoned.  Ever available are workers of the health unit to care for ever threatening tuberculosis, malaria, childhood diseases, etc.

If by some quirk of genetic inheritance the child's capabilities lie outside the realm into which he was born, he will not here be limited by this accident of birth.  In Christ we are neither Jew nor Greek bond nor free, made not female; there are to be no dividing lines of hostilities; we are all one in Him. (Galatians 3:28; Ephesians 2:12-17.)  One in the promise of inheritance, the potential of eternal values.  However, genetic code does not determine motivation and within the framework of Kulpahar a child will be encouraged, assisted (and disciplined with love) to go as far as capabilities determine.  Schools, colleges, and training centers around the country are available for trades and professions.  In this way these babes can grow into responsible young adults, continuing their Christian role into professions and married lives. Thus the Kulpahar Kids will hopefully be building a healthier community wherever the leaven of their lives may be felt.

After more than three weeks among these kids, some observations become more firmly impressed upon me:  the open joy on their faces at play or study, the uninhibited toddle toward open arms of an "Aunty" or older sister; the unfearing eyes of a young adult facing an uncertain future with confidence.  To attempt an adequate description of these reactions to the Kulpahar Kids that would be understood and appreciated by Western readers would necessitate a comparative and contrasted description of the millions of wee lives encountered along the streets and gutters of the cities and villages outside these walls."

Jim and Kay Price from Arizona arrived in February 1975, to complete the adoption of a little girl.  One night I took them to a Hindu wedding.   Of course, we were the only white people there. During the wedding, some little children sat in front of us.  They stared and stared at us.  We were served very sweet Indian candy.

I went to New Delhi to pick up the final adoption papers. Jim, Kay, and the child were  to follow to pick up the completed papers before they returned to the States.  I had hoped to get the papers so we could see them off and then welcome the Rostvit twins, but it didn't work out well at all. I went to the appropriate office to get the papers, but the official told me that he could not give them to me until the next day.  I pleaded with him to try to get them to me that day, but to no avail.

Meanwhile, I wanted to buy an engagement sari for Sheila, one of the  nurses who was to be engaged soon.  I don't remember how it came about, but I ended up on the back of a motor scooter going to a place where a man told me I could find the prettiest saris at the best price.  I hung on for dear life as we flew along the Delhi streets.  I was exhausted by the time I got back to the Y.W.C.A. where I was staying.

I had another problem: I had enough money for only one night in Dehi.  But since I would not get the papers, I would have to stay another night.  I laid down to rest.  Not long after that I heard a knock on the door.  It was Mr. Lal who had been sent by Leah and Dolly with money when they had gotten word of my delay.  God once again provided.

But I had still one more problem.  I had to send the Rostvit twins to Khajaraho by themselves since I still had to get the papers for the Prices and see them off.  I knew the driver would be expecting me, so I made a sign with his name on it for the Rostvits to hold up.  There was no way they could communicate since he didn't speak English and they didn't speak Hindi.  When they got to the airport, he was about to leave when he didn't see me.  But a man who knew him told him that there were two ladies holding up a sign with his name on it.  So they made it to Kulpahar.

I succeeded in getting the papers for the Prices and saw them off to the States.  I finally returned to Kulpahar a day later than I had planned.

Janice and Faye Rostvit were a real blessing to everyone at Kulpahar.   The only disappointment was that the visit wasn't long enough.  The children and adults enjoyed hearing them sing in Hindi, English, Urdu and Tamil.

They went with me to Larpur, and the school children and adults were fascinated by their musical instruments.  Soon

138

quite a crowd had gathered to hear them sing.  After they sang, the people gathered around as they presented a flannel graph lesson on Jesus in the temple.  Goodwin translated .  When they finished the flannel graph lesson, they brought out their puppets Big Mouth and Big Nose. The people were fascinated with the puppets and the lesson they gave.

On the way home from Larpur, they held the puppets out the window of the ambulance.  People on bicycles turned completely around to look at the puppets, not even watching where they were going.  Prem Sheila laughed so hard she said to me, "Aunty, tell them to stop, I am hurting from laughing so hard."

They also used the puppets for programs for the children with some of the young people assisting them.  In the two short days they were with us, they won the hearts of all the folk at Kulpahar.

I welcomed my mother and Marie Rayls, a long- time family friend and neighbor, to India on July 9, 1975.  I flew to New Delhi to meet them.  After spending a night in New Delhi, we went to Kulpahar.  This was quite an unforgettable experience for both of them, especially my mother who had never been in an airplane before.  They had a lot of time to rest, read, and play with the children.  When they sat on the front verandah, they would soon have a large group of children around them.  Two little girls spent a lot of time on Mom's lap.  I also  put Mom to work doing a lot of mending.  She also crocheted and made beaded necklaces.

I took them to visit a nearby fort and one day took them for a drive through the village.  After seeing all of the people and the crowded streets, they decided not to get out of the car.  I had to laugh one day as Marie was eating a meat ball made from goat meat.  Mom had told her she would be eating goat.  I think she had forgotten.  She said, "Is this goat meat?" I told her it was and she said, "It's good," and ate another meat ball. On our way back to New Delhi, we stopped one night in Agra so they could see the Taj Mahal and the Red Fort and do some shopping to buy gifts for their families and friends in the States.

Eleanor Daniel, Shirley Smith and Ruth Morgan visited in December 1975. We had hoped that Eleanor would come to assist Dolly with the school, but she didn't feel called to that work. But ever since that visit I have had a good friendship with Eleanor and Shirley.

And all too quickly, it was 1976, and the end of my first term in India was drawing to a close. I looked forward to furlough—and to my return to Kulpahar in 1977.

*Guests - the one on the right is Madonna's mother*

140

# Chapter 15

# Furlough—Not A Vacation!

It was with anticipation, yet sadness that I began my first furlough from India in March 1976. I knew how much I would miss my work, the staff, the children, and Leah and Dolly in the year I would be gone. But I looked forward to seeing Martin and Evelyn Clark in Japan, meeting the Japanese Christians who had been sending me regular support, finding new missionary friends, and meeting and visiting with those in the U.S. who had faithfully helped me with their prayers and gifts for the previous five years.

I was shocked when I heard the flight attendant announce that the temperature in Osaka was 48 F. when we landed in Japan. I had not anticipated this. I was wearing a pant-suit with short sleeves, and my sweater was packed in my suitcase. My second shock was to find out that I should have had a visa to visit Japan. But Martin Clark came to my rescue. We signed several papers—and finally four hours after my arrival, I received the necessary permission to stay in Japan for as long as two months.

My visit to Japan was a real blessing. I was impressed with the ministry of Osaka Bible Seminary. I also was able to attend the all-Japan Christian Convention and share the love of Christ that I saw on the faces of those in attendance. I showed slides of the work at Kulpahar and spoke both to Japanese Christians and the missionaries about the work in India.

After I reached the States, I participated in eight different churches in DVBS during the summer. I taught the children to say good morning and good afternoon in Hindi. They enjoyed learning that if they weren't good, I might give them a "*put-put*," that is, a spanking. Each day I wore a different Indian outfit and used some of the children to model Indian clothes. By the time I wrote my newsletter for May-July of 1976, I had traveled over five thousand miles by car and plane.

I also participated in four weeks of Christian service camp—two in Indiana and two in Oregon. I was the camp nurse as well as the missionary for two of the weeks. I enjoyed my time at the camps, although I got a little cold in Oregon. The water in the ocean was freezing! Each day I wore a different Indian dress and the children enjoyed that.

I attended the North American Christian Convention in Denver. While I was in Colorado, I especially enjoyed meeting Shallini Menge. Originally a resident at Kulpahar Kids Home, she had been adopted when she was five years old by Mr. and Mrs. George Menge of Rangely, Colorado.

At the end of the summer, I began visiting congregations in Iowa, Illinois, Michigan, Ohio, West Virginia, Virginia, Kentucky, North Carolina, Tennessee, Georgia, Florida, Missouri, Kansas, Oklahoma, and Arizona. I also visited with Christian friends in New Mexico. By the time my furlough was over, I had traveled over 20,000 miles in my little Volkswagen.

After having lived in Africa and India, I no longer enjoyed the cold Indiana winter. I experienced enough snow during December, January, and February to last me for a long time. One Sunday morning, I was scheduled to speak at the Faith Church of Christ in Burlington, Indiana. When I went out to start the car, I had no success. I called the minister of the church to tell him. Because of drifts on the country road, a neighbor brought his tractor to take me to meet a couple from Burlington who had a four-wheel drive vehicle. I must have been a sight in my boots and sari as I climbed up the small ladder onto the tractor. I spoke in the morning and showed the slides. The wind chill factor that morning was 60 below zero. Yes, I had enough cold weather to last me for a long time!

An exciting piece of news during that furlough was the birth of Goodwin and Sheila Herbert's first baby, a daughter Glory. Sheila had a C-Section, but everyone did well.

I met Dr. Steve Plettner, who would later join the team at Kulpahar, at the National Missionary Convention. God seemed to put us together on many different occasions. He felt a call to serve as a medical missionary. And that call eventually was focused on Kulpahar. He would complete his residency in internal medicine in June 1977.

The second son in a family of four boys, Steve had grown up in Sutton, Nebraska, from the time he was four years old. His parents and another family were instrumental in starting the Christian Church in Sutton. He wrote: "It was here that I received much sound Bible training and I think my parents for their wisdom." Steve had been baptized when he was eight years old at a Christian service camp.

He graduated from high school in 1965 and attended the University of Nebraska for his pre-med studies, continuing his medical training at the medical school at the university. During his college years, he became an active member of the Benson Church of Christ in Omaha. The elders of the church later wrote of him:

> Steve has been responsible for starting a college age Bible study group that is thriving. He has served on the Missionary Committee and is Chairman of our Evangelism and Missionary Committee this year. He is our song leader and also a member of our Church

choir. He attends a mid-week Bible study and is a member of our Church Board. We feel Steve's greatest talent lies in his concern and desire to make everyone aware of the Good News of our Lord.

Steve had spent six months in Rhodesia at the Chidamoyo Christian Hospital. He felt that it was there he began to mature spiritually. He was highly recommended by Dr. Jim Frasure of the Chidamoyo Christian Hospital.

He completed his residency in internal medicine in Omaha on June 30, 1977, and started working on July 1, 1977, with Dr. Garland Bare at the Student Health Center at the University of Nebraska in Lincoln. Dr. Garland Bare was well known as a missionary who had served in Thailand for twenty years. He taught Steve much about working in an Asian country. He recommended Steve highly.

My last week of furlough was spent packing boxes to take to Missionary Services, Inc. in Wheaton, Illinois, to be repacked for shipment to India. Several people had given me baby clothes andTupperware. The women from Michigantown (IN) Christian Church gave me two hundred bars of soap and nearly that many wash cloths.

After three or four days in Germany with the Sid Allsbury family on the return trip, I flew to New Delhi, arriving early in the morning of March 9. I had no trouble with immigration, but customs was another story. Since I was not Indian, the officials thought I had to be a tourist. They kept shifting me from one line to another. Before I finally got someone to help me, I had been back and forth to six different agents. But I didn't have to pay any customs, so I guess it was worth it!

My plane the next day was delayed leaving New Delhi, arriving in Khajuraho nearly an hour late. There were so many tourists on the flight that I waited a half-hour for my luggage. The mission driver was sick with malaria, so Leah had arranged for another driver from Kulpahar to pick me up. We stopped in Chhatapur to pick up Dr. Singh for her routine visit to the mission. After tea at her house, we had driven to within sixteen miles of the mission when the back axle of the vehicle cracked. We were fortunate that a truck from Kulpahar came by about ten minutes later and gave us a ride to the mission. Needless to say, I surprised everyone when I arrived in a big truck! I laughed and told them that since I had gained so much weight, I had broken down the ambulance and it had taken a truck to get me home.

But I was home again!

# Chapter 16

# Second Term at Kulpahar

### Day-by-Day Life

I was happy to resume my ministry at Kulpahar. On my first Sunday back, Mr. Maclawrence Lal asked that we thank God for the service that Mr. and Mrs. Goodwin Herbert had rendered in my absence. They both continued to be a blessing as they worked in the dispensary. All the staff was also blessed when Goodwin translated portions on the book of Matthew into Hindi from *Halley's Bible Handbook*. These were shared in our morning devotions before we began work each day.

An important ministry for Leah and Dolly was to find good Christian husbands for the girls. In October, November and December, three weddings occurred. One of the baby room workers was married to a young man from Kanpur in October. Then one of the auxiliary nurses was married in November to a young man from Roorke in Northern Uttar Pradesh. She had been in nurses' training with his sister, so she knew his family. Finally, one of the registered nurses was married in December to a young man who taught in the Christian Inter-College in Jhansi. She would work at the Christian hospital in Jhansi where she had taken her nurses' training.

Debbie Unruh from Dodge City, Kansas, served at Kulpahar from October 1977 through most of March 1978. She assisted with office work, taught shorthand to the secretary in the dispensary, helped teach the fourth and fifth grade girls' physical education classes, helped me with my twirling classes, and went with me on most of my mobile dispensaries. Debbie brought a ray of sunshine into our lives in the nearly six months she was with us.

Linda Stanton, a registered nurse, arrived in 1978 to work mostly with Leah in taking care of the children. We had prayed fervently for her to receive a visa. She had been turned down once, but had tried again and this time received a visa. Her presence allowed Leah to do more of the administration of the entire mission. However, since she was a nurse, she freed me from some of the work with the children in the orphanage, allowing me to work more with the village work and the dispensary.

One of my unforgettable experiences was the time I hit an ox with my bicycle. Prem Sheila and I had returned from a mobile dispensary, she on the back of the bicycle. There was a wall to my left as I cycled out the gate. Unknown to me, two oxen were running on the other side of the wall. As I went through the gate, I hit one of them. Prem Sheila was able to jump off the bicycle and was not injured, but I ended up with a big hematoma on my leg. It eventually had to be drained, and I was in bed for a week.

## The Doctor Is Coming!

Steve Plettner felt God calling him to Kulpahar. I had told him that it would be best if he were married when he came to serve in India. We were all praying for him to find a good wife. He did, and he and Ann Tolliver were married on April 29, 1977. Ann was a niece to Charles Selby, a missionary serving in the Philippines. She had been working with Charles as his secretary since 1969. His loss would be our gain!

One day in 1978, when Ziden and Helen Nutt were visiting, a man from Hamirpur came to investigate the application for a visa for the Plettners. I decided to wear my white sari that day. I had to make a trip on my cycle, and the sari got caught in the chain, leaving it soiled with grease. Fortunately, Helen solved the problem by using shortening to remove the grease. Since the sari was a lightweight material, it dried quickly. I showed the official around the outpatient building and explained about the number of patients. He said: "I believe you could use some help!" Not long after, our prayers were answered when Steve and Ann, as well as Linda Stanton, received their visas. It is interesting that this particular official was in that position for less than a year, but long enough for the visas to be granted. God surely put him there for a special time.

Steve and Ann arrived the last part of 1978. I had worked on the house where I was living to give them their own big bedroom-office and bathroom. I used what had been the dining room for my bedroom and had my own bath. The living room was used for a dining room. Many people advised that it wouldn't work for a single woman and a married couple to live in the same house. But we respected each other's privacy and got along quite well. Ann liked to clean house, but didn't like to cook' I liked to cook, but didn't like to clean house. So Ann did the cleaning and I did the cooking. Steve wrote a friend about how well it was working out, saying: "Madonna likes to cook and Ann likes to clean house and I like to eat and I like a clean house."

The name of my newsletter was changed from "Message from Madonna" to "Medical Evangelism in Kulpahar, India—Teaching, Preaching, and Healing," using the Scripture from Matthew 9:35. Steve wrote most of the articles for this joint newsletter.

In January-February 1979, Steve wrote about his work in the clinic and one of our mobile dispensaries:

> The process of receiving health care brings a person into contact with a number of different people. For our patients here, the same is true when they come to the Kulpahar Christian Dispensary. The patients are greeted by the secretary who gets their charts ready; then the nurses record their vital signs; then they are seen by the doctor and then go to get the medicines prescribed. The patients pay a token for these services and pay the cost of the medicine unless these medicines are donated and then they are given to them free. We intend to use the Dispensary and proposed small hospital only as a base for outreach programs in the villages. Many of the nearly 100,000 people who live in and hear Kulpahar have no idea who the Lord Jesus Christ is—"'And how shall they believe in Him whom they have not heard?'" Traditional medical missions have placed most of their emphasis on the hospital. This has been an effective witness in the past; however we feel that with the thousands and thousands of people in rural India who are as yet unreached by the Gospel we will be able to reach more people if we go to them. The real fruit for evangelism will be with the contacts we make in the surrounding villages. Madonna has developed already four sites for mobile dispensaries. Our vision is to greatly expand our involvement in these villages and others taking with us the good news of Christ, forgiveness of sin and eternal life.

Besides staying busy at the hospital and the mobile clinics, Steve and Ann were able to find Mr. Victor Lal to teach them Hindi. They spent April through June 1979 studying Hindi in language school at Landour, north of Kulpahar. It had been hard for them to study and work; this allowed them to make more rapid progress in speaking Hindi.

# Faithful Staff Workers

One of the faithful staff members was Gideon Singh, the son of Dr. Grace Singh who had come to Kulpahar to help since even before I had arrived. He was an electrician and had taken some Bible courses, allowing him to fulfill three functions—electrician, evangelist, and driver. One time we were going to a mobile dispensary when some young men stopped the ambulance and told him that if he continued to play Christian music, they would kill him. He calmly looked at them and said "O.K." He knew it was an idle threat and stayed calm.

I mentioned before the many preparations Leah and Dolly made for weddings for the Kulpahar Kids. On October 29, 1979, it was my turn to make the preparations. Gideon S. Singh and Punitha Carunia were married that day. Punitha had worked for me as a secretary since July 1974, and Gideon had been my driver, electrician and evangelist since September 1977. In India, most marriages are still arranged by the parents, but by 1979, especially in the case of Christian young people, their parents let them choose their mate. Punitha was reared in South India at the Dohnavur Fellowship which had been started many years earlier by Amy Carmichael. So when she came to me one afternoon and told me that she and Gideon would like to marry, it was necessary to write to her "Aunties" in Dohnavur to tell them of her desire to marry and to tell them about Gideon. I also asked them to write to Dr. and Mrs. Singh, Gideon's parents, who lived in Chhatarpur. I was very happy to be able to help arrange this marriage. I had to admit to both the folks at Dohnavur and to Dr. and Mrs. Singh that part of the reason for my happiness was purely selfish.  Punitha had been such a blessing in the office.  I had feared that she would marry someone from South India and leave Kulpahar—and that would mean I would have to teach her job to someone else.  We had also learned to love and appreciate Gideon so much.

After the appropriate correspondence, the engagement ceremony was held in the living room of our house in May.

I had attended many weddings at Kulpahar, but I had done little to help with them. But I knew what a job it was to get the food supplies ordered for the wedding dinner and to make the other preparations.  Fortunately, Leah loaned us many of the plates, cups, and cooking utensils that we needed and gave us her food supervisor to help me to plan the food order.  Mr. Lal and his young men decorated the church building for the wedding, and Linda Stanton and Sosan John helped get the flower girls ready.  Steve was the wedding photographer.

On Monday morning, October 29, the day of the wedding, the bus that Gideon's parents had arranged to bring the wedding party from Chhatarpur arrived with a sick groom. Gideon had run a fever of 103 since Saturday, but since the banns had been announced, the wedding had to take

*Madonna escorting Punita down the aisle at her wedding*

152

place. Mr. Lal brought some chairs so that the couple could sit for part of the ceremony. And with Gideon's big smile, one would never have known that he was sick. Many of Punitha's sisters who worked in the Kulpahar area and one of her Aunties from Dohnavur came for the wedding. It was a happy reunion for them. Punitha had asked me to walk down the aisle with her, and Christina, her Aunty from Dohnavur, stood up with her. It was a beautiful wedding in spite of the groom's illness.

## Babies, Babies, and More Babies

One of the most interesting people in the village of Kulpahar was Ram Kumar Goel. His wife came to the clinic pregnant with her tenth child, but she also had pain in her right side. A blood test indicated that she had appendicitis. She was seven months pregnant and needed to be in the hospital for observation. But all Ram Kumar could think of was the baby she was due to deliver. He so much wanted a boy after nine girls. I could not convince him that she needed to be in the hospital. He cared nothing for his wife, but only for the baby that he hoped was a boy. I really wanted to slug the man! Fortunately, he had a nephew who spoke English. I explained the need to him, and he finally convinced his uncle that she needed to be in a hospital. Finally she delivered another girl. Now he had ten girls and no sons. He also had an eleventh daughter that the doctor named Asha, meaning "hope."

Finally he had his first son. He was so happy to have a son that he gave candy not only to the staff at the Chhatarpur hospital, but to all of our teachers and dispensary staff. (He had many of his daughters in our school.) Unfortunately, since his wife was about forty years old, the son was born mentally deficient. His wife begged me to do something to help their son.  They had been to countless hospitals trying to find help.  I had to tell her that there was nothing to be done, but to love and care for him.  When John and I visited in India in 1989, we were invited to their home for tea.

The maternity work continued to increase.  Sixteen babies were born in September 1977, and by October 16, we had already had ten deliveries for that month.  Most of these babies were born to girls having their first babies, though some women were having their eighth or ninth child.

An exciting occasion was when I delivered a son to Steve and Ann.  When Ann found out that she was pregnant, she was determined that I would deliver the baby.  I told her that I would, but first I wanted her to be checked by an obstetrician at the Jhansi Christian Hospital.  The doctor said she thought Ann would have no problems, so we planned a home delivery in one of the side rooms of our home where we put a delivery table.  Naturally, her labor pains started at night.  Steve was a doctor, but early that morning, he was acting as an encouraging husband and allowing me to take care of delivering the baby.  Wouldn't you know!  Just about the time for Ann to deliver, the lights went out.  I will never forget hearing Steve running toward the generator yelling at the men, "You need to get the electricity on—my wife is delivering a baby."  Fortunately, they got the problem fixed just long enough for me to deliver a son and to put in a few sutures—and then the lights went out again.  Our Muslim neighbors, having heard the excitement during the night, kindly brought over some tea and parathas (an Indian fried bread) for our breakfast.

I just knew that I would deliver a boy--it had been just seventeen years before on the same date that I had delivered a son to Ziden and Helen Nutt at Mashoko.  These are the only two babies I have delivered to missionaries.  Needless to say, it was an exciting time and this was only baby ever delivered to missionaries at the mission.

A week after Caleb was born, Goodwin and Sheila Herbert were blessed by a son as well. Ann had this to say about Caleb and Samuel in our September, October, November 1979 newsletter.

No, I haven't got the story wrong, Caleb and Joshua entered the promised land together, but Caleb and Samuel entered this world together—almost, and so a new story has begun. The last newsletter just informed you of Caleb's arrival and Sammy entered the scene exactly one week after Caleb was born, so in this newsletter we'll introduce you more completely to both of them, because I'm sure in the years to come you'll be hearing more about them.

Caleb Andrew Santosh Plettner—"What a long name for such a little boy" is usually the comment we get when people find out his name—but at the rate he's growing—from 7 lbs. 4 oz. at birth to 15 lbs. at three months—he'll soon be big enough for his name. My great grandfather Selby's name was Caleb and Steve's great grandfather Plettner's name was Andrew. Then, of course, Caleb and Andrew are both unique Bible characters. Caleb had enough faith in God to believe what looked impossible was possible and Andrew brought his brother to the Lord. We gave him the Indian name of Santosh because we wanted him to be proud of his birth in India. The Christian people on the mission gave their children names beginning with the father's first initial. Santosh means satisfaction or contentment, which we have wished him and pray that he will have in his life of service to our Lord. Caleb is the first missionary's child to be born in Kulpahar in at least 50 years and perhaps the very first. Other missionaries have had children, but none of them were born at Kulpahar. This was possible for us because Madonna is such an experienced and capable nurse-midwife.  Steve and I are very grateful that we could have the delivery at home.  It made everything so much nicer and much easier than having to travel 100 miles over rough roads and then having to be in a hospital.

Samuel Hal Herbert is the first son, but second child of Goodwin and Sheila, our medical technologist and head nurse.  Both are also Kulpahar Kid's.  They departed from the tradition for Samuel's name because, like Hannah, they prayed for a son and they wanted him to have a Bible name.  His middle name is also interesting.  When they were trying to think of a name after he was born, their Auntie Leah (Moshier) jokingly suggested that since their daughter's name was Glory, they should name him Hallelujah—thus Hal for his middle name.

I have known Sheila since I was quite young.  My home church adopted her and sent money support. I never imagined that that little girl I used to hear about and see pictures of on the bulletin board would someday be a co-worker in India, and not in my wildest imagination would I have thought that our sons would be playmates here in Kulpahar."

After I left Kulpahar, Ann and Steve had another son. Sheila was the midwife who delivered him.

A baby boom of sorts occurred after we opened the new hospital in 1980.  Only twenty-nine babies had been born in the old dispensary from January through April 17, 1980, but from April 18 through July 22, eighty-seven babies were born.  It was an exciting time with the new facilities to enhance our work.  One of our enthusiastic nurses put it this way, "Aunty, this is fun."  The same nurse was called one night by another nurse because two women were about the give birth to their babies at the same time.

Three sets of twins were born—two sets of identical boys and one set of a boy and girl. The three baby boys were born within six minutes. The nurse on duty called me to help her with one patient who needed the help of the vacuum extractor to give birth to the first of her two boys. The vacuum extractor was a big help in difficult deliveries. We would put a cup on the baby's head and then pump up the extractor so it would hold. As the woman pushed during a contraction, we pulled with the extractor. Sometimes this was the help she needed. It was better than forceps, requiring less space.

Women from twenty-three different villages and cities came to the hospital to deliver. Most were from Kulpahar. But one woman came from Madhya Pradesh, the state south of us. She came because she knew her sister who lived in Kulpahar could help her. Women also came from Rath, twenty-five miles away. All of them came and stayed because they wanted to use the facilities of the new hospital.

We shared John 16:21 "A woman when she is in travail hath sorrow, because her hour is come; but as soon as she is delivered of the child, she remembereth no more the anguish, for joy that a man is born into the world." Prem Sheila Rohit was on duty most afternoons from 2:00 to 5:00 P.M. and did personal witnessing to the patients. She also passed out tracts to them if they could read. Every woman left the hospital with her new baby dressed in baby clothes sent by Christian women from the States or made by Christian Indian women. When we gave them the clothing, we told them that the gifts were given to share the love of Christ. We also had our morning devotions just outside the post-partum ward so that the patients and their relatives could hear us sing songs of God's love and salvation through

Christ and could hear us read Scriptures and pray for God to help us in our work each day.

## Other Medical Opportunities

We took the mobile dispensaries to additional villages. One was at Kalmalpura.  With a population of only seven hundred, this village was much smaller than most where we went.  The village was so small that  we had to turn the Jeep around and back in the last one-quarter mile since there was no place to turn around in the village.  As Steve wrote in one of our newsletters,

> It is like going back in time a couple hundred years. You see no new buildings.  The women, if they are out of doors at all, have their faces covered.  The old Hindu belief is that a married woman should not be seen by other men.  So in Kalmalpura if we want to do some teaching about healthy babies, Madonna goes to a home where the women have gathered to talk to them—no men allowed and that includes male doctors.

For some time I had wanted to start well-baby clinics in the villages, giving babies and children their vaccination against smallpox, the inoculation to prevent diph-

*Groundbreaking for the hospital at Kulpahar*

theria, tetanus and whooping cough, and the drops to prevent polio, all given at no charge. But there never seemed to be a time when I could do it. However, with Linda Stanton's arrival to help with the hostel work, I had more time. Starting in November 1978, I was able to start five clinics. We soon changed the name to "Under-Fives" and "Maternity clinics," because I expanded our services by also examining ante-natal patients and teaching the mothers how they could give better care to their children.

The "team" for the clinics was made up of an office girl, one of the nurses, Gideon the driver to pass out tracts, the laboratory assistant, and I, better known as "Nurse Aunty." In the villages I was known as "Aunty Gee" or "Birdie Bye." "Gee" is a term of respect and "Birdie Bye" is big sister, also a term of respect.

The first clinic started was in the village of Kulpahar at the home of a carpenter at the Home. Twenty-one babies and children from six months to five years were brought for the "Triple-Antigen" inoculation against tetanus-pertussis (whooping cough)-diphtheria. The next clinic was also in a different area of Kulpahar at the request of a young man whose wife had given birth to her babies in our dispensary. More than thirty babies and children came the first day. But only about twelve returned for their second inoculation.

After this, we started clinics in Larpur, Sungra and Kamalpura, the three villages where we had mobile dispensary work. The response of children coming back to repeat their series was not good, probably because the babies had a fever after their inoculation. I always explained to the mothers that the child would get some fever for a short time, but they just didn't understand that this short, mild fever would protect their children from having the more serious disease. It was frustrating, but we kept trying.

The well-baby clinics also provided another opportunity to share God's word.  As we entered a village, the loud speaker was playing Christian songs in Hindi.  Then as the inoculations were being given, Gideon told a Bible story over the loud speaker.  We also passed out hundreds of tracts and sometimes sing choruses with the children.

# Bricks and Mortar

When I returned from furlough, work continued on the well that had been begun before I left.  The goal was to finish it before the monsoon season.  The laborers continued to remove dirt and stones, digging to forty feet.  The original goal had been to dig to forty-five feet, but the final decision was to stop at forty feet.  To celebrate the conclusion of the digging, a service of praise was held on May 5, 1977, with Mr. Lal reading Scripture and leading in prayer.

Then the masons and laborers had the formidable task of lining the well with granite stones.  This task required 600 stones, each of them weighing110 pounds.  The finished well was 45 feet deep and 19½ feet wide.  Some of the workers predicted that by the end of the monsoon season the water would be within four to five feet of the top.

The well was dedicated on September 22, 1977.  At the dedication, Goodwin read from John 4:14: "But whosoever drinketh of the water that I shall give him shall never thirst, but the water that I shall give him shall be in him a well of water springing up into everlasting life." As dispensary and mission staff, masons, and laborers gathered for the short service, we were grateful to God for the gift of water.  None of the masons or laborers was Christian.  As Goodwin read the Scripture from John 4, my prayer was that these men would seek the water that Jesus alone could give—the water that could be in them a well of water springing up into everlasting life.

*Dedication of the hospital*

The next project was to complete the outpatient building. It was dedicated on December 28, 1977. The dispensary staff, along with Leah, Dolly, Debbie Unruh, and some of the other mission employees gathered on the front verandah of the building. I cut the crepe paper ribbon, officially opening the building. As we occupied the building, Goodwin enjoyed his large well-equipped laboratory, and the two large exam rooms were a real asset for our work.

Construction of the hospital came next, though it wasn't completed for a couple of years. The new hospital was finally finished, however, and the dedication was held on April 17, 1980. The name of the hospital was *a-sha aur a-rog-ya ka ghar*, meaning "Home of Health and Hope." The mission staff, the Kulpahar Kids, and many friends shared in the service. Steve gave the welcoming address in Hindi. Fellow missionary Ralph Harter from Kanpur braved the stifling heat to travel to Kulpahar to give the sermon. He spoke about the meaning of *shalom*, the Hebrew word for peace, so effectively that for days some people in the village were heard greeting each other with "Shalom, Shalom." The choir sang, and Goodwin gave a special message dedicating the new hospital to the honor and glory of Jesus Christ.

A special part of the program was devoted to the dedication of the maternity ward to Dr. Grace J. Singh. Her son, Gideon, read a tribute to his mother written by Leah Moshier and unveiled the bronze plaque which was permanently placed at the entrance to the maternity ward. Dr. Singh and I cut the ribbon to officially open the hospital. The next morning the first patient was admitted and delivered a baby boy.

## More Than a Mobile Dispensary

Another mobile dispensary was established in a village of three to four hundred people located five or six miles from the mission. When I asked village leaders if they would have any objection to our telling Bible stories when we came, they said they not only would like Bible stories during the dispensary times, but they also wanted us to come in the evening to show filmstrips. When my filmstrip projector arrived from the States, male staff members went in the evening to show filmstrips in the villages.

We began doing mobile dispensaries every Tuesday morning and Wednesday afternoon. We alternated going to Larpur and Sungra on Tuesday. On Wednesday we went to Kamalpura. Most of the time three

*The hospital*

162

staff members went with me— Gideon, Prem Sheila Ro-hit, and one of the nurses. We had a record player to play songs, Scripture and sermons. We had two records in the Bundelkhand language, understood better than Hindi by most of the people in the area.

We continued to pass out tracts to the boys who came before their classes started at school at Larpur. One boy was beaten by his teacher because, his teacher said, he was studying the tracts more than he was studying for his school work. But the boy continued to come to get more.

One of the mobile dispensaries was in the village of Sungra about four miles from the mission. We announced our arrival by playing music and sermonettes in Bundelkhan-di over the van's P.A. system. With both Steve and me work-ing, we could see more patients. We felt that some patients came mostly out of curiosity to see the "white" doctor and nurse, but others had serious problems that were even more than we could care for in which case we recommended a hospital to them. I sometimes only translated for Steve while he saw most of the patients. While we saw patients, Gideon took the children aside to tell them Bible stories—and we always passed out tracts.

The mobile dispensary became increasingly important for sharing Christ with the village people. Steve, Goodwin, Gideon, and Michael Lal, the twenty-year-old son of the headmaster and preacher, regularly went to villages at night to show filmstrips. The good will created by the mobile dispensary provided an open invitation to do this in every village where we had a mobile dispensary. In each village someone offered the side of his whitewashed house on which to project the filmstrips. If there was electricity, they graciously allowed us to run a long extension cord into their home to power the van's audiovisual equipment. If there was no electricity, we had a battery and voltage inverter which allowed us to run it without electricity.

Ziden Nutt of Good News Productions had produced for us a series of five film- strips with coordinated cassette tapes. The series entitled "What the Bible Says explained what it means to be a Christian, how to become a Christian, how a Christian looks at the world and other people, and how an Indian Christian lives and worships.  Since very few people in these villages knew anyone who was a Christian, they had no concept of rebirth or the Christian life.  The filmstrips communicated these concepts in their own language and cultural setting.

Large crowds—sometimes as many as four to five hundred—usually gathered to watch.  We were even asked to begin showing film-strips at a second location in one of the villages because the people in that section of town wanted to see them too.  We praised the Lord for the knowledge of modern electronics being used for His glory.

## Village Evangelism

Goodwin translated a series of filmstrips on the Life of Christ into Hindi.  He and Gideon began to go to Kulpahar and Sungra to show these filmstrips.  Between 150 and 200 adults and children saw the filmstrips.  The viewers showed a lot of interest and wanted Goodwin and Gideon to show more.  We hoped to set up a regular schedule to go to two different villages each week until the series was completed.

We started three Bible schools during the last part of 1979, a result of the V.B.S. programs we had conducted earlier in these villages.  The people actually requested us to come to do the Bible schools. Steve wrote in our January-February, 1980 newsletter:

> When the children in the villages following last summer's VBS kept asking us to come back to teach them more, we realized that God was allowing us to do just what we had asked Him. We had a meeting of those who volunteered to teach. Since most of them had helped with VBS, they elected two villages as a trial. They picked Kamalpura because of the receptivity of this small village, and Sungra because there had been a very large attendance there. Since some of these teachers were already teaching Sunday School at the Kulpahar Kids' Home Chapel, and others were going to teach in both villages, we decided to go to one village on alternate Saturdays and the other on alternate Sundays.

The Bible school at Kamalpura began with about eighty children and adults, but the initial excitement wore off. However, about fifty continued to attend faithfully, including three young men who rarely were absent.

Sungra was true to expectations that attendance would be large. The most we had was 258; there were usually 150 in attendance. This created a problem because we had only seven teachers. The primary class, with an enrollment of over 100, had to be split into three sections. The real problem was with the junior high and high school boys, many of whom came only to cause trouble. I began a junior high girls' class because the boys bothered them so much. The boys also roamed around and disrupted the little younger kids' classes. Our van was also looted. The situation was so bad that many of the teachers began to dread going, but God provided encouragement. Many of the children, even after weeks, could tell the stories and recite their memory verses. When one teacher had been absent the time before, the class told her that they wanted only her as a teacher and that they never wanted her to be away again.

Satisfied with these accomplishments, we neglected the third village where VBS had been held. We thought that we might not find teachers. However, God would not let us be complacent. Some older boys from Larpur happened to be visiting relatives in Kamalpura one Sunday when we were there, and they sat in one of the classes. Not long after, when we were in Larpur for mobile dispensary, we were given a letter signed by nineteen older boys asking us to come there also. A second letter came the next time we were there. How could we refuse? Some of the teachers in the other Bible schools were willing to go to Larpur every other week. Now regular Bible teaching went on where there had never been Christian converts.

We planned to have Vacation Bible Schools again in 1980. We were prepared to increase our VBS outreach. Plenty of supplies were ordered far in advance, and the teachers were organized. But the supplies never arrived; we never learned what happened. Even if Satan thwarted our plans, we had no intention of waiting until it was too late to have VBS. With leftovers and make-do supplies VBS started. Each week we went to a different village for six days, praying each week that the materials would come. By the time school and the monsoons began in July, we had gone to two new villages and two of the three villages where we had gone the previous year. A VBS for the third was planned, but circumstances prevented it being conducted.

Twenty volunteer teachers were recruited from the small number of Christians at Kulpahar and the young men from the Kids' home. They faithfully taught six evenings a week for four weeks in spite of the heat. Each class had two to three teachers, so it wasn't necessary that they all go every time. The teachers were in charge—each week a different one was the VBS director and took full responsibility for the details for that week.

The staff gathered each evening about 5:30 P.M. By this time the beating sun was low in the sky. Even though the temperatures were sometimes over 100, it was still cooler than at midday. One or two vans were loaded with teachers and supplies to travel three or four miles to the village where VBS was being conducted that week. The music from the PA systems told the kids that we had arrived and they came running. The opening consisted of singing a few songs, an object lesson or one of Jesus' parables, Scripture reading and prayer. These children had no idea of what Christian worship was like—the only thing they were familiar with was idol worship. Following the opening, children went to classes. On the last day awards were given for the students who had memorized all their verses. The pencils, combs, crayons, coloring books and other small prizes that churches in America had sent were put to good use. Our prayer was that God would use this program and regular Bible school for the glory of His Son, Jesus Christ—that His light would be known by those living in darkness.

We had many interesting experiences in the villages where we did our mobile dispensaries and Bible schools. We became acquainted with the *sadhu* of Larpur. *Sadhus* are Hindu holy men and religious teachers, usually self-appointed, who live an austere life, receiving their food and other necessities from the people. Of course, they do no work, but since it is a thing of great merit in Hinduism to care for these "Holy Men," they live well enough. They often make long pilgrimages to "holy places," taking nothing with them but their clothes. (Since most are very scantily dressed or naked, they don't take much.) We frequently saw these *sadhus* along the road crawling on their stomachs toward Allahabad, one of the most holy places in India, located some distance from Kulpahar.

167

The *sadhu* of Larpur came to our attention the first Sunday that we held Bible school there. This seemed to be no coincidence. For the last nine years we had held a mobile dispensary only a few hundred yards from where he lived, but had never seen him before the first day of Bible school. He yelled and jabbered in obscene language to try to disrupt the teaching. He sat in the primary class, definitely not for the purpose of learning. Once he tried to unnerve me by stripping naked in front of me while I was teaching. He was certainly an agent of Satan.

The villagers told us that he had been crazy for twenty years, but we thought his behavior was put on. His grandfather had been an extremely wealthy man who owned the entire village. The village folks described his wealth as being so great that the money piled up would be taller than a six-foot tall man. The grandfather had done something evil to one of the village Brahmins (a Hindu caste which is supposed to be the priestly caste most worthy of Hindu salvation). He and many of his relatives had been poisoned for this. The family wealth began to dissipate until by now the *sadhu* was the only one left—with nothing. Years earlier his only sister had gone crazy and died mysteriously. The Larpur boys said he was under a curse.

He finally gave up disrupting mobile dispensary and Bible school and became quite sane. We were told that he had done this two other times in the previous twenty years only to return to his insanity. But for the time being, he now sat and spoke with us intelligently when we talked to him about the one God who gave His Son on Calvary.

Larpur was the one village where the boys really listened to the Bible stories with interest. What was unique was that the women asked me to teach them. This was a wonderful opportunity, for Hindu women generally are not allowed to be in public very much. But in order to respect the customs,

I taught them in the courtyard of a home near where the children's classes met.

Another Bible school was in the small village of Bamori, near Larpur. We were asked by a couple of men from the village to do the Bible school. We were grateful for the opportunity, and the Lord provided the teachers.

## The Missionary's Best Friend—The Forwarding Agent

The missionary's forwarding agent is significant key to the ministry overseas. Mine were especially important people. Janice Reed served as my first forwarding agent from August 1960 until 1965, when Gene and Mary Helen Sandefur assumed responsibility. When Gene became too busy in his ministry to help Mary Helen, she did all of the work. She was amazing. Besides serving as forwarding agent, she cooked breakfast in a restaurant, had a full-time job as housewife and mother, and kept a spic-and-span house, and was an excellent cook. She also went calling with Gene. I was thankful for her ministry.

It was a shock in late 1977 to receive a telegram from Dr. Eubanks, President of Johnson Bible College, telling me of the tragic death of Janice Day Reed. Janice and I grew up together in the Normanda Christian Church, and we both graduated from Prairie High School. I was four years older than she, but because I did my nurses' training and worked a year before going to J.B.C., we started college together and graduated the same year. Even after Janice gave up being my forwarding agent, she continued to write articles about my ministry and also wrote the book *To an African Drum* about my years in Rhodesia.

# Blessings from Visitors

We at the mission looked forward to another visit from the Rostvit twins in February 1978.  They had been with us for only two nights in 1975, but this time, they were scheduled to stay for a week.  As the ambulance sent to meet them arrived, I didn't see double.  Only one twin was in the vehicle. I was sure one  had stayed at the gate to play a joke on me, but it was no joke.  We were sorry to learn that Janice was in traction in the Christian Hospital in Bilaspur with a pinched sciatica nerve.  We were happy that Faye was willing to leave her and come to experience her first time of singing and telling stories with her puppet alone.  She said: "I only feel half here."  But she blessed us with her singing in Hindi and English and other Indian languages. I joined her for a song in Shona.  Everyone fell in love with her puppet and the stories she told about Christ.  She also took several pictures that were used for Good News Productions (Joplin, MO) to produce a filmstrip for our use.  Since Faye wanted to get back to be with Janice as soon as possible, she was not able to stay for a full week.  Though we had to change dates from the original schedule, she still went to the villages, one day even going to two villages.

I was especially happy to learn that Ziden and Helen Nutt of Good News Productions and their daughter, Karolyn, who had just completed her first year at Ozark Bible College, would arrive in India on June 6, 1978.  Ziden and Helen were to stay until July 18, Karolyn until August 15.  Ziden's primary task was to construct the boxes for holding the equipment such as the filmstrip projector, loud speaker, and tape recorder so that the new ambulance would not only be equipped for mobile dispensary work, but could also be used for village evangelism.  Faye Rostvit had given Ziden the pictures she had taken when she visited.  He hoped to bring some filmstrips in which these pictures were used.  I also hoped to get some valuable advice from him about building since he had constructed much of the hospital at Chidamo-yo. Leah and I had several projects lined up for Helen and Karolyn. Little did we know how timely their arrival would be.

The day after the Nutts arrive, the wind started blowing dust into the house. We hurried to get clothes off the line and the windows closed. Helen asked, "Do you have tornados here?" I said, "No." But about two or three minutes later while I was closing the last of the windows, Helen and Karolyn heard a large crash. Then one of the laborers was at the front door with the news that the roof of the back verandah of the outpatient building had been blown off. I told him to see if there was any other damage. He returned to tell us that the roof of the drug room had also been blown off. We got our umbrellas, and Karolyn, Ziden, Helen, and I hurried over to the outpatient building and pushed the medicines to the back of the cement shelves to try to keep them dry. There was a leak in the laboratory, but it did not affect any of the expensive equipment. A very large tree had been uprooted on one of the other compounds.

Ziden had another job to help the carpenter repair the roof. He also showed the carpenter how to do it in a way that would prevent the winds from ripping it off. Once again God had blessed, for I had enough funds to complete the repairs.

After the roof was repaired, Ziden was able to get started on the cabinet for the equipment. Goodwin and Gideon were eager for him to complete the installation of the cabinet for the new ambulance. They had already been out to four villages in the old ambulance, sometimes using electricity for showing the filmstrips and sometimes using the battery and inverter. Ziden had to use equipment that he was not used to, but he managed with the drill operated by running a heavy string. Gideon was able to see how he put in the panel with the electric outlets, both for 110 and 220 volts. After the cabinet was completed, Ziden showed Gideon and Goodwin how to operate the equipment. Ziden was disappointed that the new ambulance was not ready so he could install the cabinet in it to see it at work. However, he was able to see the ambulance, for it was nearly completed when we went to New Delhi for their departure. He asked the man doing the body work to mount the brace for holding the loud speakers.

The week after Ziden and Helen left, the driver and I went to New Delhi to bring the new ambulance back. My carpenters cut out the place on the cabinet where the wheelbase and diesel tank were. Before Karolyn left, she was able to see it in operation so that she could assure her dad that everything was working well.

Ziden brought the series of five filmstrips that had been produced by Good News Productions. While he was at Kulpahar, Maclawrence Lal translated the English commentary to Hindi and put on tape the commentary for the first filmstrip, which showed what the Bible says about God and His Word. Ziden added some instrumental music and singing by our young men and women to the tape and showed the first filmstrip for one of the prayer meetings before he left.. Mr. Lal was able to finish the translation for the other four filmstrips and get them on tape so that Karolyn could take them home with her for Ziden to complete.

Not only did Ziden keep busy, but Helen and Karolyn did as well. Helen typed my contributors list, updated my contributor's cards, cleaned out my files, and updated my address book. She also cooked many delicious meals. Karolyn worked nearly every day in the baby room, giving bottles, feeding cereal to the babies and changing wet and dirty diapers. She also went with me on mobile dispensaries. Karolyn was also a good cookie baker. Between Helen's good meals and Karolyn's baking, I managed to gain nearly ten pounds in ten weeks.

We were really happy to welcome Steve and Ann's parents in January 1980. They had come to see their new grandson. I moved into the Indian nurses' quarters while they were there so they could stay in the house. They enjoyed going to the surrounding villages with us for the mobile dispensaries and Bible schools. They made delicious apple butter, painted signs in Hindi, typed up cards for a new drug order system, and repaired some of the electrical appliances. They taught me a new card game and then I proceeded to win the games, leading Ann's dad to call me "Ace".

After Steve and Ann's parents left, I decided to stay where I was in the nurses' quarters. I knew they worried that Caleb's crying at night would keep me awake. I continued to eat all of my meals with them.

Mr. and Mrs. Harvey Beard and Bill McClure also visited in 1980. Both Harvey and Helen taught classes to the children of the orphanage. Bill was Dolly's nephew and also the director of Gospel Broadcasting Mission. The opportunity to begin a Hindi broadcast beamed at North India from Manila in the Philippines opened up, so Bill came to get us started in producing tapes for the broadcast in Hindi. We worked with Vijay Lal from Damoh, India, to produce a daily fifteen-minute program. Our Kulpahar Kids and staff produced the tapes and sent them to Manila for broadcast. This was a wonderful opportunity to reach thousands around Kulpahar, not to mention the millions in the rest of North India, most of whom could not read, but were able to hear.

Linda Williams, the librarian at Johnson Bible College, also visited. We had hoped she would return to help Dolly with the school work, but she didn't feel called to that ministry. While Linda was there, we had floods and the roof leaked in the house where I was living.  We had to put buckets in various places to catch the leaks.  Linda remarked that she was happy God said he would never destroy the earth again by floods.

# The End of An Era

For many months before the dedication of the hospital I had an unsettled feeling that I would not stay at Kulpahar. Early one morning in February 1980, during my time of Bible reading, I read Psalm 143 which led me to write the following:

>Teach me to do Thy Will, Oh God,
>Help me to know which path to trod.
>Hide not Thy face from me, Oh God,
>For in Thee only do I trust.
>Cause me to hear Thy loving voice,
>Morning, noon and night time too,
>Teach me to do Thy Will, Oh God,
>Help me to know which path to trod.

The next morning as I was praying for all of my friends in Zimbabwe, it seemed that this was the path God was telling me to follow.  That entire day I prayed and thought about this.  The next morning as I was praying again for Zimbabwe and my friends there, I felt that I just must not delay writing to the Central Africa Mission Board asking to be reinstated as a member.  It was not an easy decision to make.  I wrote the letter to the chairman of the board.  As I sent my resignation to the Church of Christ Mission in Kulpahar, the tears streamed down my cheeks.  But in spite of the heartache of leaving Kulpahar—I loved my work, my friends and especially my co-workers—I felt a peace and contentment that I had not felt in many months.  I wrote to all of my supporting churches, except for my home church and two women's' groups, to ask them to continue to support the medical work at Kulpahar. I explained that Steve and Ann would need the support to continue to operate and to expand the growing work. There was no question in my mind that they would be excellent stewards of the Lord's gifts.

The day before the dedication of the hospital, I received a letter from the Central Africa Mission board telling me that I had been reinstated as a member. I also had an invitation from Jack and Peggy Pennington to work among the Indian population in Salisbury since I had mentioned I would like to be able to use my Hindi if possible. I knew there were many Indian people in Zimbabwe. Dr. Pruett had also written that there were plans to reopen the Mashoko Hospital and invited me to join those who would go there. Gladys Jongeling offered me a place to stay in her home in Salisbury for a time as I studied Shona, which I was determined to learn as well as I had learned Hindi. I asked for prayers that I would follow God's leading to where I should serve when I returned to Zimbabwe.

It wasn't easy as I spent my last days at Kulpahar. I loved my ministry, but I knew it was time to move on. I was given a wonderful farewell party where many tears were shed. And I was ready for the next phase of my life.

# Chapter 17

## Back to Mashoko

### Another Transition

I planned to leave Kulpahar around October 15, visit the congregation in Japan that supported my ministry and arrive in the States in time for the National Missionary Convention. I hoped to leave for Zimbabwe in June 1981.

Before I left India, Aunt Blanche had written that Dick Sprague of I.D.E.S. wanted me to consider going to Honduras. He had been there after Hurricane Fifi and had seen the need for medical help. I told her to tell him that I knew the Lord was calling me back to Zimbabwe. Then while I was at the National Missionary Convention, I saw Bob Pate who was a missionary in Honduras. He said, "When you get things straightened out in Zimbabwe, come and help us in Honduras." I just laughed, for I had every intention to spend the rest of my life serving in Zimbabwe.

As I waited for my resident papers for Zimbabwe, I visited all of my supporting churches, encouraging them to support Steve and Ann in India. About one-third of them decided to support Steve and Ann, one-third decided to support me, and the final third decided to support both of us. God provided for both of us in a wonderful way!

The resident papers arrived in good time. I left for the field the last part of June. On my way, I stopped in England to visit Sylvia and Keith Golsby. Sylvia had been the first secretary at Mashoko and was now married and living in Lancaster, England. From there I took the train to Kircaldy, Scotland, to visit Maggie Waters, 92 years young and still going strong. She with her husband Archie had been missionaries in Bulawayo during my first stint in Rhodesia.

From London I flew to Johannesburg where I spent just over a week before I could buy a pickup truck. I visited Aletheia Christian Center and showed slides of India at their Sunday evening services. I visited primarily with Bill and Verna Weber, good friends of Steve and Ann who had just started their missionary work in South Africa in January.

Finally on July 9, I acquired my vehicle and drove up to Zimbabwe. I got through customs very quickly and drove to Fort Victoria where I spent the night with Doug and Frances Johnson. The next day I went on to Salisbury to the home of Gladys Jongeling.

God provided in a wonderful way for a Shona teacher. I had hoped to make arrangements to study at the university, but the classes there met for only an hour a week. On my first Sunday in Salisbury, I was happily reunited with Enos Bhonda, who had worked for me when he was a schoolboy at Chidamoyo. He now worked for the government in the Ministry of Labor and Social Services. He graciously agreed to teach me when I could not make other arrangements.

While I was in Salisbury, I attended the Greencroft Christian Church and enjoyed the fellowship. It was good to renew my friendship with Dr. Gloria Cobb who lived in the building where the church met. I was able to take her twice to visit Chidamoyo Mission. The hospital there had been repaired and looked beautiful with the new paint. But it still needed to be equipped before it could be placed in operation. The second time we went to Chidamoyo; we stopped in Sinoia and loaded the truck with hospital supplies stored there.

178

On September 11, with the help of Gladys and two African men, I loaded my pickup truck with a gas stove, refrigerator and groceries and began the trip to Mashoko. I went only as far as Fort Victoria the first day and spent the night with Doug and Frances Johnson. Early the next morning, I started for Mashoko. Everything went well until just after I passed through Bikita. There I found slippery, muddy, messy roads left after an unseasonable rain. I hadn't gone far from Bikita when I met a car, went too far to the side of the road, and got stuck in the mud. Four African men were kind enough to push me out.

When I told my rescuers that I was going to Mashoko, one of them asked if I was Sister Burget. He needed a ride and could go on with me. Since he wasn't impressed with my driving on muddy roads, I let him drive. Soon after we started, we were stopped again when we couldn't get up a steep, slick hill. This time Dr. Bill Vennells and two others from Mashoko came along and gave us a push. Bill thought I should turn back, but I wanted to get to Mashoko. We continued on the wings of prayer. As we drove, I found out that the driver had been a patient at Mashoko in 1965, which was why he had remembered me. He got out at his home about twenty-five miles from the mission. Even though I continued on muddy roads, I arrived at "C" cottage about 12:30 P.M. The headmaster of the secondary school sent some boys to help me unload the truck and I began getting settled right away.

## The Work Begins

It was a blessing to be in church at Mashoko on Sunday morning, the first time I had worshipped in the large building that had been built after I left in 1967. It was a bit of a shock when the students burst forth into their first song. It was such a change from the way the Indian people sang, but beautiful because the Africans sing in harmony. It was sad, though, to find so few adults in the service.

*Mr. Makuku, hospital evangelist*

My work at the hospital started on Sunday night when Dr. Vennells asked me to help him with a C. Section. Dr. Bill Vennells was from England and was with an organization named Oxfam. The government had sent him to Mashoko. I had not been in surgery for twelve years, but it all came back to me.

The days flew by as we worked to get the hospital back into full operation. Slowly, but surely, things began to look better around the hospital. The kitchen was not yet in operation, resulting in a lower patient count than if we could have fed them. Even so, we averaged about fifty patients.

The outpatient department was really busy. I spent most mornings seeing from forty to sixty patients. Often someone who looked familiar to me came in. When the person gave me a big smile, I knew it must have been someone who had been in the hospital back in the '60s. One day when I was helping with a labor patient, she told me that I had delivered her first baby in the hospital in the '60's. This was now her eighth baby. The maternity department stayed busy. In one two-day period I delivered four babies.

180

One of my first visitors was Augustine Makuku, the hospital evangelist. He was eager to start morning devotions on the wards. He had not done so earlier because he didn't want to interfere with Dr. VennellS' schedule. We started two days after I arrived, finishing before the doctor started his rounds. Dr. Vennells was not a Christian, so he didn't join us for devotions. In the beginning I joined Mr. Makuku for the devotions on the two wards, but I had to take over the drug room, making it possible for me join him only on the female ward. Soon four patients gave their lives to Christ and were baptized.

Mr. Makuku had been faithful to his ministry even during the war. During the war, he often went to the hospital to have a service with the women who were expecting babies. One evening he remembered singing the song *Rock of Ages* and having prayer with the women. When he opened his eyes after the prayer, he looked up to see three guerillas standing there, each with a gun. They didn't threaten him, but instead asked him to have the women sing *Rock of Ages* again. After the women sang the song, the guerillas asked him to pray for them. In telling me this story, he told of how God protected him during the war.

We started having services each Wednesday night either in the hospital chapel or in one of our homes. At the Wednesday night service in the hospital many patients joined us. At our homes usually five of the primary school teachers, the postmaster, the chaplain of the secondary school, Simeon Kumutsana who was in charge of the nursing school, an untrained orderly who worked at the hospital, Mr. Makuku, and I attended. We prayed especially for those employed on the mission who needed to return to the Lord.

I had resigned myself to the fact that I would have to be the one to start up the medical assistant school again. But all the time I had been praying that God would provide someone else to do it. My prayer was answered with the arrival of Simeon Kumutsana. Simeon studied high school at Mashoko, did his medical assistant training also at Mashoko, and then went to the States where he received his B.S. in Nursing at Berea College in Kentucky. He arrived at Mashoko a week after I did and was immediately busily at work in the nursing tutor's office sorting materials and getting ready to open the school in March.

One of the most frequent questions I was asked after returning to Mashoko was, "Will there be others who will return to Mashoko?" Those who asked were thinking about the missionaries such as me. My reply was that I was praying for others to return. We had a need especially for a male missionary to work with so many of the men who had turned from the Lord during the war. We also needed more nurses, a medical or laboratory technician, doctors, a maintenance man, and a secretary. Though some were concerned that I had moved to Mashoko, where there were few non-Africans, it was quite safe and I had no fears living there.

The days were long and I was busier than I had ever been. We were short of staff, and I spent many long hours at the hospital. And some of the employees weren't very competent. I just had to trust God that people would receive good care. Some late evenings as I walked up the hill from the hospital to my house, I thought of the song "The old grey mare ain't what she used to be." But God gave me strength for each day.

The months flew by as the hospital was cleaned and painted. The staff was increased. The Medical Council of Zimbabwe also gave official approval to re-open the medical assistant school. The first class was comprised of eight women and six men. It was encouraging to see them on the wards assisting the medical assistants. They would soon help by making beds, taking temperatures, and in other ways to give the patients good care. Simeon Kumutsana was busy giving lectures, and one day a week I taught a class on Christian living. The very first Sunday the students were on the mission, they sang a special number in English at the afternoon worship service.

I enjoyed going with Mr. Makuku to visit village churches. Five churches in one area not far from Mashoko had been having meetings in which they joined together for a Sunday worship service. They had a good time of fellowship, singing, meeting around the Lord's Table, and hearing the preaching of God's Word. The host church then prepared a meal for those in attendance. Mr. Makuku and I enjoyed attending these services. I couldn't go every week, for I had to take my turn being on call at the hospital. Attendance increased both in the village churches and at the mission church. The major weakness in all the churches was the lack of men.

One of the most faithful staff members was Mrs. Effie Gwinj, better known as "Mai Gwinji" or "Mother Gwinji." She had served at Mashoko for twenty-two years. She was not sure of her exact age, but she must have been around sixty years old. She was still quite vigorous in her work. On one

*Students in the lab*

busy day, for example, besides her regular duties of giving medicines and patient care, she also examined over one hundred pregnant women and delivered a baby.  It was she who had worked so faithfully all through the war years to keep the hospital open.  She saw patients in the outpatient department, delivered babies, and admitted some patients to the general ward.  This faithful Christian woman was loved and respected by people for many miles around.

It was like Christmas in January when the drums with my possessions finally arrived from the States. I shared some of the food items given to me by L.A.M.S. (Ladies Auxiliary of Mission Services) with the other missionaries.  Three of the drums had been opened and some things taken out, but the things I needed most, such as my electric typewriter, were there.  I had also brought items for Dr. Gloria Cobb.

A blessing of being back in Zimbabwe was seeing some of my former medical assistant students.   In Salisbury, I had a meal at the home of Earnest Gwangwadza and his family. He had been a student in the third class of medical assistant students in 1965.  He was very proud that he was a graduate of the Mashoko School of Medical Assistants.  He had left nursing and was by now the manager of the baby food products of Nestles, Zimbabwe.

## Visitors Blessed Our Lives

Visitors were always welcome at Mashoko, especially those who helped us.  Gladys Jongeling, who had originally set up the laboratory in 1962, came to help get the laboratory cleaned and also taught some classes to the medical assistants.   She left notes for Linda McClintock who planned to return to Mashoko in 1983.

We really looked forward to August when Dr. David Grubbs, his wife Eva, their oldest son Andy, their daughter Miriam, a friend of Andy's, and Linda Ruth McClintock were to visit.   Linda Ruth was the medical technologist who worked with Dr. Grubbs at the hospital when they had to leave Mashoko during the war for independence.  The Grubbs and Linda were praying about returning to Mashoko. Many of us were praying that the Lord would lead them back. They were needed at the hospital, but also to help to strengthen the churches.

In 1982, a medical student from Ohio served for a few months at Mashoko.  Bill Polinski was Catholic, but really enjoyed going to the village churches. One time as the congregation took the Lord's Supper from a common cup, he observed that his priest would be shocked.  Bill did a lot of running and he enjoyed a good meal.  I think he thought that he would be eating ants and other odd items while he was at Mashoko.  Margie Pemberton, who lived in Chiredzi, would save up ice and send it to me so we could make ice cream.  Bill loved ice cream and gladly cranked until it was ready.  He was a joy to have around and we stayed in contact for many years. John and I visited him and his wife and three children several times in Mansfield, Ohio.  A few years ago his wife died of stomach cancer and, unfortunately, we have now lost contact with him.

An amusing incident occurred when I invited the staff to my home for a Christmas tea.  I served Indian samosas and doughnuts.  At the time two female British medical students were visiting.  They asked me where I bought the doughnuts.  Here we were in the Zimbabwean bush and they asked where I bought doughnuts!  I told them that I had made them myself to which they replied, "You can make doughnuts?"  They were obviously city girls.

# It Wasn't All Medical

Evangelistic efforts were renewed.  In 1982, 147 people from the Bambaninga congregation were baptized.  This came about after I had a well-baby clinic there.  After the Scripture lesson, 39 school children went forward to give their lives to Christ.  When we returned to instruct and baptize them, 108 more gave their lives to Christ and were baptized.

One day Angie Vennells mentioned that she wished we could have a Sunday School at Mashoko so her little girl could attend.  The next Sunday we had so many little ones at church who were not really enjoying the service.  I bought material and about the same time one of my supporting churches sent some crayons.  So Louise, the doctor's daughter, joined the other children for Sunday School each week.

# Working With A Non-Christian Doctor

It was not easy working with a doctor who was not a Christian.  On one occasion others from Oxfam gathered at the Vennells' home for a party.  They had invited African dancers and drank beer.  It broke my heart to see this happening.  I went to the party, but didn't stay.  I had promised Angie that I would bake biscuits for them for breakfast the next day.  When I took them to her, she said,  "It was bad, wasn't it?"  I agreed that it was very bad.

Dr. Vennells seemed to have more interest in feeding programs and the vaccination clinics than he did in caring for patients at the hospital.  I was left to do most of that work.

He also had been very slack with three of the staff who had been ex-guerilla medics.  They often arrived very late for their work in the out-patient department, making the patients wait for a long time to get their medicine. I tried to get him to be stricter with them, but he didn't seem to care. Finally, his wife helped me to convince him that two of the workers needed to be fired. One of them was very responsible, but the other two were most irresponsible. We wrote a dismissal letter. Though we both signed the letter, they knew that it would not have been done if I had not been there.

The day after they were fired, they came to the outpatient department where Simeon and I were seeing patients. They wanted me to go outside. I was determined not to go because I knew they wanted to beat me up. I put my arm around the bench and refused to move. The ringleader— I don't think the other really agreed with him—hit me. I quickly removed my glasses, bowed my head, and started to pray for them. That made the ringleader even angrier, and he hit me once more in the face. One of the untrained orderlies forced him to stop. I had only a slight bruise on my face, so I was not harmed. By not acting afraid I allowed those who still feared the ex-guerillas to have courage. That morning I had awakened early and had a good prayer time. I know that gave me the strength to handle what happened.

I asked the headmaster if I could sleep at his house that night, for no one wanted me to sleep alone at my house. He refused to allow me to sleep there, so both Simeon and I slept at Bill and Angie's house. The next day Bill took the offenders away. Some felt that the headmaster was behind what had happened because, they said, he had resented me since before I had arrived. He felt in charge of the entire mission, including the hospital. When John Pemberton found out what had happened, he fired the headmaster. Later Timothy Tembo filled that position, and we worked together very well. Later the Minister of Health apologized to me for what had happened. About a year later, when Mr.

Makuku and I were visiting a village church near the home of the non-aggressor, he approached Mr. Makuku and asked if he thought I would talk to him. He apologized for his part, although he really had not touched me.  The stories about what had happened were quite exaggerated.

## Other Service in Zimbabwe

I flew to the clinic at the Maranda Mission regularly. John Mark Pemberton picked me up and flew me to the site.  The flight was less than an hour while driving took 5 ½ hours! A Zimbabwean nurse was there, and she was always happy for my visit.  In 1983, when Jim and Joyce Mouer and their family came to Mashoko, I spent a week at Maranda since Joyce was a nurse and could take care of things at Mashoko.  I had fun cooking on a one-burner kerosene stove and "roughing" it for the week.  The Zimbabwean nurse needed a vacation and I was happy to fill in for her.  John Mark checked on me a couple of times.

## More Equipment, More Personnel

Toward the end of 1982, needed medical equipment arrived from F.A.M.E. of  Columbus, Indiana.  The shipment included four hospital beds—the kind that can be cranked up and down, bassinets for babies, bedside tables and lots of stainless steel equipment such as urinals, emesis basins and water jugs. The staff was fascinated with the adjustable beds.

In February, 1983, the Vennells returned to England. Just before they left, Jim and Joyce Frasure and their family came for about six weeks. From then until David and Eva Grubbs returned in October, six different doctors and their families came to help.  Frasures were followed by Bill and Jeannie Nice, Dwain and Marilyn Illman, and Mike and Sue Bishop. All of these doctors had served either at Mashoko or Chidamoyo in the '70s.  Dr. Tommy and Phyllis West and Dr. Jim and Joyce Mouer also came for short periods.

During the time a doctor was present, I fixed an Indian meal.  One of the dishes was a vegetable dish with spices. The Frasure children let me know that they didn't like eggplant.  But this dish just had to have eggplant in it.  With the other vegetables, it was well disguised.  During the meal, their mother wanted to know what vegetables were in the dish.  The children had already had one serving and were enjoying it until I turned to them and said, "It has their favorite vegetable."  One of them looked at me and said, "You didn't!" and refused to eat any more.  I also always made doughnuts when they were there.  One day I made some chocolate doughnuts.  Mike Bishop's daughter was helping me and she didn't realize they were chocolate and thought I was burning them!

Bill and Jeannie Nice and their three girls were there on April Fool's Day.  Early that morning, they called me to the hospital for a C-Section.  I got to the surgery, but no one was there.  So I went over to the maternity section and nothing was going on there either.  I knew that Bill had played an April Fool's joke on me so I fixed the locks in the doctor's office to prevent him from getting in when he came to the hospital.  One of his daughters asked me if I was angry at their dad and I told them that I wasn't:  that I didn't get angry; I got even!!

Tommy West was doing a residency in Obstetrics-Gyn and loved delivering babies.  One thing I had learned to use at the Frontier Nursing Service was a vacuum extractor.  Especially with a young woman having her first baby, it was helpful in delivery.  To use it, a suction cup, which could be pulled as the mother had a contraction and was pushing, was placed on the baby's head. One evening, a young lady was having a difficult time. Tommy had used forceps, but he felt that he was making no progress. I asked him if he would like me to try the vacuum extractor. He was willing and delivered a healthy baby. A few nights later, Tommy called, asking me to go to the delivery room to show him how to use the vacuum extractor. He decided it was better than the forceps. When Dr. Jim Mouer came, I learned that he was one of the few obstetricians who regularly used a vacuum extractor.

## Frustrations and Blessings

I delivered my second set of triplets at Mashoko during my second year back. This delivery of three boys was easy. Some of the African people still had superstitions about multiple births, and the mother refused to feed one of them; he died in the hospital. We learned later that the other two died at home. It was so unnecessary because all three were healthy. But that was one of the frustrations in dealing with the superstitions. Fortunately, that would not happen now.

But there were blessings too. One Sunday Mr. Makuku and I were out to visit churches. On the way home, he stopped. A man came up and Mr. Makuku asked him if he knew who I was. The man said he didn't, so Mr. Makuku told him that I was Sister Burget. The man got so excited that he made a noise that is hard to put down on paper, but it was like "Eh, eh, eh." It turned out that he was the father of the twin I had delivered five days after her brother. Men didn't usually go to the hospital with their wives, so he had never met me. He told me he would send his daughter to the hospital to see me, which he did. After twenty years I was able to see her.  That was just one of the many blessings I received from being back at Mashoko.

# A New Call

I don't remember exactly when I began thinking about Honduras, but knowing how much a nurse was needed there, I began to pray that God would send one nurse to work there.  I was not interested in going to Honduras: I had planned to spend the rest of my missionary life in Zimbabwe.  But as I read *Horizons* to see if a nurse had gone yet and found that it hadn't happened, I realized that perhaps God was calling me to go.  Once David and Eva Grubbs returned to Mashoko, there would be a permanent doctor at the hospital.  Simeon Kumutsana was doing a good job with the nursing school, and staffing was adequate.  I realized that the work I had gone to Mashoko to do was finished.  I remember telling Mike Bishop that I felt the Lord was calling me to go to Honduras and he said to count on him to help with support.  (He was true to his word and continues to support us financially and with his prayers.)

Dave and Eva arrived in October and I made plans to leave Mashoko in December 1983.

The last months at Mashoko seemed to fly by.  It was a sad time for me—I have never liked goodbyes.  The hospital staff arranged a farewell party for me. I also celebrated my fiftieth birthday at Mashoko before I left.  Eva Grubbs baked a cake for me.  Since there was a piece missing, Dave always said Eva had baked a different kind of cake.  He said that she always had to check the cake out to make sure it was good.

I took the long way back to the States. Doug and Frances Johnson, Gladys Jongeling, and I traveled to India to visit Kulpahar. It was a blessing to be back with Steve and Ann for a short time. Gladys and Frances thought I was crazy when I packed some cans of green beans for Ann. They don't like green beans and couldn't imagine anyone else wanting them, but when Ann saw them, she was so excited. We visited the Taj Mahal on the way to Kulpahar. I was able to bring back my Hindi enough to keep some of the merchants from cheating us when we bought souvenirs. At Kulpahar, I met Mike and Robin Keralis who were visiting Steve and Ann. Mike taught us how to play Speed Uno. We have continued to keep in touch through the years.

I arrived in the States in January 1984 and began visiting my supporting churches. I can't say enough about how the churches have been so faithful to continue supporting me with my moves to India, back to Zimbabwe and on to Honduras.

Since I was going to Honduras without being under an existing mission organization, I.R.S. regulations required that all of my funds go through a church or that I form a non-profit incorporation. My home church agreed to allow the funds to go through them. Because of this, I needed to find a member of the congregation to serve as forwarding agent. God answered my prayers when Norma Alderfer agreed to serve. She had been a friend for years; when we grew up, we had lived only about 1½ miles apart. Norma, her husband Larry, and her three children were all active in the Normanda Christian Church. She was highly recommended by the minister at the time.

The details had fallen into place. I was on my way to Honduras.

# Chapter 18

# A New Work

## Getting Ready To Go

My new chapter in life was about to begin, though many preparations had to be completed. I had been advised by a couple of Latin American missionaries that it would not be good for me to go to Honduras as a single woman. I might have understood their concern if I had been a young lady, but I was now fifty years old and it wasn't likely that I would be a candidate for marriage to any Honduran man. So the preparations for Honduras began.

Being very sure of God's will for me to go to Honduras, I began assembling my papers for residency to live and work in that country. I had to have a health certificate, a certificate from the law that I had never been arrested, a letter from the church assuring the Honduran government that I would have enough money to live on, and my birth certificate. I found out what they mean by "red tape" when I took my notarized papers to the State Department at Washington D.C.: on each paper there was a red ribbon! After I had all of the papers, I went to the Honduran Consulate in Chicago.

An interesting incident occurred on the way to Chicago. At a rest stop I saw an Indian man, who it turned out, was from Pakistan. I said a few words to him in Hindi and he asked me to wait at the ladies' restroom and greet his wife in Hindi. He wanted to see her face when this tall blond American began speaking to her in Hindi. The look on her face was one to remember!

In Chicago, I left my papers and received a visitor's visa to go to Honduras. They would send my papers to Tegucigalpa, the capital.

Meanwhile, during the time I was in the States, I was honored at Johnson Bible College on February 15 when I was given the Distinguished Service Award. Then in May I was given the Outstanding Nurse Award by the Ball State University Nursing Alumni Association.

I had hoped Bob Pate would be in Honduras when I went to get my residency, but he was out of the country. I made plans to go in May, not knowing anyone there and speaking very little Spanish. My prayer the morning before leaving for Honduras was that God would allow me to meet someone on the airplane who could help me in a special way. My prayers were answered when I met Malcom Matheson, the director of a coffee exporting company in Honduras. We were seated in the same row. I told him why I was going to Honduras and he told me he knew of a lawyer in Tegucigalpa who was very good at getting residencies for Americans. He arranged for me to have an appointment with him after I had spent a few days in San Pedro Sula. Malcom's wife knew of Ruth Paz, an American lady married to a Honduran, who could help me find a place to room in San Pedro Sula as I studied Spanish and found the site to start my ministry.

On Sunday, I attended the Evangelica Reformada Church where I met Delia Cristine Russell who translated for me. I also met Ramon Guzman who took me to find the Church of Christ in the city and gave me a New Testament which had Spanish in one column and English in the other.

I located Ruth Paz and she found a very kind lady, Luisa Julia Kipps, who was willing to rent a room to me. She was a widow who had been married to an American, and she spoke perfect English.

On Monday evening I flew to Tegucigalpa. Malcom had called the Rhonda Hotel, where I stayed, and the lawyer with whom I met on Tuesday morning. It was amazing. I could hardly keep up with him as we went to various offices. We found out that my papers had not been sent from Chicago. After going to various offices on Tuesday, Wednesday, and Thursday, I found myself back at the hotel on Thursday afternoon with my residency papers in hand. It was obvious God wanted me to serve in Honduras. I remember feeling like the people who had prayed for Peter when he was in jail, then couldn't believe it when he appeared at their home. I was in a daze, but God had answered my prayers. I flew back to the States and made plans to return to Honduras in August.

When I arrived back in the States after my trip to Honduras I was the missionary for five Vacation Bible Schools. I also visited many friends and relatives in between going to supporting Churches.

I had so many blessings. This one I wrote about in my May-August newsletter.

### Dorcases of Macedonia Christian Church

Back in June of 1980, just before I was ready to leave for Zimbabwe, I realized I had no nurse's uniforms. I had bought some material and a pattern, but sewing is definitely not one of my talents. On a Saturday morning, only about a week before I was to leave, I called my good friend, Ada Johnson, and said: "Help, Ada, could you possibly make me a couple of uniforms next week?" Ada is always very busy, but if you want something done, ask those kinds of people. She said she might be able to do two for me. Then, on Sunday morning at the Macedonia Christian Church, Kokomo, Ind. where she attends, she saw some other women who also sew. They had mentioned they would like to do something for me, so she challenged them with the uniforms. On Monday, Kathleen Cannon cut out eight uniforms and in less than one week, I picked them up, all very well done and ready to wear. Ada Johnson; Kathleen Cannon; her mother, Bessie Lovejoy, and Suzanne Terrell had made those uniforms in record time. In May of 1984 while on furlough, I spoke to the women at Macedonia and they wanted to do something for me again. The uniforms they had made before were still in good shape, but I needed some summer cotton clothes and some lab coats. One Saturday morning I called Kathleen Cannon and again asked for help—in picking out patterns and material. Kathleen joined the Joanne Fabrics Club and that day by joining, we got 25% off on all material, patterns, etc. purchased. For $99.60 we bought the material and patterns for three dresses, two skirts, four blouses and two lab coats. Kathleen managed to get three more blouses made out of the left over dress material and picked up "just a little remnant" to make another blouse to go with a blue skirt. This reminded me of the Scripture in Acts 9:39: "And Peter arose and went with them. And when he had some, they brought him into the upper room; and all the widows stood beside him weeping, and showing all the tunics and garments Dorcas used to make while she was with them." Truly, Kathleen Cannon, Ada Johnson and Gladys Ellabarger were Dorcases from Macedonia Christian Church.

## Learning to Live in Honduras

My plane reservation to leave for Honduras was set for August 27, but I had needed a new prescription for eyeglasses which did not come in time. I delayed my departure until August 29. All I could think was: "I wonder what surprise God has for me this trip." I found out while I was in the waiting area at the Miami airport. Who should I see but Malcom Matheson! In July, he and his family had moved to Connecticut, and this was his first trip back to Honduras since then. He was now the Director of Purchasing for the Lonray, Inc., New York City Company and traveled to Central American to purchase coffee. He remembered that I had planned to move to Honduras in August and again was willing to take me to town from the airport. However, Ruth Paz had arranged for her husband to meet me and take me to the home of Mrs. Kipps. But Malcom had his former secretary fill out the forms for getting a post office box.

God really blessed me when Ruth Paz found Luisa Julia Kipps with whom I could room. She was kind to me in many ways. My luggage didn't arrive with me in Miami, so it was two days late getting to San Pedro Sula. Mrs. Kipps made a trip with me to the airport. Since she ran a travel agency, she knew customs officials and they told her they would call her when the suitcases came. She then arranged for her daughter to take me to pick up the luggage when it finally came. One Sunday she took me with her when she went to visit relatives and I enjoyed a swim in the Caribbean Sea. She offered me the use of her postal box until I could get one and made me feel welcome in her home. I had a spacious bedroom, my own bathroom, and the use of her desk in the study. My rent included room, all of my meals, and my laundry.

My first Sunday in Honduras, Luisa Julia took me in her car to the Church of Christ in Barandillas to make sure I would find it. One of the first people I met that Sunday was the son of the minister. I asked him if he knew of anyone who could help me learn Spanish and he volunteered. He had learned English when he attended school in the States during the time that his dad studied in Texas. He came to Luisa's home three days a week to help me, put phrases on my tape recorder for me to memorize, and taught me some of the customs in Honduras. Luisa found a lady, once the principal of a junior high school, who could help with the grammar. This woman didn't speak English, so I had to listen carefully to her Spanish. It was also helpful that I attended the Church of Christ in Barandillas five times a week and learned Spanish from my new Christian friends.

The church was sixteen blocks from Luisa's home. I walked there on Sunday morning, but rode the bus in the evening. I got on the bus only about two blocks from where I lived and then get off only about four blocks from the church.

I started the process of getting registered as a nurse in Honduras, but this wasn't an easy process.

Through Ruth Paz I learned about groups coming to Honduras through Interplast, a group bringing medical personnel to Honduras each year to repair cleft lips and palates, do skin grafts on burn victims, and perform other plastic surgery work. She asked me if I would like to help them when they came. I was most happy to do so and made many friends. The first time, I mostly helped with records since my Spanish wasn't very good, but when my Spanish improved, I did a lot of translating for the doctors. I also met Mercedes, an auxiliary nurse, who later helped me with medical Spanish. She also helped me to get permission to work in the hospital so that I could be registered as a nurse in Honduras.

I continued to study Spanish, using the method recommended by the book Language acquisition made practical (L.A.M.P.). I often rode the bus and attempted to talk to people on the bus to practice my Spanish. One day as I

198

was walking, I met an older lady, originally from Nicaragua, who liked to walk, but often had no one to take her. I volunteered to walk with her. That gave me someone else with whom to practice Spanish. I practiced with Louisa's maid as well and even got her to go to church with me occasionally.

## Finding A Ministry Location

While I was learning Spanish, I was also praying for the Lord to show me where I might begin a medical ministry. Luisa had put me in contact with a man who worked for the newspaper. One Saturday afternoon I took a trip with him and another person to the city of Coyoles, located near Olanchito where I had seen a picture of an unfinished hospital. The mother of the newspaperman lived in Coyoles, so we would stay with her while I checked out the possibility of helping to finish the construction of the hospital.

The trip to Olanchito took us north and west. Even though this was supposed to be the best road to Coyoles, it reminded me of some of the roads in Rhodesia. I hate to think was the bad road was like! We didn't arrive until 11:30 P.M.

Coyoles is the home of the Standard Fruit Company. All along the way to the city, I saw banana plantations with tree after tree of bananas. I had never seen so many banana trees in my life.

On Sunday morning I went to see the unfinished hospital. It turned out to be much larger than it appeared in the newspaper picture. As I walked through it, I knew that my idea of helping to finish it would not be feasible. It was far too elaborate for the area. After talking to a deputy in Congress, I found the cost for completing it would be $700,000.

The deputy said she wished at least enough of it could be finished to help women and children. After talking to her, I went to see the mayor of the city. He asked if I would consider returning to Olanchito to start another health facility. He also asked me to write up a list of proposals to send to him. Soon after my return to San Pedro Sula, I typed up a list of proposals and Luisa translated them into Spanish. The newspaper contact picked the list up to take to the mayor. After two months without hearing from the mayor, I concluded that my ministry would be elsewhere else in Honduras.

Later Louisa's god-daughter and I visited San Nicolas in the State of Copan. Jackie's aunt had an available house that looked as if it could be fixed up for a clinic on the first floor with living quarters above.

Even as I prayed about San Nicolas, I could not forget the need in the mountains near San Pedro Sula. As I prayed, several different people indicated that they thought this was an area that really needed help. Salvador Canahuati, one who had told me about the need in the mountains, had not contacted me again, so I went to see him. It seemed that he was just waiting for my visit. He asked me several questions about my church background and wrote down my name and telephone number. In less than a week I had a contact from a Mr. Venegas who worked for the Texaco Company. He wasted no time in arranging for me to visit Peñitas Arriba, an aldea in the Merendon Mountains. I found out from the driver that he went up twice a day all year. Mr. Venegas had a store in the mountains and also received money from an organization in the States to help the children in the area. He also had a small building where he kept medicine. He tried to get some of his doctor friends to go with him to see the sick, but visits were not on a regular schedule. It was only about a thirty- to forty-five-minute drive from the city, but I had the feeling I was going straight up—it was high. My ears popped for three to four hours after I returned to San Pedro Sula.

Mr. Venegas introduced me to a lady who took me walking to visit four families. She told them that I might move there to help them. At the first home I learned that nine *aldeas* (villages) were located in the area with Peñitas Arriba being central to the others. The homes in the village were not very close to each other. We went down the mountain and then back up to get to the homes. By the time I returned to see Mr. Venegas, I was huffing and puffing.

The people literally "took me in." I really felt that I had found my place for a ministry, but I told them to give me two weeks to think and pray about it. They told me they would also be praying. As the two weeks came to a close, I couldn't help but wonder if it would be like Olanchito and I would hear nothing more. But exactly two weeks to the day Mr. Venegas came to see to me to learn what I had decided. I told him that if he could help me get the necessary permission from the Minister of Health, I would go, but that because I had finally heard from the Colegio de Professionales de Enfermeria, I would not be able to go until the end of March. He said getting permission would be no problem because he knew the Director of the Leonardo Martinez Hospital who, he knew, would help. Another businessman had promised to help me get a house built where I could live. It seemed as if I had come full circle. The first place I had heard that needed medical help was the Merendon Mountain area. It was the last place I visited, but I had no doubt that this was where I should begin my service to the Lord in Honduras.

I felt that I could write a book on all of the exciting things that had happened to me in my first 5½ months in Honduras. And all this came about in answer to my prayer to meet someone who could help me in some way when I went to

Honduras to get my residency papers. It was evident that many were praying. It was through Malcom Matheson's wife that I met Ruth Paz who then made arrangements for me to live with Luisa. Nearly every Friday morning I walked to Ruth's house so she could get on her amateur radio to give her call HR2RP to KD9GZ who was Byron Bezdek at I.D.E.S. in Kempton, Indiana. Thanks to Byron he could call Aunt Blanche; my forwarding agent, Norma Alderfer; and my mother and hook up his phone patch to allow me to talk directly to them.

Ruth Paz was a blessing to me in so many ways. It was because of her asking me to help Interplast that I met Mercedez Rodriguez who then helped me with medical Spanish and I helped her with English. But Mercedes helped me in a greater way when I was trying to get permission to work in the government hospital which was a requirement for me to receive my card as a Professional Nurse in Honduras. I had received a phone call from the Colegio de Professionales de Enfermera to tell me that I needed to report to the hospital to Martha Rodriguez to received her permission to work in the hospital. After several visits, she told me she could not allow me to work in the hospital until I went to Tegucigalpa to get permission from the Minister of Public Health. Mercedes felt that this was not necessary, so she went to work for me and came to the house late one night with a letter written in Spanish for me to type up to send to the acting director of the hospital. Early on a Friday morning I went back to the hospital to talk to him and was given permission to work. I started working in the pediatric ward on February 11, 1985.

But that was just the start of my attempt to get registered as a nurse. The first week went well, but then I was to work in the maternity ward. The head nurse gave me a nice welcome, but one of the doctors asked her why I was there and insisted that I bring him a letter from the director of the hospital showing that I had permission to work. Back I went to his office. He gave me the letter and apologized for the problem. The third week I worked in Consulta Externa or the outpatient department. At first the head nurse was hostile to me as if she thought I wanted her job. Eventually she realized that I only wanted to work to be recognized as a Professional nurse in Honduras. The final week I worked at a big government health clinic—and finally I had a week when I was given a warm welcome and had no problems. Now all that was left was for me to do was to go to Tegucigalpa to take the written exam on March 15. I wrote this in my newsletter of March-May, 1985.

## Carnet de Colegiacion

Thank you so much for your prayers for me on March 15th, the day I took my exam. As I looked at the test I had to take that day, I was reminded once again that my timing is not always best. Had I had to take that exam when I first arrived in Honduras, I would never have passed it. The exam was 200 multiple choice questions in Spanish. I would like to share with you the three ways I feel God provided in answer to your prayers for me to be able to pass the exam. First, it was a multiple choice exam, so all I had to do was circle the correct answer which meant I didn't have to write in Spanish. Second, there was a nurse there who could speak English and she was allowed to tell me meanings of words and questions I did not understand. And, finally, I only had to get 50% to pass the exam. My score was 63%, and ordinarily I would not be very happy with a score like that, but this time I was delighted and thankful. There was a panel of three nurses there as I took the exam and they graded the test and discussed what I had done and then called me in to tell me the good news. They were all very kind and helpful, and one, who was the

Director of the School of Nursing at the University in Tegucigalpa, gave me a lot of materials to read on nursing in Spanish.  It took me just over four hours to complete the exam and they gave me the results in the afternoon.  Thank you again for your prayers.

The first person I met at the Iglesia de Cristo in May was Ursina Toro.  At that time I did not know her name, but soon after I arrived in Honduras, I had been told that she was in the hospital.  I started visiting her when I worked with  Interplast and continued to visit her at her home which was only 41/2 blocks from where I lived.  Her grandson had stayed with a friend from church while she was in the hospital, but had moved back into one room with her and his father when she went home.  I started taking him to church with me.  When Ursina felt well enough, I often got a taxi on Sunday night and took her to church too.  Later she had to move because the owner planned to build some apartments where she had lived, so she went to live with her sister outside of San Pedro Sula.  The boy's father moved to his office to sleep and the boy lived with the daughter and her husband of a family for whom Ursina had worked for many years.  Since he moved only about five blocks further down the street that since it was on our bus route from church, I continued to take him to church.  When I moved to the mountains, another lady from the church started taking him to church.

Just before I moved to the mountains, Hermana Ada, the minister's wife, asked if I would teach one of the Sunday School classes for the children.  I said I would if someone would help me in the event  the children could not understand my Spanish.  I also told her that I would not be able to teach for very long since I would be moving to the mountains.  No one came to help me the first week I taught, but I told the nine children they would have to listen closely and later asked the women to find out if they understood me.

The second week a lady sat in on the class. I was happy to have her since I had more children, some of them younger ones. She helped me out a few times when the children did not seem to understand. I was thankful that when I had been in Tegucigalpa I had bought some teaching material from the Honduras Bible Society.

The preparations complete, it was time to turn my attention to establishing a medical ministry—the purpose for which I had come to Honduras.

# Chapter 19

# Ministry in the Merendon Mountains

### A Place to Live

I moved to the mountains the last of April where I lived in a little room on the side of the house where the lady lived who ran the store. My first night there Dalila decided that the room was too small, so she moved the bed in a room next to where she and her children slept. Unfortunately, she left her radio on and I couldn't sleep. I moved the mattress to the little room further away and the next day moved my bed. I had a shower with cold water—and I do mean cold! I ate with the family and had a diet of beans and tortillas or beans and rice day after day. Finally after having some bad diarrhea, I bought a one- burner electric hot plate and started fixing my own food. Dalila wasn't the cleanest person; I felt I was better off doing my own cooking.

A real obstacle to sleep was Dalila's youngest son who cried out at night. It was a long time before I had a complete night's rest. Finally, when he started crying, I would call, "Be quiet, Chele," and he would stop. There was only a screen door separating my room from their bedroom. I also learned to fight cockroaches and mice. And I learned to overcome self-pity, remembering to be thankful for a room of my own and my own bathroom. To help Dalila out, I sometimes cooked the Sunday dinner on their wood stove. It took me awhile to get used to using their type of stove, but I think they enjoyed a change in diet. Their favorite was spaghetti. I learned to bake a cake on the top of my stove by using a big cast iron container.

Dalila never taught the children to say please or thank you, so I worked on that. They never minded my discipline.

In fact, they would have lived in my room had I allowed it.  I would sometimes pop popcorn which they loved.  The Spanish word for popcorn is *palomitas de maiz*.  The little one came to the door of my room and say, "Madonna, *paomitas*," his way of asking for popcorn.

One time Dalila had a bad kidney infection, so I tried to keep up with the clinic work and do the cooking for the family.  One day after our noon meal, I rocked the youngest to sleep.  When he went to sleep, I went to their room to put him to bed, but there was a hammock in my way.  With the child in my arms, I tried to step over it, but my foot caught in the hammock and I fell down.  I wasn't hurt, but the child started to cry, Dalila woke up and I was laughing.  There was never a dull moment living with Dalila and her four children.

# Beginning Clinic Work

My first clinic was in one small room and a shelter on Mr. Vanegas' property.  The shelter had some benches where patients could sit as they waited.  The Saturday before I moved to the mountains, I started painting the inside walls to make the room a bit more cheery and easier to clean.  Three young girls wanted to help; they painted the two doors and the walls.  This was my first time to do any extensive painting so I had a good laugh when the teacher of the Peñitas Arriba School, pointing to a wall I had done, told one of the girls that she hadn't done a good job.  I think he was a bit embarrassed when I told him that I had painted that area, so I hurriedly told him that this was my first time to paint and laughed so he would know he had not insulted me.  We did not finish on Saturday, so when I went up the following Tuesday morning, he sent three school boys to finish the painting.  It was good that he did because though

208

I thought I would have a couple of days to put things away and to clean, patients started coming that first day. In fact, at the end of the first week, I wondered how I could keep up the pace. But after the first week, the patient load began to slow down and I also had hired a girl to help me.

In my first week most patients came from aldeas (villages) of Peñitas Arriba and San Antonio del Perú. However, after the first week I saw patients from eight aldeas and a few times from two more distant aldeas. I visited some of the people. The paths to their homes were very steep. On some of them I didn't even look down because I didn't want to see where I would go if I fell. Yami, Dalila's oldest daughter, usually went with me and always got tickled when I crouched down and tried to find a stone or something to steady me on the steeper paths.

During my second day in the mountains, one of my patients was a girl whom I thought had malaria. I treated her for that, not realizing that in the mountains, there is no malaria. The next day she came back and was worse and I realized that she had meningitis. I gave her a shot of penicillin and told her mother she needed to get her to the hospital in the city. Since I didn't have a vehicle and no others were available, her mother had to carry her all the way to the city in a hammock on her back. I thanked God that she got there in time and fully recovered. Two months later her father became very sick with asthma and pneumonia. A few days after he came to the clinic, I was told he was much worse, so I went to visit him. As I walked the path to their home, I wondered how he ever got up the hill to the clinic when he was so sick. But when I arrived, I found him much better.

I had many opportunities for personal witnessing in the clinic. Many times the opportunity came when a patient noticed the Bible on my desk. I also passed out tracts. I had a little card with a Scripture on the back printed so that each patient could have his/ her own number. I found that just like in most countries, a lot of illness came from being in an unhappy situation. When women asked for medicine for their "nerves," I gave them a verse of Scripture and encouraged them to pray more and to study the Scriptures at home. I didn't even keep tranquilizers in the clinic.

One of my best publicity agents had always been Aunt Blanche who died June 7, 1985. I wrote the following tribute to her in my June-July 1985 newsletter.

### AUNT BLANCHE

On June 7th, 1985, Aunt Blanche Burget went to be with the Lord. She is going to be missed greatly by so many, but in the past year had been sick so much and I was not surprised by the news that came via telephone to Luisa by my sister, Marilyn. Aunt Blanche faithfully supported me not only with her finances, but by showing slides to churches; sending them out to other churches to be shown; sending out display material and being the best public relations person anyone could have. From the comments I had from those where she spoke on my behalf, I think she did as good or even better than I did in presenting the Lord's work I was doing. Aunt Blanche was the youngest sister of my Dad and since she never married, always had a lot of time for her nieces and nephews and great nieces and nephews. She was my music and art teacher at Prairie High School and used to take me to a lot of the basketball games. I always get so sleepy riding and would often drift off to sleep on the way home, but not for long. Aunt Blanche would honk the horn, put on the brakes and scream and I would come out of my seat like a bullet. I have to confess that I have pulled the same trick on others. having been taught well by her. For many years she was the nurse at Hanging Rock Christian Assembly and is still known affectionately by many preachers and former campers as "Nursie." Many people thought she was a nurse, but she was first a music teacher and later went back to Ball State and got her Masters Degree in English, so taught English until she retired. She was also popular at Hanging Rock for the way she could sing "There's a hole in the bottom of the sea." Aunt Blanche was always at our family gatherings for holidays and it won't be quite the same without her, but we will still have the memories that can't be taken away and I am just thankful she is free from pain.

When I moved to the mountains, Camilo Vanegas asked me to help him with his work with Holy Land Christian International, an organization based in Kansas City that had sponsors for many of the children living in the mountains. Before long I was doing all of the work—taking pictures of the children, getting them to write letters to their sponsors which I then translated into English, going to their homes to update information, and using the money to help with feeding programs at the schools. I did a lot of hiking in the hills getting the information I needed and visiting the schools to make sure the children were getting their meals. Sometimes when money ran out from the organization, I used mission funds to supplement so the children got at least one good meal a day.

## Laying the Foundation for A Church

On my first Sunday in the mountains, I started a Sunday school and soon had more than twenty children coming. They ranged in age from five to fourteen. Some of the younger ones didn't try to do the work in the books I had—but they enjoyed singing and listening to the Bible story. I tried to show some filmstrips I had from Good News Productions, but many people came to the store to watch television and were not interested. One night when it was raining, I was able to show the filmstrip to about eight people, but I had to wait until I could find a quieter place to show them regularly.

The first Sunday in August, I started a second Sunday School at the school building in the next village, San Antonio del Perú. It was interesting that at Peñitas Arriba I had mostly girls and at San Antonio del Perú, I had mostly boys.

Soon three of the girls from my Sunday school class made the decision to give their lives to Christ. Camilo Vanegas loaned me his pickup and another man drove us down to the Church of Christ in San Pedro Sula where one of the elders of the congregation baptized the girls. The girls were Yami, the oldest daughter of Dalila, the lady where I lived; Maria Anita Rivera, the youngest daughter of a family I had visited when I first moved to the mountains; and Suyapa Martinez, the daughter of the lady who ironed my uniforms. The following Sunday we started having worship services so that the girls could partake of the Lord's Supper. I had started attending the afternoon services of the Catholic Church where they had a Bible study They gave me permission to use the church building in the morning for our worship services.

I continued to conduct the two Sunday schools and the worship service. I also started a Bible study with some of the women on Wednesday. However, the first Wednesday, no one came. Knowing what it was like to climb up the steep mountain paths, I decided it would be easier for one person to do the walking than for several of them to do it. The Bible study alternated between two homes.

212

Sometime later, after I had my truck, a man from Laguna told me that he believed in Christ and wanted to be baptized. So I took him and a pickup truck full of people from our little congregation in Peñitas to the Church of Christ in San Pedro Sula where he was baptized. I hoped to get a congregation started there soon.

# A Part of the Community— and Expanding Opportunities

I learned that the Honduran people were most generous, expressing it in a variety of ways. In my work with Holy Land Christian International, I needed to buy shoes for the children in the program. I took a measurement of their feet to get the right size. The cousin of a good friend owned a shoe company. The friend called his cousin and the result was that I bought fifty-five pairs of shoes of very good quality at below wholesale price.

My first Independence Day in the mountains was on a Sunday. As a result of the programs at the schools, I had only six girls for my Sunday school at Peñitas Arriba. I went to the program at the Peñitas Arriba school and was pleased when the teacher said in his speech that I had told him that God should always be first if they wanted their country to prosper. In the afternoon I walked to San Antonio de Perú for the Sunday School class and found that the village people were still celebrating Independence Day. One man was passing out hard candy to the children when I arrived. I was given a warm welcome and ta ken into a room where music was playing. I hadn't been there long when one of the children came to share a piece of candy with me. The next thing I knew I had a steady stream of children sharing with me. One child brought a small packet of cookies. Later the teacher told the children who wanted to attend Sunday

School to go to the classroom where I was sitting. I had books for only twenty-five children, but close to forty were there in addition to several parents. We had prayer and sang some choruses and I told them the story in the lesson and pointed out that Independence Day should not be a day of independence from God. One of the men who led the Catholic Church had a closing prayer.

I mentioned earlier about the feeding program sponsored by the Holy Land Christian International. We had hoped they would send more money to sponsor a *comedor* (dining room) at a village about four miles further up in the mountains, but they did not respond. Seeing the need for the children at Laguna de Tembladeros, I wrote to Byron Bezdek of International Disaster Emergency Services in Kempton, Indiana, asking them for $500 monthly to help get a *comedor* started in Laguna. I told them that if that sum wasn't enough, I would supplement it from my mission funds. I am a believer in "preventive" medicine, and even though I.D.E.S. was for emergency needs, I pointed out that providing this one good meal a day could prevent malnutrition in many children. I.D.E.S. responded and the *comedor* was started in October 1985. I learned the road well up the hill to Laguna de Tembladeros—from 3200 feet to 5000 feet. I closed the clinic on Wednesdays to check on the *comedor*. I took my Bible and gave a Scripture lesson to the children before their meal and emphasized many times that it was the love of our Lord that prompted people to share with them.

Life was always interesting, full of surprises and challenges. One day I heard gunshots nearby. I quietly went outside and saw a man in front of the store pointing a gun in the air. Dalila was terrified. I slowly walked to the store and saw that the man was drunk. Someone had once told me that the best way to sober up a drunk was to get him or her to drink strong coffee. I went back inside, made a cup of strong coffee and took it out to him. Remember, I am very

214

tall, taller than he, which apparently intimidated him. I insisted that he give me the gun—and he handed it over! But I am terrified of guns and I had no idea if it was still loaded. I took it and gingerly placed it on a table. Later a man who worked for the owner of the store came to see what was happening, and he took the gun, for which I was thankful. Later the drunk was fired from his job. Some of the men who owned property in the mountains teased me by saying that no one would mess with Madonna now! Oh, well, just another day in Honduras!

Another afternoon as I walked up to the clinic from the house, I startled a young man from the Peace Corps as he was driving to San Pedro Sula after a visit to another Peace Corps worker at Laguna de Tembladeros. He told me he had been listening to tapes as he drove and that when he looked up to see an obviously American nurse in a white uniform with her nurse's pin, he could hardly believe his eyes. He told me of Matt Housman who was working in Laguna de Tembladeros.

The first time I went up to that village, Matt had gone to San Pedro Sula, but the second time, he was home, so I went to introduce myself. It was nice to be able to talk to someone in English. In one of our conversations I was able to share some Scriptures with him from my Spanish Bible. I remember him saying that he didn't think the devil existed. I encouraged him to read the book of Job and told him after reading it, he would change his mind.

Before Matt had gone to Laguna de Tembladeros, he had worked in El Negrito where he met Suyapa Flores Assaf. She moved with him to Laguna. Matt, or Carlos, as he was called by the Honduran folk, was teaching the people how to better utilize the land to grow flowers and vegetables.

I had often been reminded of how God answers prayers in unexpected ways. I was reminded of that again when Matt and Suyapa moved to Peñitas Arriba. I had prayed for a missionary to come to help the people with agriculture, but God provided someone else. Now living in the house were Matt and Suyapa—using one of the back storerooms; Don Rosa; Dalila and her four children; a new girl who was helping Dalila; and me. The same day Matt and Suyapa moved in, I baked a chocolate cake and Matt said it had been two years since he had had chocolate cake. He not only enjoyed the finished product, but also enjoyed cleaning out the bowl in which I had mixed it.

I gave Matt an English Bible and Suyapa a Spanish Bible. I also gave her the booklet in Spanish that goes with the Good News Productions filmstrips. Matt read the Bible, and he and Suyapa attended some of the Sunday worship services. I was praying for salvation for both of them.

My work in the clinic kept me busy as people came from more villages. One day I had twenty-one patients from La Cumbre, a village southeast of us. Later I would go there to have a vaccination clinic. The people could walk the mountain paths to get to the clinic, but to drive to La Cumbre, one had to go down to San Pedro Sula, then drive another road up to La Cumbre. I was now seeing patients regularly from fourteen different *aldeas* with people coming occasionally from five other villages.

A family had said they would give land for the clinic, but changed their minds. However, Mr. Vanegas said he would give the land where I was now working. Since it was a small area, I would have to look for another place to build my home.

I continued to work with Interplast. In November, I once again worked with them and sent them two patients who

216

needed surgery. As my Spanish improved, I translated for the doctors.

Thanks to a generous donation from the Lincoln (IL) Christian Church, I.D.E.S. sent $2,000 to help in the feeding program at Laguna de Tembladeros. Since it was such a large amount, with the help of leaders of four villages, we picked out seventy of the poorest families and provided them with supplies to make their Christmas special. Before we distributed the food, Matt helped me write a note on a Christmas card notifying them of the date the food would be available. We used I John 3:17: "But whosoever has the world's goods and beholds his brother in need and closes his heart against him, how does the love of God abide in Him." We explained that it was the love of God that prompted Christians from the U.S.A. to share the gifts.

It would not have been possible for me to get all of the provisions without the help of the Vanegas family. Mr. Vanegas and his wife brought all of the food to the village where we divided them according to the numbers in the families. He also provided pork at a very good price and helped cut it up and weigh it. The families were given twenty different items including pork, a chicken, bread, eggs, flour, sugar, rice and other items necessary to make the special food for Christmas. Mr. Vanegas' son took me to two of the villages the Sunday before Christmas to distribute the food in those two *aldeas*. The families from San Antonio del Perú and Peñitas Arriba came to the store to get their food.

## A Place for My Home

I had been praying for a place to build my home. I was thankful for my little room, but I looked forward to having my own place.

One Sunday when I was at Sunday School at San Antonio del Peru, Emma Reyes, the mother of some of the children in my class, brought me bananas. She and her family had been frequent patients at the clinic. The next to the youngest in the family had been brought twice with a very bad attack of asthma. One Sunday, even with the adrenalin injections, she didn't improve. I had prayer with her and her father and then told him I thought she should be admitted to the hospital. I found out later that he did not take her, but that she had improved after she got home.

The Wednesday following the Sunday that Emma had given me the bananas, I decided I would bake the family a banana cake and take it to them. I also wanted to look for a piece of land where I could build my house. and I had to get letters collected from there for the sponsors of the Holy Land Christian Mission International. I first walked to look at a piece of land that I had thought might be a good place to build, but after looking more closely, I decided it was too small. As I headed down the hill to take the cake to the family, I saw a piece of land below the Catholic Church that looked like it would be a good place to build. I had no idea who owned the land, but it wouldn't take me long to find out. I delivered the cake, and one of the daughters went with me to show the way to some of the homes where I needed to collect letters.

At the first home, I saw a man whose name I didn't know, though I thought he was the man who owned the first property I had looked at. He told me who owned the land below the church. To my surprise, I found it belonged to Rosalio Martinez, the husband of Emma, to whom I had just delivered the cake. I asked his daughter, who was with me, to ask her father to come to see me. He did, and he agreed to sell me about 1.7 acres . Others had asked to buy that piece of land and he had refused. I felt certain that he sold it to me because he was grateful for the medical help I had given his family.  It was located only about a kilometer from the clinic and about a twenty- minute walk from where I was living.  We would have to clear the land, but I was happy to know that soon I would have my own home.

## Visitors—A Blessing Indeed

Berry Kennedy of F.A.M.E. and Bob Devore of Lifeline Christian Mission visited in February 1986. The god-daughter of my former landlady knew of a house in  San Nicolas that we could buy—it had belonged to her aunt.  Since Bob was someone who knew construction, he, Berry and I went to San Nicolas to check out the house.  Bob concluded that because of termites there were too many problems with the house to convert it into a clinic.  After visiting the government clinic and seeing that they had a good nurse, we felt this would not be a good place for F.A.M.E. to build a clinic. After our return, Berry said,  "Let us help you build your clinic."  So F.A.M.E. approved $65,000 to build and equip the clinic.

While he was with us, Berry  had the joy of taking the confession of faith of Matt and Suyapa and baptizing them in the water tank outside the clinic in the presence of many from the Catholic Church.

Dr. Alan Handt and John Kenneson from the Trader's Point Christian Church, Indianapolis, and representing Lifeline Mission, visited in April 1986.  As usually happens with those who visit, they fell in love with the people.  Alan and Yami, Dalila's daughter, really bonded, and he wanted her to go to the States to study. After much work we were able to get a passport .  A visa application needed the signature of the father, but Dalila and Yami had no idea where the father was. But I persisted and finally got the passport. When we went to Tegucigalpa to get the visa, we were walking down a street when Dalila exclaimed, "There is Yami's dad." We could not believe it. Here we were in the middle of the largest city in Honduras and who should we see but her father. Dalila blurted out to him that Yami hoped to go to the States with Alan. We hoped he would not object; he didn't. Alan had hoped to get a visa so Yami could study in the States, but he could get only a three-month tourist visa. However, Yami did get to spend from September to November 1986 with the Handts.

Brenda Smith, a registered nurse from Ann Arbor, Michigan, was the first of many missionary interns to work with me in Honduras. She arrived on May 22 and was busy from the time she arrived. She cleaned and organized the clinic while I saw patients. I had never had the time to sort through the equipment I had received from F.A.M.E. and it had been a long time since I had had time to clean cupboards and get the medicine in order. The second day that Brenda was with me, a doctor from the city came to see patients. I don't know how I would have managed to keep up if Brenda hadn't been there. She also studied Spanish and taught Yami some English.

Brenda was a special blessing when a team of ten people from Colegio Biblico arrived to hold a Vacation Bible School and to conduct meetings in the evenings. It was a major challenge to cook for that many people on a one-burner stove. Some of the local women helped by making corn tortillas, and the group really liked the Honduran food better than my American dishes.

The clinic was also very busy while Brenda was with me. We saw 421 patients in only eighteen days in July. Because we were getting so tired, I changed the clinic days to Monday, Wednesday and Friday and every other Saturday after-

220

noon when two doctors, both of whom I met through Inter-plast, came to see patients.

The group from Colegio Biblico was a real blessing. When I had attended the missionary reunion in Mexico in March, John Cary, the president of Colegio Biblico, had asked if I would be interested in having a group from the college to come to Honduras.. Since I had no home yet, we had to solve the problem of finding a place for ten people to stay. My good friends, the Canahuatis, allowed the girls to stay in their home and the Catholic congregation allowed the men to sleep in the church building. We also had our evening meetings in the Catholic Church building.

The group went calling in the mornings, conducted Vacation Bible School in the afternoons, and led meetings in the evenings. At night the building was full of people for the meetings. An accordionist and a guitarist led the singing and provided special music. The men took turns preaching. The final night we showed the movie *Jesus*, based on the Gospel of Luke. Two people came to Christ as a result of the meetings.

Many tears were shed as we bid farewell to this group, for everyone had come to love them for their enthusiasm for the Lord. There were times when they had to wait for their food—we had to cook most of it on my hot plate. One day we had no water, so they couldn't have a bath nor even have water to drink. It was tiring as they hiked to visit homes. Some of the men had helped in the fields for two days. We continued to see fruit from their labors as soon four more people came to the Lord and were baptized.

Gerinne Dudley arrived in early September. That same day I had a vaccination clinic planned at Las Crucitas and had promised one of the nurses working at the government health care center in San Pedro Sula that I would take her to Las Crucitas to talk to the people about selecting a health care worker in their village. Unfortunately, my messages had not reached the people, so there were no babies or children to be vaccinated and only a few children at the school.

When Gerianne arrived, Suyapa Flores was living with me. She helped Gerianne with Spanish and Gerianne helped her learn more English.

When Alan Handt returned in the autumn to take Yami to the States, I put him to work in the clinic. One day he saw sixty patients. Once he treated a man with a machete wound. Alan sutured the deep wound and one on his knee.

# Transportation!

It never ceases to amaze me at how the Lord works. I had been trying for some time to get a *dispensa* to bring a Toyota pickup to Honduras. I found out that I could get a 60-day permit at the border when I drove the pickup into the country and then work on getting the *dispensa* after I got the car into the country. A couple of alternatives had emerged to get the vehicle into the country. Bill Baker from Span-

*A way to get around*

ish American Evangelism wanted to visit Central America and had indicated that he might be able to tow the pickup to Honduras. Norm Dungan had suggested that I attend the missionary reunion in Mexico. I had been praying about going and the money was provided. I decided to call Bill

*Madonna teaching in Laguna de Tembladeros*

to see if he could drive the pickup to the reunion and then drive me to Honduras afterwards. He said he could, so my forwarding agents drove the pickup to El Paso for Bill. I flew into Mexico City a week early: the dates of the reunion had been changed and I didn't have time to change my ticket. I had the missionary directory with me and called the first name on the list to see if they could host an unexpected guest. When I called Rich and Leta Atkinson, I had no idea what a blessing it would be. They welcomed me and that was the start of a beautiful friendship. The reunion was a blessing with Don Richardson, author of *The Peace Child,* as the speaker.

Bill and I drove through forest fires through Mexico on the trip to Honduras. I was reminded of Isaiah 43:2: "When you pass through the waters, I will be with you; And through the rivers, they will not overflow you. When you walk through the fire, you will not be scorched. Nor will the flame burn you" (N.A.S.B.). When we arrived near the border between Mexico and Guatemala, the police could not believe that we had made it through the fires. God certainly had protected us, but it was a bit scary seeing all of the flames on both sides of the road.

It was a blessing to have regular transport from the mountains to San Pedro Sula.  I had depended on rides, but now I could go when I needed to and return quickly.  I used the pickup for trips to the city, to travel to El Peru and Laguna de Tembladeros to check on the *comedors*, to take nurses from the government health clinic to vaccinate children, and to see how construction of my new home was progressing.

Once I had my pickup, I was able to visit the *comedor* in Laguna Tembladeros more often.  One week when I drove up the mountain, I took a visualized Bible story and shared the story of Elijah and the prophets of Baal with the children and passed out some tracts.

## Expanding Evangelistic Outreach

I hoped to get permission from the Department of Education to have regular Bible lessons with the children.  In February, when Bob DeVoe from Lifeline Mission had visited, he heard of the need in Laguna, so Lifeline Mission sent money for me to buy school books, notebooks, pencils, crayons and other supplies to help the children have a better education.  Because of the aid from Lifeline Christian Mission and I.D.E.S., I was also able to provide new school uniforms.  I was happy when a man from the village came to tell me that

he believed in Christ and wanted to be baptized.  I took him and a pickup truck full of people from our little congregation in Peñitas to

*Construction of the clinic*

224

the Church of Christ in San Pedro Sula where he was baptized. I hoped to get a congregation started there soon.

# Construction Begins

Before construction could begin on my home, I had to arrange for a bulldozer from San Pedro Sula to clear enough space and do leveling for the house. While the bulldozing was being done, a place for the clinic was cleared and leveled too. The house would have a kitchen, living-dining room area, three bedrooms, and a bathroom. Construction moved along well, and I was soon able to move in. I surely enjoyed the greater amount of space.

# The Medical Work Goes On—and On

My first maternity case in the mountains was a fifteen-year-old young lady—her son was born on her fifteenth birthday. She had pre-eclampsia. I tried to persuade her to go to the hospital in the city, but she refused. I managed to deliver the baby fine, but then she started having convulsions. This was before I had my pickup, but I was able to find someone to take her to the city. She recovered quickly and soon returned to her home.

That same day I did my first home delivery in the mountains. This mother was sixteen years old. She lived down the mountain, so her sister-in-law prepared a corner of her house where I could deliver the baby. I went to the home about 5:30 P.M. and delivered the baby five hours later with the light of one candle and a small flashlight. I was on my knees at the side of the bed which was too low for this tall nurse to bend over.

A few months later, I hiked down a mountain path to do a second home delivery for an eighteen-year-old woman. This time I had only the light of a candle. Again I had to do the delivery on my knees. I was so tired afterwards that I didn't think I would make it back up the mountain. I am sure the new father thought the same when, as he walked back with me, I had to stop to rest a few times. I knew I would be happy to have the new clinic completed so I would have a good place with good light to deliver babies.

## Clinic Construction Impeded

Clinic construction was stopped by D.I.M.A., the water department, in June. I had a number of meetings on the problem in San Pedro Sula.

The following was in my newsletter of August-September, 1986.

### D.I.M.A. STOPS CLINIC CONSTRUCTION

One day toward the end of June, the builder told me it was rumored that D.I.M.A. (Division of Water Municipality of S.P.S.) was going to stop the clinic construction. An employee of D.I.M.A. suggested I go down to see the engineer working in this area. I went to San Pedro Sula to see Domingo Larach (the contractor) and he said he had not obtained approval for the construction of the clinic because he didn't think it was necessary for a rural area. But we found out that the land in the mountains was actually owned by the municipality and under the control of D.I.M.A. We also found out that the head of D.I.M.A. had said there was no way he would approve a clinic for that site. That was when I called my friend Donna

Webster and asked her to contact Berry Kennedy
at the N.A.C.C. that was being held in Indianapolis,
Indiana, and request prayer that the construction
would continue.  I might have been over-estimating,
but I told the people in the mountains that 30,000
people were praying about our need and for the
head of D.I.M.A., Gabriel Khattan.  The Scripture that
sustained me was Exodus 14:13,14: "But Moses said
to the people, 'Do not fear! Stand by and see the
salvation of the Lord which He will accomplish for you
today; for the Egyptians whom you have seen today,
you will never see them again forever.  The Lord will
fight for you while you keep silent'".  On July 8, I had
a visit from a man who owns property here in the
mountains and he said if I would see the mayor, he
would approve the construction.  I literally danced for
joy, but I danced a bit prematurely.  It just was not
that simple.  For one thing I had a lot of unforgive-
ness in my heart toward Gabriel Khattan.  His reasons
for disapproving the clinic construction were valid and
involved a large water conservation project for the
Sula Valley, but I disagreed with some of his meth-
ods.  At the mayor's request I attended a meeting on
this subject and much to my dismay got into a bit of
a word battle with Mr. Khattan.  He kept accusing me
of being political and this puzzled me.  I only found
out a year later why he said this.  Then the mayor
kept putting me off when I tried to see him.  Finally,
through a friend I learned that the mayor also disap-
proved the clinic construction on the present site.
But I still felt certain our prayers would be answered.
One morning when I was praying about the situation,
I felt the Spirit leading me to go see Gabriel Khattan
myself.  Although it was a Saturday morning when
most of the offices are closed, I knew that if this was
the Spirit leading, I would find him.  He was there and
I sat down to wait; I had my Bible with me.  Other

227

people were also waiting; one was an older man who sat beside me and asked if he could practice English with me. I was happy to comply and during our conversation he said he knew I was a happy woman as I was reading my Bible. It turned out that he was the father of a woman who works in the travel agency with Luisa Julia, my former landlady, and I knew his daughter. During our discussion about the Bible I was also able to give a Scripture reference to a lawyer who was with him. Soon Gabriel Khattan came into the office to take a phone call and when he had finished, his secretary told him that I wished to speak to him. Rather abruptly, he said, "Tell me what you want." I started by asking his forgiveness for some of things I had said in our verbal battle. When he realized I was not there to do more battle, he sat down and we had a very amiable discussion. The last things he said were: "I am not the man you think I am," and, "We can work together." He promised he would come up to the mountain and look the situation over. He did not come, but the next week I took the clinic plans to his assistant and left them along with the application for permission to build. His assistant, Jorge Milla, told he didn't think there would be any problem. I said I was willing to make the building smaller and also donate the building to the municipality if in 15-20 years there were no people living in the mountains. The following Saturday I was told that the work could continue and so the construction continued.

Now for the rest of the story. It was a year later that I went to visit a businessman who owned property in the mountains. He asked me how my friend Gabriel Khattan was. Then he told me that a year earlier, he had called his friend, the President of Honduras, and asked him to tell Gabriel Khattan to allow me to continue the clinic construction.

This was why I had been called political, but I had known nothing of what had been done. When I went to apologize, he realized this, making it possible for him to give me permission without feeling that he was forced to do so. As I told people later, I had requested prayer to our

*A farmer on his way to market*

Father in heaven and it was answered when someone talked to the head of the Honduran government!

As work continued on the new clinic, we had to move from room to room as workers completed a room, painted it, and moved on to work on another one. The clinic consisted of a large exam room, a smaller room for storage of medicines, a small office, and a room for delivery of babies. Viewing the clinic from the road, the left side was composed of two rooms—a large one where we could have worship services and a smaller room we could use for Sunday School classes.

## More Medical Opportunities

It was definitely God's leading that helped me persist in working toward achieving registration as a professional nurse in Honduras. When Berry Kennedy had visited, we went to the government health care center in San Pedro Sula to see if they would permit me to have vaccines to start some vaccination clinics. At first the nurse would hardly even talk to me, but when I pulled out my Professional nurse I.D. card, the attitude changed completely. When she saw that I had

worked to be registered in Honduras, she was very coopera-
tive and that led to good cooperation with the government in
many different ways.

Once I had my pickup, I took some of the nurses from the
government clinic to do vaccination clinics. Later, when I
had my own supply of vaccines, the Centro de Salud would
loan a nurse to help. I later did the vaccination clinics on my
own and submitted a government report on what vaccinations I had done each month. I was also able to take medicines from the Centro de Salud to one of their government
health care centers to Santa Marta further up the mountain.

## Life's Little—and Big—Challenges

Challenges always came along—some of them not good.
As I explained in my December 1986 newsletter:

JAIME

After Brenda came, we made a trip to Tegucigalpa to
see about the customs on my pickup. We were gone
three nights and when we got back, Camilo Venegas
told me that he had some bad news for me. The bad
news was that someone had broken into the house.
What a mess both our bedrooms were as drawers
had been pulled out and left and clothes and other
things thrown on the floor. After putting things back,
I found only my radio-tape recorder missing and later
found some jewelry missing. About two weeks later,
our thief came back, this time coming on a Saturday
night when we were sleeping. He opened the door
to my room and then went into Brenda's room and
took her purse. She must have awakened just as he
left. She called to me and told me she thought there

was a rat in her room. Then she heard someone go out the back door and I got up to investigate. I found the back door wide open, but found that our thief had come in one of the front windows by taking out some of the window panes and then breaking the screen. I went out to replace the window panes and found he had left his shirt, so I put it in the house. It wasn't until later that Brenda discovered her purse was gone and then I remembered that Camilo was sleeping at the store, so I decided to go get him to see if he and some others could catch our thief. When I went out the second time, there was Brenda's purse on the porch. We were thankful to find he had left her passport and travelers checks, though he had taken some credit cards, checks, cash and her camera. Camilo woke up several men of the village when someone recognized the shirt and said it belonged to Jaime Orellana, a young boy who had a history of stealing. One of the men who went out looking for him was his older brother and he found my tape recorder in Jaime's house. Later I learned about Jaime's history.

When Jaime had been about a year old, his older brother had to have surgery, so his mother left Jaime with the eldest brother while she was at the hospital with her other son. When she finally returned, her eldest son asked to keep Jaime as he had no children at the time and had learned to love him. But, when Jaime was 12 years old, his brother was injured in an automobile accident and later died from his injuries. None of Jaime's other brothers wanted him and his mother had moved to the city after separating from his father. Jaime felt forsaken and turned to crime.

I had been praying for him and began to pray even more earnestly. The day he returned to the village and the word got out he was back, I had to laugh as a man and another boy sat on my front porch guarding me with their machetes.

Jaime had come to apologize and ask my forgiveness and to ask for work so he could pay me back for what he had stolen. I told him that he had been forgiven and that I had been praying for him. Before this, his mother had sent back Brenda's camera and the cash he had taken plus some other items.

I gave him a cup of coffee and a doughnut and every day that week he came by after I got home from the clinic for a cup of coffee and something to eat. I always tried to keep on hand some goodies for visitors. The second day I gave him a Bible and the booklet that goes with the filmstrips from Good News Productions and encouraged him to study the Bible and then we would discuss Scripture when he came to visit. At the end of the week, he told me he wanted to become a Christian. The following Sunday night we went to San Pedro Sula where he was baptized into Christ. I gave him some work at the house for a short time and then he worked with the building crew at the clinic. He later worked as a night watchman at the clinic. Unfortunately some people in the village did seem to be happy that he had changed, so his temptations were many. I prayed that he would be able to withstand the temptations and grow in Christ.

# Christmas 1986

Christmas in the mountains in 1986 was a special time, thanks to Lifeline Christian Mission and I.D.E.S. Dean Cary, Director of Latin American Expansion for Lifeline, brought toys and candy for the children at Laguna de Tembladeros. A teacher at the school who was paid by Lifeline Mission told the children the meaning of Christmas and led his Bible study class in some choruses he had taught them before the gifts were distributed.

Later I went back to Laguna to help the women as they passed out sandwiches of chicken, cabbage and tomato to the children—believe it or not, this was a special treat at Christmas—and provisions were given to the families for special food on Christmas Day. Food was also given to some of the families in Peñitas Arriba, San Antonio del Perú and Perú. I bought 400 pounds of chicken, 150 loaves of bread, rice, tomato sauce, peas, cabbage and tomatoes. Besides the food, toys provided by Holy Land Christian Mission International were distributed. It made for a busy week, but I had several good assistants. On Christmas Eve we had a candlelight service at the clinic, singing some Christmas songs. Then on Christmas Day we also had a worship service.

Right after Christmas, Wilda Rush from the Walton Christian Church in Indiana arrived along with Cheryl Noel, a student nurse from Marion, Indiana. Cheryl came to do an inter-cultural study in nursing. Berry and Amy Kennedy also came for Berry to speak at the dedication of the clinic. Christine Kelley also came to obtain a visa to live in Honduras. We all had to laugh one day when we were at the home where I used to live when the man who lived there said there was an invasion of the white people.

# Clinic Dedication

Many people assisted in preparing for the January dedication of the clinic. Chepe and Chela Canahuati had their employees finishing cupboards; Gerianne and Cheryl organized and put up medicines; Christine, Rosalinda, Gerianne, Wilda and Cheryl cleaned thoroughly; Dean Cary and Berry Kennedy put up towel racks, soap dishes, etc.; Dean, Gerianne, Cheryl and Christine did last minute buying. Luisa Julia Kipps, my former landlady, found her punchbowl for us to use. The day of the dedication, Dean brought meat pies

*The completed clinic*

and cookies from the bakery. Salvador Canahuati brought sherbet for the punch and his wife and daughters worked all morning making delicious pastries to add to our other refreshments. Anwar Zummar and his wife brought a cooler of Cokes and sambusas. As the others were working on getting the last of the cleaning done, Amy Kennedy was a typical grandmother taking care of babies so I could examine their mothers.

Dedication day was a beautiful day. We had a record attendance of seventy-one in church with many also there for Sunday School. Berry preached for the worship service with Dean translating his excellent message. Berry also gave an excellent message for the dedication, again with Dean translating. We had between three hundred and four hundred in attendance. Even though we borrowed more beaches from the Catholic Church and from Dalila, many people had to stand. At the close of the service, I called on all of my helpers to assist me in cutting the ribbon. How thankful I was to F.A.M.E. for providing the funds for the clinic-community center and to all of those who helped to make it a very special day.

But the day wasn't over yet. We had a wedding in the evening. Matt and Suyapa had been married in a civil ceremony at the Municipality, but they also wanted a Christian wedding. Since Berry Kennedy had baptized them, they wanted him to marry them as well. Gerianne, with the help of a Peace Corp worker, a teacher from Laguna de Tem-

234

bladeros, and Cheryl transformed my living room to make a beautiful setting for Matt and Suyapa's wedding. Berry did the ceremony in English with Dean again translating into Spanish.

# Visitors Come and Go

Cheryl Noel was an asset in the clinic. She shared a room with Gerianne at my house and Gerianne shared her love of Christ and her knowledge of the Scriptures with Cheryl. As a result, when a young boy made his decision to come to Christ and be baptized, Cheryl made the same decision. Dean Cary baptized them both in the water tank at the clinic.

We sadly bid farewell to Gerrianne Dudley who was leaving after six months to return to the States to complete her medical training. She was always happy and full of love. The people learned to love her. She learned Spanish quickly and did so well communicating that she saw patients alone on Wednesday mornings, giving me a morning to do other things. We had a surprise farewell party for her the day before she left.

We were sad to see Gerianne go, but Wilda was still with us. A retired nurse, she had arrived in January and would stay for almost a year. She gave nearly all of the vaccinations in the clinic and also went out to the vaccination clinics. She did the sterilizing in the clinic after Alan Handt brought us an electric sterilizer. She never learned much Spanish, but she talked to the patients in English whether they understood her or not. Dean Cary said that Wilda might not learn Spanish, but she was teaching the people a lot of English. She described her experiences in one of my newsletters.

The plane landed at 11 P.M. on January 2, 1987, in San Pedro Sula, Honduras. Customs was no problem, but when we walked out of the airport and no Madonna Burget, I thought: "What is an old woman like me doing out here in the middle of nowhere?" Madonna showed up in a few minutes and that thought has not had time to cross my mind since. The next day was the first Saturday of the month. Dr. Garcia comes to the clinic on the first Saturday of the month, so we went to work early that A.M. and have not let up yet—five full months later.

The warm, friendly people of the Merendon Mountains accepted me, a non-Spanish speaking, old Gringa, and have made me feel so welcome and needed that I have no need to get homesick. Oh yes, I miss my family, but the adorable kids are so very curious as to what goes on around Madonna's house and the clinic, they keep us company.

Kerosene lamps, candle light, and cold showers awaited us each evening for three months; then the long promised electricity arrived at our house—what a joy! Cold showers are still the only kind available, but when you can see what you are doing they are bearable; one gets used to them eventually.
The clinic keeps us busy 3½ days a week, averaging around 30 to 35 patients a day. I

*Feeding program for children*

have had the privilege of assisting on three deliveries so far at the clinic.  To me it is still a miracle—those beautiful newborn babies and I get to clean them up and dress them.  The first one, Grandmother had to help me dress him for they dress them differently than we do at home.  Can you imagine putting a newborn male in a red cloth for a diaper, a red shirt, red cloth for a band and red socks, then mummying him in a bath towel—oh yes, they put a knit sock cap on him.  (Neither it nor the towel were red.)  I have learned you dress newborns in what is available, be it red, white or blue.

The people who come to clinic sometimes walk for as long as six hours to get there.  Why?  They hear of the care and the medicines they get there; for often, in the local government clinics there is limited medicine, if any at all.  They sometimes get rides in open pickup trucks (people trucks) for a price.

Every day brings something new.  Example:  today we were to do "well-baby clinics" in an aldea that had two schools.  We knew where the one on this side of the valley was and Madonna thought she knew about where the other one was.  We drove down, and around hairpin curves, up and around on this very narrow rutted, rocky road for what seemed like ages—when we came to the end.  There was a house there so we asked about the school.  There was no road—only a foot path to it and it was about 1.8 miles farther.  To top it all off, the teacher wasn't back from attending a meeting in San Pedro Sula the day before. We turned around and went back on the same road. We had planned to leave the Public Health Nurse from the Centro de Salud of San Pedro Sula at the school, but all three of us went back to the school on the other side and did what vaccinations we could.  There was a measles epidemic, especially in that area of the mountains and we were anxious to give measles vaccine to as many children as possible.

Not all the work here is medical. The clinic and medical work give an excellent entry to the spiritual needs of the people in the area. Many seem starved for attention and love. There are three Sunday Services plus two Sunday Schools and two evening services during the week and all are well attended. When there is a minister available, he does the preaching.

How does a non-Spanish speaking lay person help in all this? You support the one who is ministering by being a sounding board; doing small tasks such as keeping track of song books, turning tape recorders on, seeing that the room is ready for showing film strips, being flexible enough to adapt to any situation. Madonna says she will use all the help she can get; carpentry, sewing, teaching, calling, dishwashing, etc. although we now have a housekeeper who eases or work load considerably.

Whenever Madonna gets a free day, we go calling on the people who live on the mountainside. We walk the paths they walk—they are narrow, steep and sometimes slick. It is always a fun experience and I have even come to the place where I can eat beans and tortillas on a dirt floor kitchen where dogs, hens and chickens and kids run in and out. We visited one home which was nice, big and clean. We were in the kitchen talking when the chickens and ducks came in to be fed. I was amazed. I'm always surprised to find the distances and steep paths some of our faithful members have to walk to come to church two times on Sunday and once during the week.

This has been a wonderfully full five months. Not only have we kept busy in the mountains, but we have given our services to help a couple of times in San Pedro Sula. We helped with the World Health Organization vaccination push on Sunday, April 5. Because of a strike of some of the medical help at the Centro de Salud (clinic), they were short of help; for the city-wide vaccination campaign. Madonna had a visiting minister to relieve her here in the Merendon, so we both spent the old day vaccinating children (150) in a poor section of town. Another interesting experience was helping the Interplast group from the U.S.A. in their performance of plastic surgery on the indigent children at Leonardo Martinez (Govt.) hospital. What a rewarding experience to work in the recovery room and take the children back to their awaiting parents on the post-op wards. The happy smiles of the parents when they saw the beautiful repair of their child's cleft lip was worth the many hours of hard work. All work and no play make even a nurse and a missionary dull, so we take time off for renewal once in awhile. A week in Guatemala City and Mexico was fun and a day once in awhile at the beach on the Caribbean Sea helps immensely.

If any of you reading this are retired or have time on your hands and are in good health, I would encourage you to contact your favorite missionaries to see if they could use your services. It is a wonderfully rewarding experience; I have learned that I can grow experientially and spiritually even at the age of 67.5 years. Madonna Burget is a beautiful role model and I have learned the power of faith and prayer from her. I'm sure that there are missionaries on the other fields who would use help and who are as faithful in their work as Madonna is here. If one knew the language you could be of more help, but that is not absolutely essential.  There are always jobs that can be done in any language.  Try it, you might like it.

In February, Dr. Alan Handt, his wife, and their two daughters, visited again.  They were accompanied by John and Kim Kenneson and their daughter.  They were with us for ten days.  Alan saw patients each day, giving me a vacation from clinic work, and John preached.  The two women held classes for the women and children each evening.

In March, four men whom I called the "Four Stooges" visited.  Gordon Clifford from Christian Mission Press, Campo, California; Larry Weaver from Chandler, Arizona; Ron Cochran, President of El Paso School of Missions and Fred Briggs from Michigan were the four.  With their trailer full of New Testaments and used clothing, they had quite a time getting through customs in Mexico, Guatemala and Honduras.  Only they could tell how two customs officials nearly came to blows over a soccer ball they brought.  Gordon brought three movie projectors and a series of twelve films on the Life of Christ plus tracts to pass out with the movies.  He also brought Daily Vacation Bible School material in Spanish.  We showed the movies both at the clinic and in Laguna de Tembladeros.  There was no electricity at Laguna, so my friends Chepe and Chela Canahuati loaned us their electric plant so we could show the movies.  Between 100 and 130 saw the movies at Peñitas and close to 310 at Laguna de Tembladeros.

Just before the "Four Stooges" arrived, the top of our septic tank broke.  Larry and Fred went beyond the call of duty to clean it out and fix a new top for it.  We called their work an example of real Christian love!!  Ron led the Friday night Bible study in the city that I did for Dean Cary when he is was gone; he also gave messages to the people at the movies.

Before Matt and Suyapa returned to the States, Matt had the joy of baptizing Maximo Diaz. Maximo, affectionately called Don Mancho, was the night watchman now for the clinic. A widower whose wife had died of cancer, he brought his children and his brother-in-law to the church.

I looked forward to welcoming Christine Kelley to the ministry in August. Christine would begin language study Honduras while spending the weekends in the Merendon Mountains. By January 1988, she was engaged in full time ministry. Christine came from a family dedicated to Christian ministries. Her grandfather, Harrold McFarland, founded Mission Services. Her parents, Chuck and Carol Kelley, served in Zimbabwe (1965-1972) and then at Butler Springs Christian Assembly near Hillsboro, Ohio. In 1985, Christian had been on a six-month internship in Zimbabwe. Upon returning she began correspondence with me, and I invited her to work in Honduras.

## God's Biggest Surprise

I could not have anticipated that 1987 would be such an unforgettable year. In my December 1986 newsletter under "Laborers for Honduras," I closed the article with: "See what happens when we obey Christ's command to pay for laborers!!" Little did I dream that as I prayed for laborers, God would send one to become my husband. Through the Holy Spirit leading and Floyd Clark's efforts, I had begun to correspond with John Spratt in November

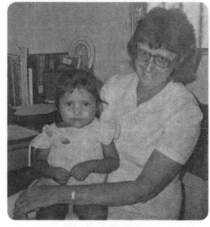

*A tiny Patient*

241

1986.  It was difficult for me to think of the stern long time Dean at Johnson Bible College as a cupid.  John had been praying for a wife since 1983, but had told no one.  I am sure it came as a surprise to him when Floyd wrote to tell him that he thought he needed a helpmeet and gave him my name and address and one of my newsletters.  Dean Clark told him that he thought I would be a good helpmeet for him.  So began a unique courtship by correspondence.

John was originally from Clinton, South Carolina, but had gone to college in Maryville, Tennessee, and was led to Christ by Floyd Clark.  He married his first wife, Louise, in Maryville, and for many years he ran a Christian bookstore. Louise died in 1981.  They had no children.  After Louise died, John eventually sold the bookstore and worked with World Mission Builders doing short term mission work in Haiti, the Philippines, and India.  Later he did volunteer work with Colegio Biblico in Eagle Pass, Texas, and at Johnson Bible College and Mission Services near Knoxville, Tennes-see.  In 1983, he had begun serving full time with Habitat for Humanity in Americus, Georgia.  In March of 1986, he had gone to Papua New Guinea to work with Habitat's project there.

John and Louise supported me when I was in India, so I had met him on two different furloughs—once when I spoke a First Christian Church in Maryville and once when I went to his bookstore to thank him for their support.

Since I was pretty certain from John's first letter why he was writing, I had to do a lot of praying.  Three years earlier I had been so very sure that God did not intend for me to marry.  But when John wrote in April 1987, asking me to be his wife, I knew God had a different plan and I accepted his proposal.  The "icing on the cake" was that when John wrote that letter, he also told me he would plan to come to Hondu-ras to serve with me.  I had accepted the fact—with diffi-

242

culty—that I would have to join John in Papua New Guinea, yet another move.    Habitat had freed him from his commitment as of October 1.  John was—and is—a wonderful committed servant of the Lord and I knew I would be getting a jewel for a husband.  Many of our mutual friends confirmed this.  We planned to marry in the chapel at Johnson Bible College on October 17, 1987.

I had not told Wilda that I was corresponding with John, so after he proposed, I told her one day that I had something to tell her and that she had better sit down before I told her.  She was very surprised, but happy for me when I told her I would be getting married.  Wilda, and later Christine with her, would go to San Pedro Sula for Spanish lessons and I would go to my former landlady's house to wait for a call from John from Papua New Guinea.  So you could say we had a courtship by correspondence and phone calls.

The reaction from my many friends was interesting, but the funniest  came from Sara Stere with whom I had worked in Rhodesia.  When I wrote letters to my friends telling them that I was getting married, I told them to sit down before they read the next paragraph.  Sara replied:  "You told me to sit down.  You should have told me to take a tranquilizer and wait 30 minutes before reading the paragraph."

Another funny reaction was from some of the people in Zimbabwe.  Dave Grubbs told me that their comment was: "Why is Sister Burget getting married?  She is too old to have children."

## Before the Wedding

A new missionary arrived on June 9, 1987, when Ana Gricel Martinez came from Mexico.  Ana was born in Zacatecas,

*A baptism*

Mexico in 1962, the tenth of seventeen children. She gave her life to Christ and was baptized when she was seventeen years old and continued to serve the Lord by teaching children, youth and women in the church. For four years she had prayed about going to Colegio Biblico to better prepare to serve the Lord, but her parents had not wanted her to go. Finally they gave their consent and she began her studies in 1983. During her four years at the college, she helped in different churches, mostly in the Almoral Christian Church in Piedras Negras just across the border from Eagle Pass. During her last year at Colegio Biblico, she had begun to pray that God would show her where she could serve. A friend at the college suggested that she might be able to serve in Honduras. She started corresponding with me in 1986. I provided her air fare and a salary from my service link funds.

Ana wasted no time in getting busy after her arrival. Her second day in the mountains, I took her for a visit to meet some families and she found out how exhausting it could be to hike the mountain paths. She taught some classes to patients who came to the clinic her first week that she was in Honduras, but later she kept busy calling on the people in the village, leading three home Bible studies, a class for young girls and two classes for women, plus leading a youth meeting and two literacy classes a week.

In July 1987, we hosted our first large work team from Trader's Point Christian Church, Indianapolis. Along with that group came a couple from Deming, New Mexico, and a woman from East Chicago, Indiana. A major obstacle was getting their luggage out of customs. Their suitcases had come on a cargo plane that landed shortly after they did, and the customs officials insisted that they would have to wait until the next day to get the luggage. But the lady from East Chicago spoke fluent Spanish and successfully convinced the officials that the group had to have the luggage because it contained air mattresses they needed for to sleep that night. In the meantime, it started to rain. Alan Handt, his daughter, and I were sitting in the truck out of the rain waiting for the visitors. When they finally got through customs, it was really pouring. They shoved all of the suitcases in the back of my pickup to keep them dry. Two of the women got in with me and Alan put as many as he could in the front two seats of the pickup we had borrowed. The rest had to sit in the back and get drenched. By this time it was getting dark and Alan headed up the mountain road first and I followed.

We got probably one quarter of the way up the mountain when Alan came to a slick hill he could not get up. He told me to back up. As I backed around a curve, someone noticed that the back of my pickup was open and were sure some of the suitcases had fallen out. We had heard nothing, so Alan proceeded to back down the mountain to look for suitcases while others ran after the car. I went on to the clinic-community center, and some of the young men at the youth meeting helped unload all of the suitcases. I went back down the mountain to see if I could bring back some of the

*An asthmatic patient*

245

people, but I met Alan coming up. We transferred some to my pickup—and finally everyone arrived at the clinic-community center. Alan was not interested in driving the Ford pickup any further, so we took two trips to get the people to my house where supper was waiting for us.

On Monday we, along with the Water Department, were supposed to get started planning trees on Chepe and Chela Canahuati's property. The men from the Water Department did not come, so the group started painting. When the men from the Water Department finally arrived, they showed us where they wanted the trees planted. The tree-planting crew had the help of some men from the Water Department, some of Chepe's employees, and two men from San Antonio del Peru. The goal was to plant 1,200 trees, and they almost succeeded by planting 1.100. The project of planting trees was to show the Water Department, which had halted the construction of the clinic, that we also were concerned about the water supply in the mountains. It also showed them that Americans could work. The men from the Water Department were especially impressed at the hard work of the women. The hillside where the trees were planted was really steep, and one day the official "camera and canteen carrier," slipped in the middle of a pineapple field and rode a pineapple down the side of the mountain. While some planted and some painted, three of the women, along with Wilda, took care of the clinic work.

Every day classes were held for the women and children of San Antonio del Peru and Peñitas Arriba. After the evening meal the men from both villages had a Bible study, and some of the men learned carpentry skills.

Dr. Handt gave lectures to doctors, medical students and nurses at the Martinez Hospital every morning and afternoon. The doctors were so impressed with his lectures that they asked him to also give lectures for three nights at the

246

Medical Society. Since there was no nephrologist in San Pedro Sula, his lectures were very much needed. He later worked to help to get dialysis machines sent to the hospital so that people won't have to go to Tegucigalpa for dialysis.

I wanted to find a Honduran minister to lead the work in Peñitas Arriba. The Lord answered that prayer through Amable Rivera. Maria Anita Rivera, his sister, had been one of the first three Christians in the mountains. Later her father, mother and his brother also became Christians. He had been attending a church in San Pedro Sula, but was happy and very faithful when we started having services in the mountains. I had been praying that God would call him to be our minister. I wrote to John Cary, the President of Colegio Biblico in Eagle Pass, Texas, to ask for a college catalog to see if Amable would qualify for admission. The day the catalog arrived in the mail, I met him going home from work and gave him a ride. I gave him the catalog and asked him to read it and to pray about going to Colegio Biblico to study to become a minister. He read it and felt that God was leading him to do this.

With some help and many delays, he got a passport on August 11. But he still had to get a visa from the American consulate in Tegucigalpa. We had hoped he would be able to travel to the States with Dean Cary, but time was running out. Amable and I took a 2:00 A.M. bus to Tegucigalpa on a Wednesday morning to get his student visa. The guard at the Consulate said it would take two days, but people were praying and a very kind man told me to go in with my American passport and to take Amable with me. We filled out the application and were fortunate to find a kind man who asked Amable why he wanted to study in the States. He told the man that he wanted to study to be a preacher so he could return to Honduras and serve his people. The man told us to return at 4:00 P.M. to pick up the visa. We returned to San Pedro Sula on Wednesday evening so Amable could pack. On Thursday morning he left with Dean Cary for the States!

In September, Delmar and Eileen Debault visited. They had visited me twice when I was in India. Delmar gave several lessons from the Bible and preached. Eileen brought my contributor's list up to date for 1986.

We bid farewell to Matt and Suyapa the last of September. They had been quite involved in the church and they would be missed.

And soon it was time for me to go to the States to be married!

# Chapter 20

## Time Out For The Wedding

It was soon time to go to the States to marry John. But before I went, I needed to find a place for us to live. God provided a small house up the hill from where the single women were living. I didn't know if the owner would be willing to sell the house, but he was. I bought it, knowing that John would keep plenty busy remodeling it. In the meantime, we would share the home with the single women.

Just before I left Honduras, my former landlady and now dear friend, Luisa Julia Kipps, and her daughter hosted a bridal shower for me. The international group composed of Hondurans, Americans, Germans, and Brits, gave me a beautiful set of china.

Wilda Rush had agreed to cover the clinic during my absence. I arranged for some Honduran doctors to visit the clinic regularly to see patients while I was gone.

John flew to the States from Papua New Guinea, arriving on October 1. I flew to Atlanta where he met me. We drove to his sister Betty's where we stayed and also visited his sister Frances and met some of his nieces and nephews. From there we drove to Indiana where John met my family. John stayed with my younger sister who would say that after staying with her, "John still married Madonna." After a few days in Indiana, we drove to Tennessee where John stayed with friends in Maryville and I stayed with my friends Fred and Patsy Moore and later with David and Margaret Eubanks.

One day Patsy and Fred went to work and, forgetting that I was there, locked me in the house. Margaret Eubanks was

*Our wedding party - Patsy Moore, Madonna, John, Jimmy Kellar*

coming to pick me up so we could go shopping. But I couldn't get out of the house. I called Patsy who said the only solution was to climb out the kitchen window. I managed to do it, hoping all the while that their neighbors would not see me and think I was climbing in to rob their house!

Our many friends in and around Johnson Bible College planned our wedding and reception. Patsy and her two daughters decorated the chapel with magnolia leaves; Margaret Eubanks planned the reception and arranged for the cake; and Dr. and Mrs. Black made the punch. John's sister Betty made mints and someone else bought the corsages for me and my matron of honor. As John said, all we had to do was "SHOW".

After the wedding rehearsal on Friday evening, the wedding party, our families, and several members of First Christian Church in Maryville were treated to a wonderful dinner by the ladies of First Christian Church in Maryville. After dinner, Jimmy Kellar, John's best man, presented us with a big card and cash gift from the church. Then stories were told about John, and Patsy Moore, my matron of honor, added one about me. It was a wonderful evening.

God gave us a beautiful Indian summer day for our wedding. John and I broke tradition and went together in the morning to look for my prayer cave to have a time of prayer together. We never did find the cave, but we used a log in the forest that looked down on the French Broad River.

As soon as I got into my wedding sari and Margaret Eubanks and Patsy were dressed in their saris, Phillip Eubanks drove us to the Alumni Memorial Chapel at J.B.C. I had wanted my sari to be a surprise for John, so they had to get him, Dr. Floyd Clark and Jimmy back to a side room so I could go into the chapel.

Abbie Michelle Smith, my great niece who was the flower girl, was dressed in a typical Honduran dancing dress. My brother Don gave me away.

About 130 guests attended the wedding, some coming from as far north as Green Bay, Wisconsin, and some as far west as Oklahoma. The music before the ceremony was beautifully done by Clara Kellar at the organ and Becky Lowe at the piano. Karen Kennedy sang "Because" before we entered and "That's the Way" as we exchanged rings. Stephanie Young sang "My Tribute" before the vows. The ceremony went well; the only problem was when I put John's ring on—that took a bit of time. I was thankful that we had plenty of time as Karen sang. We had a good laugh after the service telling Dean Clark that he forgot to tell John that he could kiss the bride. His reply was: "You didn't tell me."

A highlight of the reception was the reunion of many with whom I had served in Rhodesia-Zimbabwe: Ziden, Helen and Tom Nutt from Missouri; Berry and Amy Kennedy from Florida; Chuck and Carol Kelley from Ohio; Sara Stere from Pennsylvania; Donna Kreegar Webster from Indiana; and Martha Raile from South Carolina.

John and I had a wonderful two-week honeymoon in Gatlinburg at the Ponderosa, an efficiency apartment with facilities for cooking. I enjoyed cooking for John, and he enjoyed eating. I also found that he was a good dishwasher. We took long hikes in the Smokey Mountains, visited Dollywood, and enjoyed just relaxing and watching football and the World Series.

After our honeymoon, the women of four congregations hosted a reception for us at my home church in Indiana. We greeted 224 well- wishers. Among the guests were some of my former classmates from nurses' training and high school; more of my former co-workers from Zimbabwe; friends with whom I had worked in India; people from nineteen supporting churches, including one who came all the way from Gentry, Arkansas; relatives from Maryland; a dear friend from Lincoln, Nebraska; Brenda Smith from Ann Arbor, Michigan; and Cheryl Noel from Marion, Indian. John even had a surprise when a cousin came with her son and grandson from Maryland. They were in Indiana visiting relatives in Logansport. And a new friend, formerly from Honduras was also there: he learned of our wedding from reading a newspaper article in the *Kokomo Tribune* and had contacted my mother. He had visited us the night before and was excited to learn that I knew some of his relatives in San Pedro Sula. We had a good chuckle when several guests commented about John, "He is tall." Some apparently worried that I had married someone shorter than I.

Before we left for Honduras, we went to Americus, Georgia, to visit the headquarters of Habitat for Humanity where John had worked before he went to Papua New Guinea. We received a warm welcome and were guests at yet another reception. We also visited our "cupid," Floyd Clark and his wife in Creswell, N.C.; Carmie and Lester Cooper in Atlanta, Georgia (I had worked with them in Rhodesia); Ziden and Helen Nutt and family in Joplin, Mo. and my Uncle Kenny and Aunt Madge and their daughter Judy in San Antonio, Texas.

252

John had a Chevy van that we loaded with much of what he had stored in a garage at Mission Services in Knoxville. It was packed full with a bed frame, washer and dryer, chest of drawers, dressing table, dishes, pots and pans, and a small refrigerator, among other things.

John wrote the following in our January-February 1988 newsletter about our trip to Honduras.

> Madonna and I decided to drive our van to San Pedro Sula. The van was fully loaded. A policeman had to accompany us, so we would not unload any of our cargo on the way. Lawrence was a very likeable fellow, so our five days of driving through Mexico were pleasant ones. Probably two-thirds of our trip was through mountains, reaching heights of close to 10,000 feet and very beautiful. For the most part the roads were good, but the traffic was something else!! Trucks would pass on curves and many times a third truck would also pass. I've never driven anywhere (even in New York City) that equaled the experience of Mexico City. The next time I drive through Mexico, I'm going to stay at least fifty miles away from Mexico City because it's impossible to enter or leave the city without getting lost! We had a nice visit with Humberto and Becky Ramirez in Queretero and worshipped with them on Sunday morning. At the Guatemalan border there was a fair amount of red tape and we acquired another guard. We reached Honduras the next day and arrived in San Pedro Sula on Thursday afternoon, December 3rd. All in all, we had a very good and interesting trip.

We thought it would be appropriate to have another wedding ceremony in Spanish in Honduras. That occurred on Saturday, December 5, with Dean Cary performing the ceremony. John had been practicing for days his "Si," and even though he couldn't understand Dean's question, he came forth with the "Si" at just the right time, bringing applause from those in attendance.

The room at the clinic was decorated with crepe paper and balloons. The place was full; many had to stand outside and look through the windows. We had people from several aldeas , most of them who had been my patients; the minister from the Church of Christ in San Pedro Sula; people from Dean's Bible study group; some of the doctors who helped at the clinic; a nurse from the government health care center; my former Spanish teacher; and many other friends. An estimated 250 people helped us celebrate.

The wedding reception was also a farewell party for Wilda Rush who had been with us for a year. She was a real blessing to all of us and a real worker!! Even though she was not fluent in Spanish, she very willingly offered to "hold the fort" while I went to the States to be married. After our wedding ceremony, she was presented with a lovely decorated cake that said: "Return quickly". Just before she left, our good friends, Salvador and Odilia Canahuati, came with another large cake that Odilia had made.

The celebrations were complete. Now we began our work together in Honduras.

*Our Spanish wedding*

# Chapter 21

## Back To Ministry

### Visitors, Visitors, Visitors

While I had been in the States during the last part of November, Wilda, Christine and Ana had hosted visitors from Zacatecas and Juarez, both in Mexico, when they came to hold Vacation Bible School and meetings. The first week they had VBS at the clinic-community center for twenty to twenty-five children from Peñitas Arriba; the following week they held the VBS for about the same number of children in San Antonio del Peru. They also called on people in the both places. Peñitas, inviting residents to the evening services that were held every evening for two weeks at the clinic-community center. Attendance was fifty to sixty each night. They drove to Laguna de Tembladeros on two different days to call on people of the community and to hold services. One lady was baptized. They were an encouragement to the Christians and many seeds of the Gospel were planted.

In December, in addition to Harland and Frances Cary, two of Christine's friends from her days at Cincinnati Bible Seminary visited. They didn't get to do as much as they wanted because of rain, but they did help some of the girls to make skirts and had craft classes for the children. They both gave lessons to the women and youth with me translating. Marina Moreno also arrived in December from Mexico to help with the ministry to the women and children.

In January, we had more visitors for a week—a doctor and nurse from the Southeast Christian Church in Minneapolis, Minnesota. I always enjoyed it when a doctor arrived so I could learn more about medicine.

# A Home of Our Own

*Our home in the Merendon Mountains*

John and I finally moved to our home early in April. Living with the single girls had been pleasant enough, but it was very nice to be in our own home. Before John started re-modeling, the house had only two rooms with no bath or ceiling and only three small windows. The house was thirty by twenty feet with a porch along the front. Even so, it was a convenient house. We put in a bath, a closet in the bedroom, a partition and cabinets in the kitchen, and another partition for our washer and dryer with an alcove for my desk and filing cabinet. We installed louvered windows, put up a dropped ceiling with recessed fluorescent lighting, laid a tile floor and added a back porch. After buying some new furniture and hanging pictures, our house had a very homey atmosphere.

# Evangelism at Work

Our Mexican co-workers, Marina and Ana, were a real blessing to the work. Ana led singing and Marina played the guitar for services. Twice a week Marina gave guitar lessons. She also gave some of the messages and was a good preacher. Ana and Marina went calling regularly and conducted home Bible studies and encouraged the Christians.

*The kitchen was tiny!*

We continued to have additions to the church, largely the result of their ministry.

In 1986, I.D.E.S. had started sending monthly funds for a feeding program at Laguna de Tembladeros. This provided a good lunch for sometimes up to 120 children, many of whom were malnourished. When I went to check on the program, I gave a Bible lesson to the children. Then with the cooperation of Lifeline Christian Mission, we were able to hire a Christian teacher for the school. Later Lifeline started a sponsorship program for the children in Laguna. That led to our having worship services in the village. At first we held services in one of the homes, but later we got permission to use one of the classrooms at the school. Christine, Marina, Ana, and I took turns going to lead the worship services. When Dean Cary was in Honduras, he preached. Several were baptized as a result of the ministry.

## The Medical Work Goes On

For over two years I regularly went to three *aldeas* for vaccination clinics. The vaccines were provided without charge from the government health care center in San Pedro Sula. The serum vaccinated against tuberculosis, whooping cough, tetanus, diphtheria, measles and polio. Naturally the shots hurt, so each child got a balloon after the vaccination; that shut off the tears in a hurry.

Roundworms are a constant health problem in Honduras, so I also took a gallon of piperazine, also provided by the government, to treat for roundworms. A few times at La Cumbre, I gave worm medicine to more than one hundred people. One of the clinics was at Las Crucitas. The road there terrible, taking us over thirty minutes to travel three miles. But when I got there, I had a beautiful view.

## 1988—Visitors Add to Ministry

The Rostvit twins spent some time with us in the spring of 1988. Dean Cary had arranged for their visit to Honduras and kindly shared them with us. They sang and told Bible stories in four schools, and we had meetings each night at the clinic-community center with them sharing in song and with their puppets. They both speak Spanish, so they could do their stories without translation. We all had a good laugh after I sang a song with them in Hindi at one of the schools when we realized later that one word in the song we sang means "to speak" in Hindi, but means "drunk" in Spanish. I picked out the song never thinking about that word.

For two weeks in May Brian and Jennifer Smith visited. Brian is my cousin. Both he and Jennifer had been in school at Cincinnati Bible Seminary with Christine. Brian had been to Haiti and Zaire on internships, but Jennifer had not yet visited a mission field. She was interested in nursing, so she wanted to observe the medical work. They gave lessons at some of our meetings and Brian preached with me translating.

The summer of 1988 was busy with work teams and visitors. One visitor was Amable Rivera, the young man we were helping as he studied at Colegio Biblico. It was evident how he had grown in the Lord. During the summer he demonstrated his desire to see his family and friends come to the Lord. He did most of the preaching while he was with us and baptized a young man from Laguna de Temblade-ros—his first baptism! As a result of his calling with Marina and Christine, and sometimes by himself, more men came to worship services. He also taught some of VBS classes.

Three different work teams came that summer. John was the supervisor of those who did construction. The first group was from Walton Christian Church, a group that had been arranged by Wilda Rush. They helped with VBS, built a partition wall at the clinic-community center, built a desk and cabinet in a Sunday School classroom, and planted a good number of trees and bushes to stop erosion on the property.

The next group, led by Glen and Carolyn Bourne, was from Florida Christian College. They planted trees, painted the clinic, built shelves, put new screens on the doors at the clinic and chapel doors, and dug the foundations for a guest house.

The final group, led by Bob Smith, was from Trader's Point Christian Church in Indianapolis. They erected most of the guest house in four days. This group included a Spanish-speaking nurse who worked in the clinic.

In addition to the work teams, Marcus Pearson, a student from St. Louis Christian College, was with us for the entire sum-mer. He was a jack of all trades and did much of the plumbing and some of the carpentry at the guest house; did some work on the pickup and van; and learned enough Spanish to preach without translation.

*Madonna and some of the children she delivered*

He also worked with the Honduran men in the fields, witnessing to them as he worked.

Karen Meade, a nurse, arrived in July for a visit. Her work in the clinic allowed me to lead a Bible study one of those afternoons and to keep up on correspondence.

I have never ceased to be amazed at God's provision. When Karen came, she brought a computer which allowed me to computerize patient records. When she went through customs, the officials wanted to charge a very high amount for the computer. She explained that she didn't have the money, adding that the person waiting for her could explain in Spanish. I was allowed me to go to the customs official. I was very surprised when the he said, "You are Madonna." I asked how he knew my name, and he reminded me that I had taken care of his little girl when she had surgery for a cleft lip during one of the times that I had helped Interplast. He had known what I was doing in the mountains and he immediately reduced the amount of customs on the computer to an amount we could easily afford.

After an extremely busy summer with the work teams and other visitors, we had no visitors for two months. Then in November, Jim and Clara Kellar and Kenneth and Helen Herron from First Christian Church, Maryville, Tennessee, came for two weeks. Jim and Kenneth preached on Sundays and during the week. Clara and Helen painted the guest house, helped with a quilting project and visited several homes. Jim, Kenneth and John even built eleven pews for our church.

We even enjoyed a good old time American Thanksgiving dinner with turkey and all the trimmings. Clara and Helen cooked the turkey and dressing; Christine, Ana, Marina, Karen and Jennifer brought the rolls, vegetables and salad.

I made the pies and Kenneth carved the turkey. Jim and John helped eat all the food!

## Celebrating A Year of Marriage

Our first year of marriage passed quickly. John wrote the following in our September-November 1988 newsletter:

> Madonna and I have been married a year and it's been the best year of my life! It seems we are perfectly suited for each other. As you know, we drove down to San Pedro Sula, Honduras last December. We live up in the mountains about five miles from the city. The people here are very friendly and poor. Some own their own land and farm, but most of them work for farm owner city dwellers. Their average wage is only $2.00 a day. Coffee is the chief crop along with bananas and pineapple. Also several vegetables are grown on a commercial basis such as carrots, radishes, green peppers and onions. Another way people earn money is by growing flowers. Every Friday afternoon we see two or three men walking down to town with a long pole balanced on their shoulders carrying several bundles of flowers. Some of the soil is so steep that you wonder how the soil and plants can stay in place during the rainy season and how the workers can keep their footing. I had a garden of corn and beans and literally fell **into** the garden time after time. We have it fenced, so I couldn't fall out!!
>
> For the first several months we were here, I remodeled, with a lot of help from visitors, our small house. Later we had several work teams from churches in the States and we did a few projects with them. The

biggest we undertook was the building of a guest house, composed of two rooms with bath and a screened in front porch. Since building supply places didn't deliver, we had to haul at least twenty loads of supplies up in our pickup.

# Furlough

Soon after the Herrons and Kellars left, John and I prepared to drive to the States for a furlough. The van we had driven down was not the right kind of vehicle for driving in the mountains, and since we could not get it cleared with customs without paying a large amount, we decided to drive it to the States and get a more suitable vehicle. Our trip to the States was much easier than
going to Honduras the year before. Since we were not loaded with furniture, we had no problems with officials at the borders of the three countries. Ana Grisel Martinez rode us as far as Mexico City so she could get the necessary papers for residency in Honduras.

As we entered Mexico City, a policeman stopped us a few minutes after we had missed a turn. He fined us 75,000 pesos ($34) for not signaling when switching lanes. Of course, he wanted us to pay the money directly to him. I told him that he could take us to the police station where we would pay the fine. I also told him we that were not "rich Americans," but that we helped the poor in Honduras. Not really believing me, he asked Ana if this was true. She assured him that it was, so he led us past the police station, got us on the right road and sent us on our way. We paid no fine! We found out later that the fine should have been only 500 pesos.

We visited with Rich and Leta Atkinson and family until Sunday when we drove to Queretaro where we spent a night with Bill and Margy Hoff. After a two-day trip through the rest of Mexico, we arrived at Eagle Pass and visited a couple of days with the Carys before going to San Antonio. In San Antonio, I spoke at the Harlandale Christian Church, and we stayed a few days with Aunt Madge. We stopped in Joplin, Missoui, to visit Ziden and Helen Nutt before arriving in Indiana where we were to stay with my mother. We thanked God for safety on our 3,700 mile trip.

We spent a few months in the States seeing family, friends, and churches. In February, we attended Homecoming at Johnson Bible College. It was the thirtieth anniversary of my graduation from J.B.C. In March, we participated in the Georgia Missionary Rally and visited former missionary friends—the Kennedys and Cooopers—with whom I had worked in Rhodesia. We shared with churches in Indiana, Maryland, Virginia, West Virginia, North Carolina, South Carolina, Tennessee, Florida, Arkansas, Missouri, Illinois, Iowa, Minnesota, Wisconsin, Michigan and Kentucky.

In the midst of all the busyness of furlough, 1989 was a sad year for me when three of my former co-workers in Rhodesia went to be with the Lord. They were all special to me, but no one was more special than Sara Stere. She had gone with me to India when I was making the decision to move from Rhodesia to India. When she retired to the States to take care of her parents, I always tried to visit her. John and I were thankful to have visited with her in April before she went to be with the Lord on June 28. The other two missionaries who went to be with the Lord were Doug Johnson and Lucy Pruett.

John wrote about our furlough in our July-December 1989 newsletter.

Madonna and I have just completed seven months at furloughing, a real eye-opener. We traveled 16,373 miles through 23 states visiting in the homes of many nice people. Madonna spoke a whopping 79 times. We found almost everyone very interested in the work in Honduras. Of course, Madonna presents it in such a way that it would be hard not to. We appreciated the hospitality shown in many homes. We slept in 66 different beds and one night recently I found myself counting beds instead of sheep!! It was good for Madonna to renew old friendships and she took pleasure in her MAN. One highlight of our trip was when Sara Stere took us to Horseshoe Curve in Altoona, Pennsylvania, and seeing two trains passing each other.

Obviously, a furlough is not a vacation!

# Chapter 22

# Around the World in Ninety-Three Days

### Europe

We had received many cash gifts for our wedding. We decided to use the money to take a trip around the world to visit friends and missionaries we knew—mostly those I knew—and, as John liked to say, to visit my single women friends in Zimbabwe to "give hope." If Madonna could marry, there was hope for them.

Leaving Indiana on August 1, we began our trip of a lifetime. Believe it or not, we took only two large suitcases, a tote bag, a cosmetic case and another small bag! We flew from Indianapolis to Chicago to catch an overnight flight to London. From London, we took a train to the home of John's niece and her husband where we spent two nights with her and her son, saying only hello to her husband when he returned the morning we left.

We went from there to the Church of Christ in Buckie, Scotland, which supported us. We visited the church on Sunday, showing slides of the work in Honduras in the evening service. We also did a bit of sightseeing and on our way back to Inverness. At Inverness, we took the train to Kirkaldy, Scotland, where we were met and taken to the Maggie Watters' apartment to spend the night. Maggie was in the hospital, but we

*Visiting Maggie Watters in Scotland*

visited her for a short time.  Maggie had celebrated her one hundredth birthday in April.  Her eyesight and hearing were poor, but her mind was as sharp as ever.   I was reminded of her hospitality in Bulawayo when she insisted that we were to stay at her flat.

From Kirkaldy we took the train to Sheffield, England, where we spent the night with Dr. William and Angie Vennells and their two children with whom I had worked at Mashoko from 1981-83.  It was a blessing to learn that Bill and Angie and the children were attending the Church of England and had even had Sunday School classes for children in their home.

We then visited a few days with Keith and Sylvia (Mehinnick) Golsby in Lancaster.  Sylvia and I had also worked together at Mashoko in the early '60s.  While we were with them, we were able to work out a mini-family reunion with John's sister, Frances, three of her daughters, a son-in-law and grandson came to Lancaster for the afternoon.  We were able to do some sightseeing in the Lake District before we took a bus to London to fly on to Lisbon, Portugal.

Sarah Robison and Cheri Oakley met us in Lisbon.  At one time John had been the forwarding agent for the Amazon Valley Children's Home in Brazil, when Dick and Sarah had served there as missionaries. When we left Lisbon, our plane was over two hours late, leaving us little time to change planes in London to go on to Johannesburg.   But we soon learned that the flight to Africa would be late leaving, giving us ample time to make our connection.

### Africa
It was a long, tiring flight to Johannesburg, but it didn't take us long to get through immigration and customs after we arrived.  We boarded our flight to Capetown quite easily.

Pete and Fran Laughren, our hosts, met us. We all had a good laugh when they looked at our luggage and said: "Is that all you have?"

Pete and Fran had often attended First Christian Church in Maryville, Tennessee, when they were students at John-

*Dr. Bungu and his wife at Mashoko*

son Bible College, so they knew John. I had known Fran since she was a baby. I had attended Johnson Bible College with both her parents, sang in a women's trio with her mother, and worked with her parents in Arizona. I shared in their ministry by speaking at a Wednesday night Bible study.

Pete and Fran gave us a royal tour of Capetown and the nearby mountains. We decided that Capetown was the most beautiful place we visited. On our last day there—beautiful and clear—we took the cable car up to Table Mountain. What a view!!

The next stop was Zimbabwe. Having served the Lord there for 12½ years, I was excited to be going back for a visit. I especially wanted all of my friends to meet John.

Our flight from South Africa was delayed, so as we arrived in Zimbabwe, we saw a beautiful sunset. When we arrived at Harare, we saw a special friend, Gladys Jongeling, waving to us from the airport balcony. She was our hostess while in Harare. She had arrived at Mashoko just a year after I had and was the medical technologist for about five years. Since then she had worked for the government, for the University, and now in a private laboratory.

*With Mai Gwinji at Mashoko*

Gladys had been instrumental in starting the Greencroft Christian Church.  Once when it seemed that they would have to close the doors, she and a few others kept things going until the Charles Delaney family went there to serve.  We worshiped there our first Sunday in Zimbabwe with a multi-racial congregation.  The thought that ran through my mind when I saw the large attendance was:  "The Church is alive and well in Zimbabwe."

On Sunday afternoon we attended a potluck lunch with most of the other missionaries in Harare—Penningtons, Morrises, Captains, Eastwoods, Marcia Thomson,  Midge Goldthwaite, and Jayne Free.  Margaret Dennis from Chidamoyo Mission was also there because she was recuperating from back surgery.  She generously loaned us her pickup so we could drive all over Zimbabwe to visit the different mission stations.

From Harare, we first went to Chiredzi to visit the two Pemberton families serving there.  We also visited with Watson Mabona, a longtime evangelist, and the Zebedee Togarepi family.  We also looked up Loice Chingwara, one of the first nursing students after the school had reopened in 1982.

From Chiredzi we headed to Mashoko where we spent five nights.  John couldn't get over the size of Mashoko—way out in the bush as it is.  I was impressed with how much growth had occurred since I had left in 1983.  We arrived in time to experience the baptism of one of the nurses from the hospital.  It was good to greet Augustine Makuku, the hospital evangelist, and to see his big smile again.  David and Eva

Grubbs were our hosts. Our first night there Eva invited all of the other missionary families for supper. It was a happy reunion the next day to see Mai Gwinji who had served as a nurse at Mashoko for thirty years until her recent retirement. I also attended two women's meetings and shared a devotional with the Christian women. We also worshiped with the large congregation at Mashoko. And John got a taste of village life and Zimbabwean food when we went to Zebedee Togarepi's home village to attend a memorial service for Zebedee's father who had recently died.

Bulawayo was our next stop, visiting on the way with a former nursing student and her husband in Masvingo. We also went to a local government clinic to look up medical assistants who had worked with me at Chidamoyo in the later '60s. What a road to their place, only to find out that she was not there. We did, however, have a short visit with her husband and some of their children.

Hazel Mansill was our hostess in Bulawayo. She was originally from New Zealand and led a very large Sunday School in a building which really fascinated John. She was a remarkable woman who loved her work with the children and youth. We were able to visit with other friends in Bulawayo as well.

*With Benji whom Madonna delivered by C-Section in 1968*

From Bulawayo we drove to Chinhoyi to visit the Marshalls, who had served there for over twenty years, and Judy Pickett. We worshiped with them at Hillside Chapel. While we were there, we visited two of my former students from the early 60s.

The next stop was Chidamoyo Mission to visit Dr. Gloria Cobb and other friends. We spent two nights and then drove back to Harare where we turned Margaret's car over to her. The following day we took a one-day trip to Victoria Falls and also had a boat trip up the Zambezi River. Marcia Thomson met us at the airport when we returned from the Falls, and we spent the night with her. The following day we visited Zimbabwe Christian College. Our last night in Harare we enjoyed a visit from two more of my former nursing students. We experienced many blessings during the three weeks in Zimbabwe.

From Zimbabwe we flew to Malawi, a country neither John nor I had visited. We had talked to Jeff and Karen Kennedy by phone and had told them that if they could arrange it, we would be happy to fly from Lilongwe to Blantyre where they lived. When we arrived in Lilongwe and didn't see Jeff and Karen, we went to the information desk where we received our tickets to fly to Blantyre. When we disembarked at Blantyre, we soon saw Jeff and Karen as well as Gordon and Estelle Nelson. We spent the night with the Kennedys and the next day went with them to a village church service at which Jeff preached. The service reminded me of the village services in Zimbabwe. After church we went to the home of one of the church members for a meal of what we called sadze in Zimbabwe and chicken and vegetables.

That evening I shared with the missionaries about our ministry in Honduras. Steve and Vonnie Skaggs were there. I had last seen Vonnie when she was a little girl in Zambia in 1969, when I visited her parents, Bill and Jackie Brant. It was a thrill to see two second generation missionaries serving in Malawi—Jeff and Vonnie.

The next two nights, the Nelsons joined the Kennedys and us to spend time at beautiful Lake Malawi. We hadn't been there long when I overturned a little plastic boat and gave Karen a scare—but I wasn't hurt, only dunked. I tried snorkeling, without much success, though we saw some beautiful fish. We went back to Lilongwe to continue to enjoy the fellowship of the missionaries there before we flew on to Zambia.

Our flight connections to Zambia permitted only a short time with the Byrd family. However, because of mechanical trouble with the plane in Malawi, we ended up having even less time. We had tried unsuccessfully to get a message to the Byrds, so they were not at the airport when we arrived. After trying three times, I finally got a call through to them and it wasn't long until Cecil came to pick us up. They thought we were coming from Zimbabwe and had been told that the flight would not come until 9 P.M. The next day they took us out to the training center where they worked and I spoke, with a translator, to the women. We visited their gardens and saw the rabbits they were raising, and we also enjoyed a meal of the traditional corn meal mixture with vegetables and chicken. The next morning we worshiped with the Zambian brethren. Then it was home to pack up for to go to Lusaka from where we were to fly early the next morning.

From Lusaka we flew to Nairobi, Kenya, where we were to visit with Mike and Karolyn Schrage. We drove to Lake Baringo to spend three nights with the Schrages and Harods relaxing and looking for birds. On our way we crossed the equator, so, of course, we had to stop to have our picture taken. Lake Baringo was a beautiful spot and I had fun playing with the children in the swimming pool, giving them rides on my back to the deep end. John got to ride a camel for the first time, but before he got on it, it looked like the camel wanted to have a bite of him.

We went from Lake Baringo to Kitale where the Schrages and Harrods have a team ministry with two other families. We attended one of their Bible studies and prayer meetings. I also attended a ladies' meeting were I met several other missionaries. Before we left Kitale, John was also able to visit a Habitat for Humanity project.

On Sunday morning we and the Schrages got up early and, leaving the children behind, headed for Nairobi. We visited a lake known for the many flamingos and had a devotional time by the lake and shared the Lord's Supper. We also saw some wild game as we did and again at the Nairobi game park. It had been special to spend the time with Mike and Karolyn and their family because Karolyn is another second generation missionary, the daughter of Ziden and Helen Nutt.

### India

We said our goodbyes to Mike and Karolyn and headed to the waiting area to board our flight to Bombay. The flight was very late leaving followed by another delay in Bombay. By the time we reached New Delhi, we had only a very short time to make our connections to Khujaraho where someone from Kulpahar would meet us. I didn't realize that there was a new international airport in New Delhi which was some distance from the domestic terminal. We had to take a bus to get to the domestic gates. When we got on the bus, the driver told us they would not take dollars for the fare. Fortunately, a young couple helped us and we got our rupees. We hurried in to the domestic terminal only to find out that the time for the flight to Khujaraho had been moved up, and we had missed it. After getting a confirmation for the flight the next day, we went to a hotel and got a good night's rest.

Imagine our surprise the next morning when while we were eating breakfast, Linda Stanton and her mother walked in. They had come to New Delhi to meet Linda's sister and her husband.

We had tried unsuccessfully to get a message to Kulpahar to tell them we were delayed. We were sure that no one would be there to meet us. But we were able to hire a taxi. The young man who drove the taxi was from Kulpahar and remembered me from when he had studied at Kulpahar Christian School. On our way to Kulpahar, we stopped in Chatarpur to visit a missionary friend who runs a Christian English school for the Friends Church. As we passed through the long village of Belatal, we knew for sure we were in India when we saw the cows, water buffalo, muddy roads and lots of people.

It was especially good to arrive at Kulpahar. As we got out of the taxi, I heard some of the children who remembered me saying, "Nurse Aunty has come!" I was delighted to see Leah and Dolly who looked great. These two had done a monumental work at Kulpahar—for 44 years at the time we visited. John had visited Kulpahar in 1982 and was sick for most of his stay, so he enjoyed this trip much more. Leadership roles were being assumed by the families who had been reared at Kulpahar. Naturally I enjoyed visiting with former co-workers in the hospital. And I was able to understand most of the Hindi spoken in the worship services!

One day Leah arranged for a tonga (horse drawn cart) to take John and me into the village to visit friends. I also visited the living two of the triplets I had delivered in November 1973. We had a good laugh when their father told us that when people asked him why one of them was so tall, he said it was because Nurse Aunty had delivered him.

Our next visit was to the Getters, longtime missionaries to India. Despite their many problems with their papers and having to report regularly to the authorities, they maintained their happy disposition. Bernie met us in Raigarh to take us to their home in Sitapur. On the way Bernie stopped to visit one of their schools. As we arrived, a big crowd of people met us with garlands, some of them made with popcorn. We walked a short distance with the group until we came to a stream where got back into the Jeep. While we there, we had a service with some of the children and women, presenting skits and Bernie preaching.

We were happy to arrive in Sitapur where we greeted Joan. During our visit, we visited their farm projects. I also helped in the dispensary Joan ran and one morning led the devotions for the girls' hostel. We also had a short visit with Bill and Jean Roland in Bilaspur.

We had taken an air-conditioned train from Jhansi to Raigarh. That had been a comfortable twenty-hour trip. But on our return, we were unable to get first-class accommodations because of the Hindu holy days. And what a trip! We arrived at the train with a red cap carrying our two heavy suitcases on his head. As John said, you really haven't lived until you take a second class train trip in India. We got the real thing in 28 hours—heat, dirt, overcrowding, beggars at every stop, and endless waiting for trains to pass. We even waited on freight trains. And we missed stopping at very few towns. It seemed like we were taking a roundabout way to Agra. For hours we were going south and then west. We thought we must be on the wrong train. The map showed that we

*Linda Stanton, Leah Moshier, and Dolly Chitwood at Kulpahar*

274

should go north.  Our compartment was designed for eight, but for most of the trip twelve to fifteen crowded into it.  We did have a board to sleep on, but it was only five feet long.  Enterprising beggars, such as the woman who was handing out copies of her request for money for her daughter who was getting married, were everywhere.  At the bottom of the piece of paper, she asked that we return the paper to her.  Even though the aisles were full, there seemed to be room for venders at every stop.  We didn't pay much for the trip—only $10 for a 600-700 mile trip.  We arrived in Agra on Thursday afternoon and were as dirty as could be.  I had planned to take a bath until I saw the dirty water coming from my hair when I was taking a shower.

We visited the Taj Mahal the following day.  John had not seen it on his first trip to India and he was as impressed as everyone is when they see it.  We rode in a rickshaw to visit another missionary friend who took us to the airport to get our flight to New Delhi.  Arriving in New Delhi, we found that because of the holidays all the hotels I knew were filled.  Finally a tourist helped us and another lady to find a hotel, which we reached about 1:00 A.M.  We planned to visit Philip and Margaret Ho in Shillong, but we had to go to the Meghalaya Tourist House to get our permits.  It took two trips, but we finally got them.

We flew to Calcutta and changed planes for Gawahati where  Phillip Ho met us.  Then what a trip from there to Shillong.  We followed a truck route, a winding road that climbed seemingly forever.  I spoke four times while we were with the Hos—to the women after church on Sunday, to another women's Bible study group, to show slides of Honduras,  and to the assembly of their school.  We had pictures with us of their children that we had taken at the N.A.C.C. in July.

When we left, we arranged to fly by helicopter from Shillong to Gawahati, saving the Hos that horrible road trip. Besides we really enjoyed the ride, our first on a helicopter. The scenery was beautiful. We had a direct flight to New Delhi before we left for Hong Kong.

## Hong Kong

The flight from New Delhi to Hong Kong was smooth, and William Rees met us at when we arrived. We stayed with William and Melba. Their son Benjamin and his family joined us for dinner. We were amazed at all of the high rise apartments and neon signs in Hong Kong. We were with the Rees only overnight, but we understood their ministry of hospitality, along with their other work.

## Japan

The next leg of the journey was to Kagoshima on Dragon Airlines, a small airline with few people on the flight. It took some time to get through customs in Kagoshima, but when we exited, we saw Mark and Pauline Maxey who had come to meet us.

This was my fourth visit to Japan, but my first time with the Maxeys. I had promised them on my last visit that the next time I was in Japan, I would visit them, little realizing at the time that it would be with my husband. We met their son Walter and his wife and daughter at a restaurant. John had his first experience eating with chopsticks.

We did quite a bit of sightseeing and ate another meal before we arrived at the Maxey's home. We were reminded at how the Lord provided when Mark and Pauline presented us with kimonos. Our tote bag had been stolen on a train in India and both of us were without bathrobes. Our stay was short, but we participated in Mark's English class by sharing

276

about our ministry in Honduras; enjoyed a picnic in honor of the birthday of Japanese minister who worked with Mark and Pauline  and who also had a ministry with lepers; did some sightseeing;  and enjoyed the wonderful fellowship, Pauline's good cooking and Mark's jokes.  John and I couldn't remember when we had laughed so much.

Our next stop was Osaka  where Paul Clark met us and took us to his mother's home where we stayed.  Martin and Evelyn Clark had been long time friends and an inspiration to me from the time I met them at Hanging Rock Christian Assembly in the late 1940s.  Martin had gone to be with the Lord in June; I was sorry he had not been able to meet John.

One reason I had made several trips to Japan was to visit the congregation at Moruguchi that had supported me when I was in India.  We worshiped with them on Sunday and I spoke about our ministry in Honduras.  I also spoke at chapel at Osaka Bible Seminary,  attended an English Bible study that Paul led at his mother's home, and attended the Tane-maki-kai Rally at Osaka Bible Seminar where we were able to enjoy the fellowship of many of the other missionaries serving in Japan.  At the first evening service of the rally, George and Ethel Beckman were honored for their over thirty years of service in Japan.

### Back Again in the USA
We left Japan in the middle of the rally, flying to Los Angeles via Tokyo.  We were met in Los Angeles by Tom Schneller and his son and Bill and Margie Hoff who had arrived from Mexico for the National Missionary Convention met us.  We too attended the convention before flying back to Indianapolis.  It had been a magnificent trip with God guiding all the way.  We had been on twenty-nine different flights, never losing our luggage even once other than the stolen tote bag.

## Home to Honduras

We returned to Indiana on November 9 and spent eight days at my mother's home before leaving for Honduras. We had bought a Ford pickup with a topper over the bed and packed it full for the trip. The trip was trouble free from Indiana to San Pedro Sula. On the way to

*Back to the USA*

Honduras, we spent a weekend with Ziden, Helen and Lynda Nutt in Joplin, Missouri, before going to Texas where we visited Aunt Madge and a cousin. We visited John's sisters-in-law and brother-in-law. We stopped in Harlingen to visit with friends. We crossed the Mexican border at Brownsville on November 25 with no problems —a sharp contrast to our experience at Eagle Pass in 1987. We spent a night with friends in San Luis Potosi, Mexico.

On Sunday, we drove to Queretero after church and visited Bill and Margy Hoff. On Monday morning we headed for Mexico City where we spent the night with Rich and Leta Atkinson. We had almost no problems getting in and out of Mexico City. After two more days on the road, we had a smooth crossing into Guatemala. The trip through Guatemala was easy.

When we arrived at the Honduran border the next day, we experienced the same good treatment that we had received from the Mexican and Guatemalan governments. Though we told the officials that we had three new 12-volt batteries and some other new items, we were not charged customs on any of the contents because we had been out of the country for almost a year.  Later that day we arrived back home in the Merendon Mountains.  We praised  God for such an easy trip and to be back home in Honduras.

# Chapter 23

# Back to Work in Honduras

## Visitors Soon Arrive

We immediately settled into ministry in Honduras once more. And a large part of that work was welcoming visitors who always added value to the ministry.

The day after John and I arrived back in Honduras, Janice and Faye Rostvit arrived for a week visiting churches and some of the schools to sing and use their puppets to tell Bible stories. They stayed in the guest house which we called the *casita*, "little house," but they ate many of their meals with us.

It's not common to have two sets of twins in one place, but we did for just a few days when Gloria and Naomi Martinez arrived from Mexico to work with us for five months. Naomi stayed in the city with the five girls who were studying there and Gloria worked in the mountain churches.

Students from the University of Tennessee Christian Student Fellowship came for five days in the middle of December. One of their projects was to put stove pipes in the kitchens of some of those who lived near us. Very few people had stove pipes, which, of course, led to a lot of smoke in their kitchens. One lady had chronic pulmonary problems from the smoke. The group visited in the homes of some of the Christians and ate two meals with some of the Christian brothers and sisters. They also participated in a number of worship services of the four congregations and baptized a young man from Perú.

Phyllis Mortenson from Waterloo, Iowa, also came to work. She led crafts and Sunday school lessons with the children in all four congregations, did some handwork with the women and worked with me in the clinic. She was followed by Eva Gehren, a nurse from Springfield, Missouri, who worked in the clinic. In February 1989, Wilda Rush returned and brought Ida Weber, a nurse friend from Tampa, Florida. They worked in the clinic. Then Jennifer Sharp, a cardiology nurse from Columbus, Ohio, arrived for four weeks. She was able to do all of the physical exams. During this time, I delivered six babies.

# And Back to the Clinic

Though Karen Meade had left the work in the mountains in August, Joanna Burgess continued to see pre-natal patients and did the vaccination clinics. I started work again at the clinic on December 6 , seeing from twenty to thirty patients a day. One day I saw sixty-one patients and delivered a baby! It was a long delivery: I was called to the clinic at 7:15 A.M. and didn't get home until 8 P.M. I was grateful for Phyllis Mortensen from Waterloo, Iowa. She helped by taking temperatures and weights on patients. She also saw her first delivery.

Two Honduran ladies also worked with me regularly in the clinic. When I look back on my first year in the mountains, I wonder how I ever managed without them. They did all of the recordkeeping, prepared the medicine for the patients, and cleaned the clinic. They also helped with the vaccination clinics every other Tuesday.

# Holidays—Special Days

Ana and Marina had worked with the children and youth to present several small Christmas dramas. It was a special program. A standing room only audience was present for the program. Some of the group then went to Perú to present the dramas on Christmas Day. After the service, everyone was given a treat which included an apple, a real treat for the Honduran people.

On January 1, 1990, John and I held open house. I baked 600 cookies and made 200 popcorn balls to distribute to the 161 church members and neighbors who attended. We wanted to start the year off right after being away for most of the previous year.

# Chapter 24

## Ministry Goes On
## 1990-91

## Extending Ministry

Before we had left for furlough, we had arranged for some of the girls from the mountains to continue their education in the city. We had arranged for them to room with a Christian couple in the city. But we wanted to find a house to buy where they could live. We finally found one only a mile and a half from the school they attended. It was large enough for eight girls and their housemother. It took about six weeks to close on the house. Then, of course, a lot of work had to be done on the house. John built closet spaces, kitchen cabinets, shelves, and a study table and installed burglar bars.

Once again the Lord provided for a need when He led Dalila Martinez to Honduras to be the housemother for the eight girls. A graduate of a university in San Luis Potosí in Mexico, with a degree in psychology, Dalila had attended a year at Johnson Bible College where I had met her and talked about the possibility of her coming to Honduras while I was in the States for our wedding.

Two more girls went to the city to study in 1991. Christine was also helping a young man to continue his education, so, even though he didn't live at the house, he often studied there with the girls.

Back in 1987, I had received permission from the Honduran government to pay teachers to work in government schools where only one teacher taught six grades. At the same time, I had received permission for the teacher to teach Bible in the schools. Two of those teachers were Raul Calderon who taught first at Las Crucitas and later at San Antonio del Peru. The other was Danilo Vijil who taught at Peñitas Arriba and later became the permanent teacher there. Danilo also preached at some of the services. Both of these young men had come to Christ through the ministry in the mountains.

## Visitors and Work Teams

Terri Handt visited for a week in March. She had been to Honduras before and came this time to practice her Spanish. She assisted me in the clinic. She helped me one night with a difficult delivery when I had to use the vacuum extractor and helped move the girls into the house in the city.

Jerry Everett was one of the team from Christian Campus House in Knoxville who had come in December. He returned and taught us how to computerize all of the patient records.

Two work teams came in the summer of 1990. The first to arrive, in June, was a team of twenty, mostly teenagers, from the Church of Christ at Manor Woods in Rockville, Maryland. They came eager to work and accomplished a great deal. They painted, cleaned, and made a good start on putting up the ceiling in the house for the girls in the city. Each afternoon we went to Laguna de Tembladeros where they led V.B.S. for 75 children.

The second team, an eight-member group from the Garden City Church of Christ in Columbus, Indiana, came for nine days during the middle of July. The group included four teenagers and four adults, one of whom was a real carpenter. Their efforts were focused on carpentry, painting, and insulating the house in the city. They made a so-so house sparkle. But they did plenty of work in the mountains too, working mainly on providing a steady water supply to the clinic. Two of the men preached and one of the women taught women. The young people used puppets to tell the children Bible stories.

Graduates from Colegio Biblico came often from Mexico for various ministries. In July, Elda Castillo came to take care of the girls when Dalila had to return to Mexico in response to family problems.

Gwen Wooters, a nurse from Illinois, came for three weeks in 1991 to see what it was like to be a missionary nurse. With Dr. Todd Chaffin with us as well, I enjoyed a semi-vacation in the clinic. All I had to do was sit and translate for Todd! One day at a vaccination clinic, Gwen gave all of the vaccines and I filled out the record form.

Dr. Chaffin was with us for six months. He taught me a great deal, and it was a real vacation in that I didn't have to "play" doctor. He and John vied over who could tell the most puns and silly jokes.

More work teams came in the summer of 1991. In June, a group from H.I.M. Ministries in Indiana arrived for twelve days. They painted, did some landscaping at the clinic, fixed the sewer line, put a sink in the computer room at the clinic, and did a V.B.S. with the children every afternoon.

Then in July nine men from the Valley View Christian Church in Dallas, Texas, arrived. They spent four days building a home for Amable Rivera, our minister. They also built him some furniture. The carpenters in the group also built a beautiful cabinet for the dentist-computer room. John lost count of how many trips he made to San Pedro for supplies to keep up with them.

Amy Schroeder, a nursing student from Iowa, arrived in July and stayed for a month. She could also speak Spanish, allowing her to communicate directly with patients. She served in a variety of ways—cooking, clinic, classes for children.

In October, Jeremy Nelson from Emporia, Kansas, arrived. He hoped one day to be a medical missionary and wanted to see what it would be like. He did a variety of tasks in the clinic, worked one morning with Amable in the fields to get a taste of mountain farming, and participated in all of the worship services.

Vera Mushrush from Noblesville, Indiana, visited in January 1992. I have often called Vera a missionary to missionaries. She arrived in Honduras on New Year's Day and the next day computerizing the remainder of the patient records. The script for a video Good New Productions was doing was due about that time. Since the dental chair was in the room with the computer, I relaxed in it and dictated the script to Vera while she typed. She updated records and calculated how many babies I had delivered since I had been in the mountains.

For the third time in four years we welcomed Faye and Janice Rostvit, or Victoria and Juanita, as they are known in Honduras. Again they encouraged us with their singing and Bible stories they told using their puppets. This time we held meetings three nights at Peñitas and three nights at Laguna.

# Ministry to the Body

Soon after we returned from furlough, a seventeen-year-old woman, came to the clinic with a hard lump on her leg just below the knee.  I didn't know what it was, but I knew it was something I couldn't treat.  I told her that she should see a doctor in the city.  Some months later I learned that she had been diagnosed with osteosarcoma and needed her leg amputated, but  that she was refusing to have it done.  As I talked to her husband, I was reminded of the women who spent all she had on a disease of the blood, but only Jesus could heal her.  This woman's husband had gone to faith healers and others who recommended different herbs.  He had spent a lot of money hoping she could be healed without amputation.  I made two trips to her home to have prayer, read Scripture, and encourage her to have the surgery.  I told her and her husband that  we would pay the expenses for the operation and chemotherapy.  She finally agreed to the surgery and completed her chemotherapy.  When I learned she was back home, I went to visit her and found her using her crutches as she made and fried tortillas on the stove. Soon after I visited her, her husband gave his life to Christ and was baptized.

Even though she had her leg amputated and the chemotherapy, the cancer spread.  She had more chemotherapy, but the cancer had spread too far.  One night when the minister went to their home to have services, she told him she wanted to be baptized.  It was raining and he encouraged her to wait, but she insisted he do it  then.  He baptized her in a tank at the house.  She went to be with the Lord on November 22, 1991.

I am always amazed at how God provides.  For example, both Christine and Marina had to have some dental work done. In talking to the dentist and his wife, they learned that the couple would like to do volunteer work to help the people in the mountains with their dental problems.  Back in 1987, we had been given a dental chair, so we put it and a sink in the room where we had the computer and on the first Friday in July, the dentist and his wife came to pull teeth. They didn't think they would have many patients on their first trip, but they had thirty-three patients and pulled forty-three teeth.  When they came the second time,  a cabinet had been added to the room, giving them a better place to put their supplies.  This time forty-three patients came, and fifty-five teeth were pulled.  The first Friday in September, only the female half of the team came, and she alone took care of thirty-nine people, pulling fifty-five teeth.  My sister, with the help of a dentist in Indiana, obtained dental anesthesia that was not available in Honduras.  These volunteer dentists provided their own transportation and charged nothing for their services.

## Continuing Work with Interplast

I mentioned earlier  that I worked with Interplast when the group came to Honduras twice a year to do surgery on children with cleft lips and palates and to do skin grafts on burn victims.  One time when they came, a reporter and photographer also came from the Palm Beach *Post* newspaper.  As I told these two about what I did in the mountains and about my vaccination clinics, they asked if they could accompany me to a vaccination clinic.  When they returned to the States,  a feature article on Interplast and on me was featured in the Sunday, July 8 issue.

## Ministry to the Soul

In May 1990, we started worship services in our home for the people living in San Antonio del Perú.  This would be the first of many times we tried to get a work going in this area. However, it wouldn't be until after we had left the mountains that regular worship services finally started and a building was constructed.  Several from the village came to Christ before regular services began, but never enough to have a church.  But  seeds were planted that did eventually grow into a church.

Since  only one family continued to attend worship services in Perú, that family was encouraged to come to our home in San Antonio del Perú for services.

Toward the end of 1990, a Wednesday night Bible study was started in San Antonio del Peru.  These studies were held in in different homes, including ours.  The result was that more people came to Christ and were baptized.

In the rural areas in Honduras, few people are legally married.  A legal marriage requires gathering a lot of papers to have a civil wedding, which is held on Friday at the municipality of the nearest city.  In order to set a better example, we encouraged Christians to be legally married and offered to help with the expenses.  One of the first  to marry legally was Juvenile Rivera and Julie Aldana.  We were witnesses to their marriage.  The ceremony took only two minutes—after taking so much time gathering the papers.  Later they would have a church wedding.

Soon after they were married, we witnessed the weddings of two more couples..  One bride was under age, requiring that we make a trip with them to Santa Barbara to find her mother and then go to the municipality for her to sign a paper giving permission for her daughter to marry.  The mother could not write, so she put her thumb print on the paper.

In January 1991, we also started conducting services in Las Crucitas.  Because we went there in the afternoon, we had Sunday School at our home at 10 A.M. Maritza and Marta Coto usually went with us to teach the children, and we had twenty to thirty people in attendance.

Amable Rivera came home to Peñitas Arriba after he graduated from Colegio Biblico in 1991. He was minister for the congregation in Peñitas and also helped with the congregation at San Antonio del Peru. These two congregations paid him some, but he still had to do some farming to have enough to live on.

With the offerings from the Laguna de Tembladeros congregation, some help from Lifeline Mission and our mission funds, and a lot of volunteer labor from those inside and outside Honduras, the congregation at Laguna built a block building where they could worship.

# Christmas Celebrations

John made wooden toys to give to the boys for Christmas. He said it was like being in his second childhood. He made buses, trucks and tractors. He even put a cam on the two axles of the buses, which made little heads bob up and down when the bus moved. He also made bulldozers and frontend loaders where the blade and scoop moved. Some of our friends in the city bought some of the buses and we used the money to buy dolls for the girls.

Christmas was always special in the mountains. In 1990, I started a tradition that I continued even after we moved to Las Brisas: I made popcorn balls to give with an apple for Christmas. This particular year we gave gifts only to the children. Besides the apple and popcorn ball each boy received one of the wooden toys that John had made and each girl received a doll. After some of the men from

292

San Antonio del Peru saw the toys the boys received, they decided that John should give them some too. John wasn't the only one in his second childhood!  Since John had some toys left, we continued to share with other boys who hadn't been at the Christmas program. Our co-workers, Ana, Marina and Christine once again worked with the young people to prepare and present two Bible dramas.  So many came for the program that they presented the dramas twice—for two different groups of people.

Once again, thanks to I.D.E.S. and the Lincoln (IL) Christian Church, we gave food to some of the poorer families in Peñitas Arriba, San Antonio del Perú, Perú and Laguna de Tembladeros.  We distributed 300 pounds each of flour, beans and corn, 200 pounds of pork, 270 pounds of shortening and rice, 130 cans of sardines and tomato paste,  80 heads of cabbage, 100 pounds of tomatoes, 150 pounds of potatoes and 48 pounds of powdered milk.

December was also the month for new babies.  I delivered babies on December 15, 17, 19, and 31.  We had been invited to have Christmas dinner with Tom and Toni Schneller in San Pedro Sula, so I was thankful that the women had their babies before and after Christmas Day!

## Retired?  What Does That Mean?

John was supposed to be retired, though one would never have known it.  He kept busy in the ministry doing many different jobs such as making toys for the children; repairing items at our home and at the clinic; ordering supplies; leading work teams and being the best encourager I could ever have.  One day when the group from Dallas was with us, he made four trips down the mountain and back hauling supplies they needed.  Once he made a bed for a little boy who had been taken in by a family because his mother was not taking good care of him.  He built a wall around the girls' house in the city.  Later he added a bedroom, bathroom and front porch to the house.  A rather busy retirement!

## The Changes—They Keep Coming

Early in December, Marina decided to return to Mexico to be with her parents.  She had been reared by her grandparents, and since her dad wasn't a Christian, she wanted to share Christ with him.  The day after she left, Ana received a phone call that her mother had inoperable cancer, so she too left for Mexico.  We prayed that both would return to continue their ministry in the mountains.

In December, I also had a visit from Jose Orlando Ramirez, who had at one time lived in the mountains, and his sister was one of the women who worked in the clinic.   He was now living in the small village  of Las Brisas de Chamelecon east of Puerto Cortes.  He came to talk about baptism.  He had given his life to Christ in a Pentecostal church and wanted to be baptized, but the minister had told him that he needed to be tested six months to a year before he could be baptized.   I shared with him several scriptures and asked him to study them and then if he still felt the same way, Amable would baptize him on Sunday.  And he told us about the need for medical help in Las Brisas—precursor of even more change.

## Ready for Furlough

Dr. Dan O'Neill was with us for the last three days before we left for furlough.  He saw patients in the clinic on two days and went with me to a vaccination clinic the other day.

They were going to be visiting other missionaries in Honduras, so we took him and his family to the bus station on the way to the airport. Since we didn't have anyone to operate the clinic during the furlough, Dan agreed to return to see patients once again on February 28th.

# Chapter 25

# 1992—Furlough, Ministry, and Moving

## Furlough—Short and Sweet

Furlough was short, extending only from February through May. But we made the most of it. We visited four supporting churches in Tennessee, attended Homecoming at Johnson Bible College and then returned to Indiana where we stayed with my mother until we returned to Honduras. Good New Productions had assisted us to produce a video of our ministry, so this was an easy furlough. We presented the ministry to twenty-four congregations and several women's groups. We also visited John's two sisters in South Carolina.

## Back to Ministry in Honduras

We had been back in Honduras less than a month when someone knocked on our door about 3:00 A.M. A lady in the village of Chile had delivered a baby at home around 5:00 P.M. the evening before, but the local midwife had not been able to remove the placenta. The patient had been bleeding for nearly ten hours. We didn't know what we would find as we went to pick her up. We hadn't been driving long when we met ten men who had been taking turns carrying her up a steep road in a hammock attached to a long pole. They put her in the back of the pickup and returned to their homes, leaving her short, not-too-strong husband to help us get her into the clinic.

As he helped carry her into the clinic, John was puzzled when he felt a lump beside the woman. I found out what it was when we got her on the delivery table. The midwife had not cut the cord, so it was the woman's baby John had felt. I cut the cord and did a manual removal of the placenta, which meant putting my hand into the uterus and gently pulling the placenta loose until it came out. That succeeded, but then I could not get a blood pressure or a pulse. I knew she was alive because she was talking and I could hear her heart with the stethoscope. I told John and her husband that we had to get her to the city as quickly as possible.

We went quickly down the mountain, but at one point, we got behind a pickup that didn't want to let us around. I recognized a woman riding in the back, so I leaned out the window and told her to tell the man to get over because a woman in our pickup was dying. John made the trip to the hospital in a record twenty-three minutes. Once we got her there, the nurses and doctors gave her blood. They were amazed that she was still alive. Because she had lost so much blood, she was weak and her milk didn't come in, leaving her unable to breast feed the baby. I gave her a big can of powdered milk when she needed it. Each time she came to get the milk, she brought me some fresh vegetables.

Two questions came up frequently on furlough: "How many babies have you delivered?" and, "Do you still deliver babies?" I am sure I have delivered close to 700 babies, but unfortunately, I do not have an accurate record. However, I have delivered few babies since 1992. I well remember when I decided to retire from delivering babies.

One night I was called to the clinic about 9:00 P.M. for a maternity patient. Before the woman had delivered her baby, another lady in labor, a sister-in-law of the first one, arrived at the clinic. I delivered the first lady's baby about 12:30 A.M. and the second one about 4:00 A.M. After I

298

made sure they were both fine, I went home to get about two hours of sleep before I returned to the clinic to see patients. When I got back to the clinic, a third lady in labor was there. My little delivery room was full, so I unlocked the room where we had worship services so she could lie down on the one of the benches. This was her first baby and I knew it would be some time before she would deliver.

I saw patients all morning. At noon when I was go-ing  home to eat dinner, I took the first two women to their homes. I had a rested a short time and returned to the clinic, saw a few more patients, and at 4:00 P.m. delivered the third baby in less than 24 hours. By that time, I was exhausted. That convinced me that I needed to retire from delivering babies. I was nearly sixty years old and enough was enough!

We continued to do vaccination clinics. Late in 1992, we helped the government in its campaign to vaccinate school children against measles. Rhonda Wilson and I gave three hundred vaccinations in six different schools.

## And Visitors and Work Teams Keep Coming

Once again interns and work teams arrived during the summer of 1992. I have always felt that one of the reasons God sent me to Honduras was so that I could be in a place near enough to the States that young people could come to see what it was like to be a missionary without incurring excessive expense.

The first intern was Marti Troester, a registered nurse, who actually arrived  before we returned from furlough. She worked with Lifeline Mission until the first of June. She was a big help in the clinic.

Next to come were Carlos and Patricia Cajon and Israel Cajon, students from Colegio Biblico. Carlos and Israel were from Guatemala and Pati from Mexico. Carlos and Pati helped with the congregations at Laguna de Tembladeros and Las Crucitas and Israel helped with the congregation at Peñitas Arriba.

Rhonda Wilson, another nurse, was the next to come from Goshen, Indiana, to be with us until May 1993. She was an R.N. She learned Spanish quickly and was able soon to communicate with the patients. She also taught sign language.

Another intern was Chris Conway from Converse, Indiana, who worked with the youth choir and helped with the younger children so they could sing special songs for sing-spirations. He also set up several programs on the computer and helped John lay block to build a retaining wall at the clinic.

In July, Ana Grisel Martinez returned for a time. Her mother had died and she felt she needed to be in Mexico with her father. She was an encouragement to many and we were sorry to see her leave. Our last interns for the summer were Mindy Frazier and Karen Shinn from near Blountville, Tennessee, both nursing students at East Tennessee State University, both of whom hoped one day to be missionary nurses.

Besides all of the interns, two work teams also came. A small group from H.I.M. Ministries arrived first. Wilda Rush came and worked in the clinic. One helped with VBS and John and another one built furniture for the Christians in our congregation in Peñitas.

The second group came from the Church of Christ at Manor Woods in Maryland. This was the third trip for some of them. They cleaned and painted, and the men helped John move a lot of dirt around the clinic and work on the retaining wall. They all participated in a VBS.

Trina Delph, an R.N. from my home church, arrived November 12. Of course, she worked in the clinic, taught a women's group with me translating, and became involved in all of the preparations for the wedding of Danilo Vijil and Christine Kelley.

## Even Nurses Get Sick

I am seldom sick, but just before I left India in 1980, I had a bleeding ulcer. Since that time I had been fine. Velma Held was visiting, and before she left, we had planned to take a short trip to Guatemala. The day before we were to leave, I had gone on a vaccination clinic and had felt fine. But the day we were to leave, I got up to go to the kitchen to make coffee and nearly fainted. I quickly sat down and put my head down, but I knew that there would be no trip to Guatemala. I called Rhonda Wilson and told her she would need to take me to the emergency room at the hospital. When the doctor did an endoscopy, he did not see anything because my stomach was full of blood. I was admitted to the hospital.

The doctor didn't want to give me blood because of the AIDSs problem, but my hemoglobin dropped very low, and I needed blood. Fortunately, thanks to Rhonda, a minister in San Pedro Sula and Danilo, Christine's husband, were able to give me blood that we knew was safe. I wasn't in the hospital long for which I was thankful, and I recuperated quickly.

# And The Church Grew

The congregation at Peñitas Arriba continued to grow under the leadership of Amable Rivera. The Honduran women by now were teaching the lesson at the Monday night meeting and going calling together on Thursday. Two young men were teaching Sunday school classes. Two adult women gave their lives to Christ and were baptized as a result of the witness of their women relatives in the church.

Velma Held arrived just before Tina left. She brought a knitting machine and also taught the women to knit by hand. Velma wrote the following about her visit.

> Humid Honduras! It was cloudy and drizzly when I arrived—and many more days. But the mountain scenery made up for the weather.
>
> The purpose of my trip was to teach the mountain women to use a knitting machine to make sweaters. Yes, it gets cold up there in the winter. The ladies who own the shop where the machine was purchased gave us 12 bags of all kinds and colors of yarn. The interest was amazing because none of them knew how to knit by hand (a few crochet), but more than 35 ladies and girls and one boy tried knitting by hand and on the machine. There would probably have been more if the weather had been nicer—walking up and down mountain paths in the rain is no fun, and if it had not been coffee-picking (they call it cutting) season.
>
> Teaching in Spanish was difficult. They didn't understand my English or respond when I tried Hindi, so a lot was done by "showing". Using "Lana" (yarn) and "Aguja" (needles), they now "tiger' knit and "reverse" (purl) making baby hats and sweaters. Many are

302

doing really well, and Marta and Maritsa (sisters) are able to teach the others. Knitting by machine is work and not my favorite thing to do, but the Lord doesn't ask us to do just the things we like. I'm grateful to have shared my enjoyment of hand knitting and Christian love.

## An Ailing Knee Leads to a Move

I had been having knee trouble for over a year. Todd Chaffin, a doctor who had been with us, had given me a cortisone shot that helped for a time. But he told me that I needed arthroscopic surgery. I went to a good orthopedic surgeon in San Pedro Sula who confirmed Dr. Chafin's diagnosis. When he did the surgery, he removed a lot of loose cartilage and told me that I needed a replacement. But at that time this surgery was not being done in Honduras. That led John and me to pray and to consider moving since I could no longer hike the mountain trails and roads.

John and I made one trip west of Puerro Cortes to look into the possibility of a move, but we hadn't found any place satisfactory. We decided to visit Las Brisas de Chamelecon where we were welcomed warmly. We went back again in September to meet with the community to tell them what we hoped to do if we moved there. They were very excited about starting a clinic and found some land where it could be built. A man in the community would lease the land; if ever the clinic was closed, it would go back to him. We went to the Municipality of Puerto Cortes and drew up papers to that effect. We thought it was interesting that at the meeting one lady asked if I would treat Catholics. I found out that only those from the Catholic Church would be given medicine by some. I told her that I would treat whoever came to the clinic, though I did want to share Scripture and have prayer each morning.

In September, John and I started a routine that would last until July 1993, when we moved to Las Brisas. Early every Monday morning John left for Las Brisas to work on the construction of the clinic. Our good friends, Jose and Graciela Canahuati, loaned us their beach house in Puerto Cortes where he could stay. Since they had a microwave in the house, I fixed John enough food to last him from Monday through Wednesday night when he returned to the mountains. On Thursday both of us went to San Pedro Sula to do our shopping and then on to Puerto Cortes that night. On Friday I went with John to Las Brisas. While he was working on the construction of the clinic, I held a tailgate clinic. We spent Friday night in Puerto Cortes. Then John worked on Saturday morning while I saw patients. On Saturday afternoon we returned to the mountain and rested on Sunday. Rhonda Wilson took care of the clinic in the mountains when I was in Las Brisas.

John came back one Wednesday and said, "You won't believe what I did!" To get to Las Brisas from Puerto Cortes, it was necessary to cross a lagoon at a little place called Chifia. Most of the time it wasn't too deep, but when John was on his way to Las Brisas, it was deeper than usual. Some men told him he could cross. He started out and the car went down, down, water started coming in, and he was stopped. But the Lord provided. The men who told him he could cross helped him get the pickup out. A man on a motorcycle was a mechanic and he dried the parts out and the car started. But John decided it would be better to wade across the lagoon and take the bus to Las Brisas.

When John started work on the clinic in Las Brisas, he had a lot of volunteer labor, but he finally found two builders to help. He started digging the foundations for our house

304

early in November.  The people helped us find some land on a small hill exactly one kilometer from the clinic.  Later we found an even better builder who helped John finish the house.

# The Christmas Season

At Christmas 1992, Rhonda and Christine helped me make the popcorn balls, and I also made over one hundred chocolate chip-banana-oatmeal-cinnamon bars to put in the bags for the Christmas treats for the children.  Trina had brought many bags of chocolate chips donated by the people of Normanda Christian Church.  John again made wooden trucks for the boys and the congregation from Goshen Christian Church (Rhonda's home church) sent crayons, coloring books, hair barrettes and other items for the girls.  The churches at Penitas Arriba and Laguna de Tempbladeros held a joint service from 8:00 P.M. Christmas Eve until 2 A.M. Christmas morning with about one hundred and fifty  people participating.  It was an evening of messages from the Word, special music, congregational singing, a puppet show, and fellowship that ended with a big meal of beef, pork, tamales, tortillas and coffee.

But the year ended on a sad note when one of the faithful men went to be with the Lord on December 31.  He was on his way from his home to the girls' house in the city where he was night watchman when he apparently fell at a place where a pole was loose on the path, hit his head, and died immediately.  Thinking he was at work, his family didn't miss him until he didn't return home from work.  His body wasn't found until nearly twenty-four  hours after the accident.  He was the first Christian in his family.  His wife had died with breast cancer in 1990.  He left three married daughters, one son and four unmarried daughters, all of whom were living in the house in San Pedro Sula and continuing their education. John and I drove down the mountain to bring his body up to be buried.

# A Few Finishing Details in the Mountains

In 1993, a record number of girls—twelve of them—lived in the house in the city while they studied. We had received permission to add a bedroom, a bathroom and a front porch to take care of the extra girls.

There was another happy wedding in April, but we were not able to attend. Before Ana Martinez left for Mexico, she became engaged to Raul Calderon, one of the teachers at San Antonio del Peru. They wanted to marry in Mexico at her home, but Raul was not granted a visa to go to Mexico. They had been told that if they were married, he would be granted a visa. They had a civil wedding in March, but he still was not given a visa. So they were married in the mountains in April. Ana returned to Mexico to try to get a visa for him.

Dr. Mike Richards and his wife and children and Bethany Hawes from Panama visited in March 1993. I had known Mike since he had visited at Kulpahar. At that time, the Richards had hoped to serve in India, but they were unable to get papers to serve there permanently. After learning of a need in Panama, they went there. Mike saw patients in the clinics both in the mountains and at Las Brisas. Bethany was an R.N. and had actually inquired about serving in Honduras, but Rhonda was present, and I didn't feel that there was enough work for two nurses. I recommended she contact Mike, not realizing that they had told her to contact us. But it all worked out as she was a blessing to them and still was able to visit Honduras.

Rhonda Wilson was with us for nearly a year. It was difficult to see her leave, but we were thankful for the time she spent in Honduras. We gave her a surprise farewell party—and really did surprise her. As she walked into church on Monday night, several of the children tossed balloons in her direction and she saw the sign on the wall: "Feliz viaje, Rhonda" or "Have a happy trip, Rhonda." Several of the congregation shared how Rhonda had blessed their lives and Amable gave a short devotion. One of our Christian sisters made Rhonda's favorite Honduran food—flour tortillas with refried beans and cheese and I baked cakes.

Move or no move, life went on day by day!

# Chapter 26

## Las Brisas—A New Ministry
## 1993-September 1994

## The Move

I began to see patients in the new clinic at Las Brisas, which was named *Centro de Salud, Las Brisas del Chamelecon*, on January 30.   By April, I had seen four hundred patients, even though the clinic was open only on Friday and Saturday.  I saw a lot of cases of anemia, probably caused by hookworms.  I also saw some cases that I thought could be malaria.  Other than that, most of the patients had the same problems as those in the mountains.  I found Norma Rivera to help me.  It was nice when the clinic opened and I no longer needed see patients from the tailgate of the pickup.  The construction wasn't completely finished, though it was finished about two weeks later.  After that, the work was concentrated on building our home. John hoped to have the roof on by May 28 so plastering could begin and the floor tiles laid.  We hoped to move to Las Brisas by July.

The house was finished, and we moved on July 1.  Bright and early on Thursday morning we started loading three trucks.  The trip was just over fifty miles, but with the bad mountain road and the construction of a new highway between San Pedro Sula and Puerto Cortes and the bad road from Puerto Cortes to Las Brisas, it took us two-and-a-half hours to make the trip.  The house was much like the one in the mountains, although larger.  I was really thankful for our much larger kitchen.  John built the house with double walls. We had no electricity at Las Brisas and it was very hot there.

So John used four-inch blocks, building two walls with an eight-inch air space between the walls. This kept the heat from penetrating the interior of the house. With this and good insulation, the house was very comfortable. We had a generator that could be used on a limited basis. We were just happy to be home in Las Brisas at last.

## Settling in—With Visitors, Of Course

We had been in our new home for only a week when John returned to the mountains to pick up a group from Manor Woods Church of Christ in Maryland. They had spent the first week working with Danilo and Christine Vijil, but now came to help us. They had to sleep on air mattresses on the floor in the clinic since we had only one bedroom in our home. When they came for breakfast, they had plenty of stories to tell about spiders, scorpions, frogs and other insects they had encountered.

They painted the inside and outside of the clinic and hauled fill dirt and rocks from the house to use around the clinic. In the afternoon they did the crafts for a VBS in Cerro Cardona, just over a mile from our home. By the way, after the group painted the inside of the clinic, they were no longer troubled with spiders, scorpions, etc.!

Javier Perez, a student at Colegio Biblico but originally from the mountains, came to teach one of the VBS classes.

*Some of the folks in Las Brisas*

I taught a class as did Norma Rivera.  It was a blessing to see the eagerness and smiles of the children as they learned new songs.  The ten to seventeen year olds in my class were very attentive.  One lady said "history" was made:  nothing like this had ever been done in Cerro Cardona.  We rejoiced at the end of the week when Norma was baptized in the Caribbean Sea.

In early August, Denny Stevenson, the minister of my home church, along with two young men from the congregation, arrived.  They and  John made twelve benches for the church at Cerro Cardona, painted at our house. And hauled more rocks and dirt to fill in around the clinic.  They also leveled some of the dirt that had been hauled earlier so we could plant shrubbery and flowers in front of the clinic.  In the afternoon they did crafts for a VBS that was held in the school at Las Brisas.

We were expecting at the most 90 children for the Las Brisas VBS, but 108 was the lowest attendance.  We had 120 on two different days.  Javier Perez again taught a class, and Norma and I each taught a class.  Again this was a first for the community.  We even had several black children who came 2½ miles from Bajamar each day.

The community folk were so pleased to have the visitors and appreciated what they were contributing.  They demonstrated their hospitality in various ways.  During the time work teams were present, for example, several of the women cooked the noon meal for the visitors.

Myra Harrah, a nurse from Terre Haute, Indiana, came to visit in December.  She came with the possibility of returning to work with F.A.M.E and take over the clinic work in the mountains.  She was  a widow with two sons, one of whom had been on a trip to Honduras and told her of the need.  She got a thrill as we slipped and slid and finally got stuck going up the mountain. Fortunately, some men who were riding with us pushed us out. We saw patients at the clinic and then crept down the mountain still sliding, though not as much. She hoped to return in October 1994.

## The Medical Ministry Develops

There was no doubt that the Lord led us to the ministry in Las Brisas. Besides the need for the Gospel, the medical needs were great. I saw many with such severe anemia that I wondered how they could even walk. In the States, they would have been hospitalized and given blood transfusions. I treated them for hookworm and anemia, and it was amazing how quickly they recovered.

Hookworm was a parasite acquired as the result of not wearing shoes. Once worms got into the body, they sucked blood in the intestines, causing the anemia. I also saw malnourished children and black people from Bajamar with high blood pressure.

I remember one baby who weighed only about six pounds, even though he was nearly four months old. He was anemic

*Centro de Salud, Las Brisas*

and had an infectious skin disease.  I really didn't have much hope for him.  But with prayers and the medicine, he got well.

Some people walked for half a day to get to get to the clinic.  One Saturday a man and his wife walked eight hours along the beach to bring their little girl who was suffering with diarrhea and vomiting.  I had so much joy to see the good results from the simple inexpensive treatment.  Several black people from Bajamar came on the bus every time the clinic was open.  Soon black people from Travesia, about five miles away, also came.

Because there was not yet a nurse for the mountains,  the clinic at Las Brisas was open only Monday, Tuesday and Friday.  On Wednesday morning we got up early and drove to the mountains where I would see patients all day, often sixty to eighty of them.  We spent the night in our old home.  On Thursday we ran errands in San Pedro Sula before returning to Las Brisas that night.

Soon after we moved to Las Brisas, I saw many patients who lived in several villages across the Chamelecon River. I decided to start a clinic in that area, going once a month. The first time we went, we drove along the east coast and took a boat across the river.  We then walked for about ten minutes to the school at La Barra de Chamelecon where I was allowed to use one of the classrooms for the clinic.  On my first trip I saw eighty patients.  I even had to turn some patients away because there was no electricity and it was growing dark.

Later, after the flood and when the river was higher, we were able to get the boat only a half  kilometer from our house.  It took about forty to forty-five  minutes to get to La Barra.  One day on our way home, we shared the boat with a cow!

313

One of the blessings of my medical work has been the cooperation I have had with the government. In fact, when

*Our home in Las Brisas*

I moved from the mountains, the head doctor of the Centro de Salud in San Pedro Sula wrote a wonderful letter of recommendation for me to take to the Centro de Salud in Puerto Cortes. Since there was no nurse at the government Centro de Salud in Bajamar, John made several trips to Puerto Cortés during a week in April to bring nurses to different areas to vaccinate children. The last day they vaccinated at La Barra was the same day I had clinic there. They did 191 vaccinations.

Three of the girls who were studying in San Pedro Sula decided to pursue nursing. They were accepted into the Auxiliary nursing program, a one-year program followed by one year of what was called government service. It was good to know that more Christian nurses would soon be at work.

## Ministering to the Spiritual

I started a Sunday School class in Cerro Cardona the second week after we arrived in Las Brisas. At first I taught all of the children three to sixteen years of age, but when the attendance increased to over forty, I asked a young Christian man from Las Brisas to teach the younger children. In September, I started a Sunday School for the children at Las

314

Brisas.  The first Sunday seventy-two came, so I asked the same young man to help me  there too.

Raul and Ana Calderon moved to Las Brisas the last part of February 1994.  Raul immediately started teaching about forty first graders at the school.  Ana started calling and conducting home Bible studies, and our attendance at the church services began to increase.  We started out having a service in our living room, offering the Lord's Supper to those who attended at Cerro Cardona since they never had the Lord's Supper there.  Finally, the church at Cerro Cardona got a minister, permitting us to stop going there.  We continued to conduct services in our living room until the attendance grew too large to fit.  We then had the services on our screened in front porch.  Raul and Ana also started a youth group with only girls attending at the beginning.  Three more people soon came to Christ and were baptized.

## Always Building Something

John's next building project was a guest house to be used by Raul and Ana Calderon who would provide help for our ministry.  I received permission from the authorities in the education department to have Raul teach at the school.  He had never received a visa to go to Mexico, so Ana had returned to Honduras.

*Guest house*

315

John started the foundations of the house in November in hope of having it finished by February. The house was a little more than six hundred square feet with two bedrooms, kitchen-dining room-living room area and a bath.

John always had something to do to keep him busy. He built benches for our front porch so people would have a place to sit for worship services. He also built shelves for the kerosene lamps which were used during worship when sometimes the generator didn't work. He constructed a pulpit for Raul to use when he preached.

## And The Rains Came

September brought floods. We hadn't even realized that there was a river running through the village. Before the rains came, it had been covered with water hyacinths with no water visible, but after the floods, it was obvious that it was a river. Some of the people had to move out of their homes and lived in the school until the water receded. We used some mission funds to supply food for some of those who had to leave their homes.

## Time Out for Knee Surgery

I had known since my earlier knee surgery that I would need a knee replacement. God provided for it in a wonderful way. My mother had taken out a certificate of $10,000 for me sometime earlier. I found that I could get a knee replacement for just that amount. Just after we helped with the vaccination clinics, I went into the hospital to be one of the first in San Pedro Sula to have a knee replacement. I did really well. In fact, about three weeks after the surgery, I crossed the river and walked to the school to have my regular clinic at La Barra.

# A Short Furlough

We left Honduras on May 28 for a furlough that would extend through most of September. This time we visited churches in Indiana, Ohio, Maryland, Virginia, West Virginia, Florida, Kentucky, Missouri, Arkansas, Iowa, Nebraska, Minnesota, Illinois and Michigan. My cousin gave us a Toyota pickup to use for the furlough. Later we managed to get this pickup to Honduras for Raul and Ana to use.

While we were on furlough and visiting Ziden and Helen Nutt, I played dentist by using the small pliers of John's Swiss knife to pull a baby tooth from Tom Nutt's oldest daughter. Tom had tried to get the tooth out with string, but it didn't work. I had pulled lots of baby teeth in India, so it didn't take long to give a quick twist and it was out. The funny thing was that I put the pliers on the wrong tooth the first time and Amanda said, "That isn't the one." Oops!!!

# Chapter 27

## Back to Honduras
## Late 1994-Early 1997

### Bats in the Belfry

We were happy to return home to Las Brisas. Raul and Ana took a much-deserved vacation to visit her family in Mexico.

We found that we had bats between the roof and the ceiling of the clinic building. On top of that, bats cause a dirty mess. The man who helped with the construction of the clinic had not done a good job of sealing the openings on the outside, allowing the bats to get in. John had to remove all of the boards, put in cement, and replace the boards. He also painted the front porch where we had worship services and then began making toys for the boys for Christmas.

### Visitors Continue to Provide Ministry

Julie Illman came for three weeks in October. I had worked briefly with her parents in Rhodesia. She hoped to be a doctor and was fluent in Spanish. Later she went to the mountains with Myra to help her get settled after she arrived on November 1.

Wilma Clements from Fortville, Indiana, and Ann Barringer from Indianapolis visited for a short time. I gave them a thrill when they went with me to the clinic at La Barra. The lagoon was deep. However, some men told me I could cross, but not to slow down in the deeper water. I did what they said and was concentrating on my driving, not even noticing that water splashing on the windshield. Ann and Wilma did notice, however, and they were praying that we make it across. We did.

In March, we had plenty of visitors: Dale Meade, missionary to Colombia; Gordon Clifford with Christian Mission Press in Campo, California; Patsy Phillips, Indianapolis; and Tricia Wright and Wendy Dickinson, student nurses who were doing an intra-cultural study in connection with their nursing courses at Anderson College.

In May 1995, Becky Williams, a graduate of Cincinnati Bible Seminary who hoped to study nursing, arrived for two weeks. She said that she was interested in "following me around" for two weeks to see what it was like to be a missionary nurse. Her first week in Honduras was one of the government vaccination campaign weeks. I had promised to go into Puerto Cortes each day to bring government nurses to our area to do vaccinations in a different village each day.

Two work teams came in June 1995. The first, from Indiana, dug the foundation and poured part of the concrete for a guest house in four days. The second group, from Maryland, finished pouring the cement for the foundations and laid most of the block for the walls. Both teams helped with VBS in the afternoon.

Since some of the women of the community had fed visitors, John and I started inviting by turn different families to have Sunday dinner with us. We used our best china and a tablecloth and tried to serve nourishing food our guests liked. One of their favorites was fried chicken. We always had bread and dessert. Our guests always dressed up for a special time. We wanted the people to feel welcome in our home.  Our goal was to entertain every family in the village for Sunday dinner.

We simply didn't have unexpected guests in Las Brisas. There were two reasons—one was just trying to find Las Brisas and the other was transportation.  There was bus service, but one had to know which bus to take, and even in Puerto Cortés, not everyone knew where Las Brisas de Chamelecon was.  But I did have a surprise on March 19, 1996, when a young man walked into the clinic and said, "Madonna, do you know who I am?"   What a nice surprise to see Tim Getter and to meet his wife.  We had last seen him in India when we visited his folks in 1989.  I knew that he and his wife had been studying Spanish in Guatemala and that they might come to visit, but I thought they would contact us first.  But they decided to take a break from their Spanish lessons and visit Honduras.  The guest house was finished, but one of the rooms was being used for a classroom.  We quickly moved the hide-a-bed from Raul and Ana's house to the other guest room, and even though it wasn't the Hilton, they said it was better than many places they had stayed. We had an enjoyable visit despite rain.  I enjoyed cooking Indian food which they enjoyed eating.

A few weeks later we were again surprised.  During the church service on the front porch, one of the women said to me, "There are some Americans outside."  It was Al Creel from Bloomington, Indiana, and Carol Jeffreys who worked with F.A.M.E. in Tegucigalpa.  They had also reached Bajamar by bus and walked the final two-and-a-half miles to Las Brisas.

In the summer of 1996, two work teams arrived.  The first was from the Joppatowne Christian Church in Maryland. Their mornings were spent building shutters for the new church building, doing landscaping, painting in the guest house and at the church building, and  helping John build a baptistery outside the church building. They also went with John to the Merendon Mountains for two days to rebuild the water tank that was above our house there. In the afternoon they led a VBS. I also took them with me to the clinics at Tronconera and La Barra where they worked with children while I saw patients. Part of the group also worked at the orphanage in Omoa.

Marshall and Bea Hills and Mike and Elizabeth Goff visited for just six days in August. The men helped John build ten church pews with backs and a pulpit for the church. They also did some plumbing for John—one job he does not like to do. Bea and Elizabeth did crafts with the children at the school and at the church and also did some crafts with the women at the church.

## Attention to Spiritual Ministry

While we had been on furlough, Raul and Ana hosted the meeting of the youth groups from the Christian churches in Honduras. Instead of having the usual Bible quizzes, the youth were divided into groups and went calling in the community.

We still had a small congregation composed mostly of young girls, but we finally had a family come into the congregation. This family had previously attended a Baptist church. We rejoiced when their two older sons gave their lives to Christ and were baptized. With Raul and Ana gone, I took care of the Sunday School with the help of an older girl, and I also led the youth group. We continued to show Life of Christ videos to the children on our front porch, always with a porch full of viewers.

Two faithful members of the congregation were legally married. Before Raul and Ana left, they had helped them to get the necessary papers for their civil wedding. John and I took them to Puerto Cortes for the wedding. Later in the evening, the minister from Bejamar performed a Christian wedding.

The congregation continued to have additions. In May, for example, a mother and her daughter gave their lives to Christ and were baptized.

One of the things I enjoyed doing for several months was conducting cooking classes with the women. Women who didn't come to church came to these meetings to learn to cook different dishes. We met in a different home each month. I asked the women what they wanted to learn to make. Mostly it was desserts. I taught them to make a jello cake, sugar cookies, puff balls (a type of cake doughnut that is dropped with a teaspoon into the hot oil), fritters—banana, corn and pineapple—and doughnuts. After we cooked something, I taught a Bible lesson. Even though the cooking classes stopped when I ran out of ideas, we continued to have the meetings with singing and a Bible lesson.

In September 1995, the first Conference of the Christian Churches in Honduras was held at a Baptist campground near Lake Yojoa. A group of 190, representing seven churches, were present. The confer-ence lasted two days and featured preaching, classes, a lot

*Children's Day at church*

of good singing, and a wonderful time of fellowship. People came from three churches in San Pedro Sula, two churches in the mountains, the congregation at Las Brisas, and a congregation in Tegucigalpa. After the conference, Delmar Debault, who had been one of the speakers, preached at Las Brisas for two evenings with me translating.

The congregation continued to grow with more adults coming to Christ. One of the faithful members was a dear older man. He came to the clinic one Monday morning when he was sick and I noticed that it was his birthday. So after our prayer and praise service that Monday night, we had a surprise birthday party celebrating his seventy-fifth birthday. Just after that he was ordained as the first elder in the congregation.

In August, we had a solar system installed in our home. This allowed us to show videos to the children on our front porch during Sunday School. This was much better than enduring the noise of the generator. More and more children began to come, even when we didn't show videos. In fact, so many people were coming that our congregation began looking for property where a building could be built.

With the help of a builder, John finally finished the guest house in February 1996. We used it for Sunday school classrooms and for the women's meetings on Thursday afternoon and for the men's meetings on Friday night.

Finally, the leaders of the congregation found some property suitable for a building. The offerings from the congregation paid for the land. Some of the women used machetes to clear the land. In February, John did the measuring and put the batter boards up. Then both men and women helped dig the foundations . Even I got busy with the digging. It was wonderful to see so many working together to help provide a building where we could worship. At first, there was a lot of volunteer help to get the foundations dug and later to pour the cement for the foundations.  But one day when no one came, John persuaded me to go down to do some digging.  When a neighbor came by and saw me digging, he sent his son to help John.

Just at the time when the church offerings ran out, a lady whom we had known for years  remembered our ministry in her will and it was enough to pay for the final construction of the building.  John finally hired the son of a neighbor to help him mix cement and lay the block and later another man to help him build the trusses.  We had our first service in the new building on June 23 and also held Vacation Bible School there when a group came from the States.

The little congregation continued to grow in 1996.  More adults came to the Lord and were baptized.  Before that we had mostly teenagers, but during this year we had four adult men and one adult woman who came to Christ in addition to one teenager.  Our little congregation continued to grow.

That year I also started having Bible study with one of the faithful women.  We studied a discipleship series which took us some time.  The congregation also started having cell meetings in the homes of three families who had been attending the worship services, but who weren't yet Christians.

## A Bible Institute for Honduras

The need for a Bible institute to educate Christian leaders was evident.  Bill and Margy Hoff had moved from Mexico to Honduras to meet this need.  The construction of the buildings for Christian Bible Institute was completed in 1996.  The Hoffs had looked for land for a long time.  Unable to find land to buy, they leased land at a low cost and finished enough construction to be able to accept students. The dedication was on September 14. We planned to send Mateo Valle from our congregation to the Institute when it opened in January.

# Back to the Clinic

I resumed my clinic work at La Barra on the first Friday of October. We could not drive to the river because an open lagoon was too deep to cross in the pickup. We drove to the lagoon and loaded our supplies into a motorboat and went via the Caribbean Sea. The man who took us promised he would return at 4:00 P.M. for the return trip, but he didn't come. My helper and I were tired after seeing fifty-two patients. We thought that we might find another boatman to take us to the lagoon, but his boat was out of gas. So we crossed the river in a small canoe and started walking to the lagoon. We didn't know how far it was, but we knew it would take some time. We had left most of our medicines at the home of a lady because we couldn't carry it. Soon after we started, we were caught in a rain storm, leaving us soaking wet. It was dark by the time we got to the lagoon and John was not there. We found out that when he arrived and we hadn't come, he felt he should return to get a flashlight. We waded across the lagoon and soon after we got across, we saw the lights of the pickup. What a relief to see those lights. We were wet and exhausted and thankful to get home to Las Brisas!

Myra Harrah and Julie Illman helped me the next month. I was thankful: we had seventy-eight patients! This time we could drive to the river because a bulldozer had moved dirt to make a place to cross the lagoon.

One of my favorite patients was a mentally handicapped man who had severe anemia. The first time he came to the clinic, he was so anemic that when I put his blood on my slide to test his hemoglobin, it was like water. The lowest number on my machine was 4 grams and his was lower than that. I treated him with ferrous sulfate tablets and the medicine for hookworm and told him he needed to wear shoes. He returned the next time I was there and his hemoglobin had climbed up to 6.5 grams. He also had bought some rubber flip flops, but had taken them off while he was waiting to be called. When I called him in, in his hurry to get them on to show me he had them, he had put them on the wrong feet. When his hemoglobin finally got back to normal, I told him he didn't need any more medicine. He told one of the Christian women that he would not return to the clinic because that nurse would not give him more medicine. He didn't return, but I saw him from time to time on our drive to Puerto Cortes.

The government vaccination campaign began at Las Brisas at our clinic. When the government nurse was in one room of the clinic giving vaccinations, a lady came to have me check her. She was pregnant and had fallen the day before when she was watching a soccer game. I checked her to find that she was very near delivery time. I asked her if she wanted me to take her to her mother-in-law's home where she was living to have the baby or if she wanted me to deliver the baby in the clinic. She preferred the clinic.

On Tuesday, I took the government nurse to Cerro Cardona. On Wednesday we drove to the river, crossed, and walked thirty to forty minutes to the village of Saraguayna for her to vaccinate. I had fun crossing a stream on two uneven logs. Again on Thursday, we went to the river and took a motorboat to La Sabana.

Dennis and Nora Suisse ran an orphanage for thirty-seven girls In Omoa. They asked me to help with their medical needs. I tried to go once a month. I was thankful for my experience in India cleaning out ears, for some of the girls had ears full of wax. I also checked to see if they were anemic. Some of them had problems with asthma, so I helped with that treatment.

*Another baptism*

The first week in November 1995, the Feed the Children organization brought a group of doctors, nurses, dentists and optometrists to Las Brisas for a day and treated hundreds of people from the surrounding communities. They were well organized and utilized students from the English-speaking high school in Puerto Cortes to translate, young men from the army to control the crowds, and people from the community to usher people in and out of the rooms.

In April 1996, Sandra Dias, one of the three girls who had studied Auxiliary nursing, came to work with me at the Centro de Salud. She had finished her service year in the mountains. She remained until November when she married and returned to the mountains. Having her working with me allowed me to go to other rural areas where medical care was needed. In May, we went up the Chamelecon River to Piedras Arañada. It took forty minutes to get there by boat. I had twenty-eight patients from that village and twenty-three more people who had walked from Tronconera. I eventually did clinics at both villages. Though we went by boat at first, we found out that we could go by road, so John drove and I did the clinic at Tronconera in the morning and at Piedras Arañada in the afternoon. I did this until these villages were flooded after Hurricane Mitch and everyone moved to another location.

In June 1996, I started a rural clinic at Barra de Ulua. To get there, we went in a boat down the Chamelecon River into the Caribbean Sea, then into the Ulua River where we went through a small inlet to the village. On my first day in this village, I saw seventy-four patients at the clinic which was held in the school. Later we followed the same route, going farther to Crique de Las Marias. I was led to go to these villages because of a lady who had walked for four hours to the clinic at La Barra. She was seven months pregnant and her hemoglobin was less than 4 grams. She was desperate for help. She walked to La Barra from Crique the first time I went there. Her hemoglobin was much better, but she had lost the baby. In these two villages I saw a lot of anemia and hookworm.

Myra Harrah had a fatal heart attack in June, leaving the clinic in the mountains without a missionary nurse, though an Auxiliary nurse was still working there. After Myra died, I tried to go to the mountains once a month to check on things there and to encourage the Auxiliary nurse.

Some unforgettable patients have visited my clinic. We hadn't lived in Las Brisas even a year when one Sunday afternoon a man came to our house and asked me to take care of his little boy who had been accidently cut by a machete by his older brother. They had come from Piedra Arañada, and it had taken them two hours to get to Las Brisas in a small dugout canoe. I took one look at the wound and knew it would take a doctor to repair it, so we took him to Puerto Cortés. When the doctor in the hospital at Puerto Cortés took a good look at the boy's hand, she found that the four fingers on his hand were hanging only by the skin and all he had left was his thumb. She said he needed surgery that she couldn't do, so we took him another 40 miles to San Pedro Sula to the emergency room.  It took some time, but he was finally admitted.  This little three-year-old boy did not cry during the entire trip.  When I did my first clinic at Piedra Arañada, I saw him and remembered what a brave little boy he had been.

## The House in the City

A big turnover in the house in San Pedro Sula occurred in 1995.  Three of the girls left because they had finished their nursing course. Some had left during the year.  Four girls from Las Brisas were among those who lived in the house. One girl from Omoa and two girls from the mountains were also at the house.

## A Quick Trip to Indiana

My mother celebrated her ninetieth birthday on April 7, 1995.  My sisters wanted us to make a quick trip to the States to surprise her.  It worked out that it was the week before Resurrection Sunday.  We closed the clinic that week, and John and I made a quick trip to the States to help Mom celebrate.  She really was surprised when we walked into her home. The open house was a special day for her.

## Furlough 1997

We were on furlough in 1997, this time visiting congregations only in Tennessee and Indiana—twenty-seven of them.  We started our furlough by attending Homecoming at Johnson Bible College, speaking to four congregations in the Knoxville and East Tennessee area, and visiting friends.  We visited friends in Kentucky on our way to Indiana.  For the rest of our time in the States, we made our home with my sister and brother-in-law. They lived in the house where I had been born and we stayed in the same bedroom where I was born, though we did have a different bed. We later made trips to visit John's sisters in South Carolina and friends in Ohio, Missouri, Illinois, and Michigan. We enjoyed my sister's granddaughter who was with them most weekends. She called John "John, John" and it was soon evident that John was one of her favorite people. She called me "John, John's wife." One day my sister bought some marshmallow cakes and told Madison she could give John and me one—but only John got the cake! We helped mom to celebrate her ninety-second birthday while we were in the States.

# Chapter 28

## 1997-Mid-1999

## Visitors—Always Visitors to Learn and Serve

We continued to serve as a learning center for those interested in short-term or long-term mission service. Our visitors came and went—and always made contributions to the ministry. Lois Atkinson, a student at Ozark Christian College, was with us for two months during the summer of 1997. She is the daughter of our missionary friends, Rich and Leta Atkinson. Since she could speak Spanish fluently, she was soon a favorite with the women and youth. She provided significant help in the clinic. She taught the children every other Friday and also taught the youth on Saturday afternoon. Since Spanish is different in Honduras than in Mexico, she kept a notebook with all the new Spanish words she learned.

While Lois was with us, Clifford and Judy Shaw from Littleton, Colorado, visited for a few days. They had been told by Richard Sprague of i.D.E.S. that if they wanted to see rural Honduras, Las Brisas was the place to go. Clifford preached twice on Sunday and visited some of the families on Sunday afternoon. They also made the trip by boat to Troconera for one of my clinics.

From September 24 to December 3, Tobin and Amy Hill served an internship with us as they prepared to serve under F.A.M.E. at the clinic in the mountains. Amy worked with me in the clinic while Tobin helped John with various projects. He also preached several times at the services with me translating. Tobin and Amy hoped to start language school in January and be in the mountains by June 1998.

In November, Johnnie and Vickie Orr, missionaries serving in Tegucigalpa, paid us a short visit. They had been on vacation with their children at the beach in Puerto Cortes and came on Sunday evening to worship with us.

The day after Christmas, Bill and Margy Hoff and John and I welcomed a group from Chapel Hill Christian Church and Macedonia Christian Church, both near Kokomo, Indiana. Most of the group went with Bill and Margy to lay block for the men's dormitory at the Christian Bible Institute, but two nurses went with John and me to Las Brisas where they helped in the clinic. One day they went with me to help in the clinic across the river.

In May 1998, the Rostvit twins and Dean Cary were with us for a four-night revival. The twins led the singing and while Dean preached, the children went to our front porch where the twins sang with them and told Bible stories using their puppets. On the final night of the revival the building was overflowing until the children went to our house. We had about sixty children, filling the porch to capacity.

In June, a work team arrived from Seymour, Indiana. In the mornings they helped John to build a septic tank and an outhouse near the church building. In the afternoon they did crafts for a Vacation Bible School.

Kirby Reed from Texas arrived in September with the intention of staying for two months. However, his stay was reduced to just over a month because of the hurricane. He went with me to help Interplast and stayed with them for a time. Then the floods came, and he couldn't return to us.

334

But he was a big help in San Pedro Sula to the Hoffs as they packed bags of rice and beans for the relief effort.

# Inevitably Building

As soon as we returned to Honduras after our time in the States, John began more building projects. The first was to put a door on the end of our front porch so we could get out easily to the carport. Then in front of the church building he built a wall with barbed wire on top. One day when no men showed up to help him to mix cement and lay block, the women asked if they could help—and help they did by mixing the cement and carrying it to John as he laid the block.

# Christmas—That Special Time of Year

Christmas 1997 was a special time. Two Christian sisters helped me make over two hundred popcorn balls to give to those who attended the Christmas Eve services. Our friends, Chepe and Chela Canahuati, gave us two boxes of apples that we shared with the people. John once again made wooden toys for the boys, and the girls received dolls. Raul and Ana worked with the youth and children on a very special Christmas program. We enjoyed lots of singing and several dramas. The program started with the children walking down the aisle singing to the tune of *Jingle Bells* "Feliz Navidad," or, translated, "Merry Christmas." The younger children each held a letter to spell out Feliz Navidad. When *Silent Night* was sung in Spanish, the lights were turned out and the children held sparklers as they sang. Besides the popcorn balls and apples the women had made chicken sandwiches to eat after the service.

# Spiritual and Congregational Growth

When we first moved to Las Brisas, we had worked with the Church of God congregation at Cerro Cardona. When they finally got a minister, we began services in Las Brisas. But most of the people eventually moved from Cero Cardona as the result of some revenge killing –two brothers were shot and killed, another was shot and wounded. This left very few families there. The minister left, so the people asked us to start having services there again. Raul and Ana walked there to have a service on Sunday morning, and many of them came to Las Brisas on Sunday and Wednesday nights. Three others went with Raul and Ana to have Sunday school with the children. Three adults gave their lives to Christ and were baptized. Two of those baptized were a couple who had lived together for twenty years, but had never been legally married. We helped them get their papers for their civil wedding and then we had a wedding ceremony at the church later to help them celebrate. In May 1998, Mateo Valle graduated from the Christian Bible Institute and began as minister to the congregation at Cerro Cardona.

# A Fall to Remember

The last part of 1998 was unforgettable. It began in September when John and I decided to take a vacation. I had been very busy in the clinic having seen fifteen hundred patients in just four months. But we had been at our hotel in San Pedro Sula for only two days when I received a phone call telling me that I had one week to get a passport, American visa, and papers giving permission to take Martha Lidia Valladares to the States for heart surgery. She had been born with a congenital heart condition. I had seen the caller a few months earlier and she had told me what to do to arrange for the child to have heart surgery at Children's Hospital in Boston. I had already done everything except to get her passport.

Our vacation was obviously cut short. We had to return to Las Brisas to get Martha Lidia and her parents to take them back to San Pedro Sula to get the passport. We got it rather quickly as well as the papers giving permission to take the child to Boston. But obtaining the visa was another story. I took a bus to Tegucigalpa to get the papers, but they did not give them to me on Friday as I had hoped. I stayed until Monday, but did not get the visa in time to have Martha Lidia at the San Pedro Sula airport to leave with her benefactor. When I arrived in San Pedro Sula on Monday evening, John told me that he had been instructed that I was to take Martha Lidia to Boston the next day!

We went to the travel agency, changed Martha Lidia's ticket from Monday to Tuesday, and bought a ticket for me. Then we took the child and her parents to the home of the lawyer to get the papers giving me permission to take her to Boston. The next morning we left early for Las Brisas to take the parents' home and for me to pack. I also managed to fix John some food to eat while I was gone. Back we went to the airport in San Pedro Sula. We flew to Miami and on to Boston. We were late arriving in Boston; it was midnight by the time we arrived at the hospital. They kindly gave us a place to sleep in the parents' room at the hospital. The next night Martha Lidia was in a room. I slept in her room in a chair that could be made into a bed.

The next day Martha Lidia had surgery. She did well, even though the doctors who had examined her could not believe that she was still alive at ten years of age. I was able to see her in recovery before I left so that I could tell her parents how well she was doing. I slept my final night in Boston in the parent's room again and flew back to Honduras the next day. Martha Lidia returned with her benefactor to Honduras on October 15. We met her at the airport. Each of her relatives commented that "her fingernails aren't blue anymore."

I had not helped Interplast for some time until Kirby Reed and I went into San Pedro Sula on October 23. I spent the entire day translating for the surgeons. It was dark when it was time to leave, and as I left, I stepped in a hole and fell, twisting my right knee—the one that had been replaced in 1994. I managed to get up and John came to pick me up. But by morning, my knee was so swollen and painful that it took John, Bill Hoff, and another man to carry me in a chair to the pickup. They took me to the emergency room at the hospital. A doctor drained a lot of blood from my knee which provided instant relief. The x-ray showed the replacement was fine. The doctor wanted me to stay in San Pedro Sula for a couple of days.

Since we knew that a hurricane was predicted to hit Honduras, we wanted to get home to Las Brisas. Kirby Reed decided to stay to help the Interplast plastic surgery team. We were home in Las Brisas about three days before the hurricane hit. Though we were not directly affected by the hurricane, our neighboring city of Bajamar was. Many houses were destroyed, light poles were knocked down and the village looked like a disaster area.

We had heard that there would be flooding in our village, so on October 31, John and Ana drove into Puerto Cortes to buy supplies for people in Las Brisas. They brought back the staples people would need—beans, rice, corn meal, sugar, flour. By the time they returned, flooding had begun and in some places John was uncertain where to drive. We learned the next day that the bridge they had crossed over the lagoon in Bajamar had gone out during the night. They were probably the last car to cross it.

*Hurricane Mitch destruction in Bajamar*

When we woke up on November 1, we heard a sound like a huge waterfall. We walked down the road from our house to the school where just a few feet away water was rushing across the road. The entire village was flooded below the school. About two-thirds of the families had to move to the school; some stayed in the church building. The clinic was also flooded. The road below our house that led to Puerto Cortes was flooded, and the road was out at several places between Las Brisas and Puerto Cortes. The only way to leave Las Brisas was to travel by dugout canoe to Bajamar on the flooded roads, take a boat from Bajamar by way of the Caribbean Sea to a passable road, and get a bus.

The water finally receded between Las Brisas and Bajamar. But until the road was repaired, we had to drive to Bajamar, take a boat to Travesia, then get the bus to Puerto Cortes.

For a time, the Hoffs brought food supplies to Travesia where some people from Las Brisas would meet them in a boat and return the material to Bajamar. Food was scarce for many, and one time some corn meal was stolen. But a helicopter finally flew over and dropped food. The Hoffs not only helped us, but many others. Their house became a center for members of the International Christian Fellowship to package food supplies for many different areas.

After the clinic flooded, making it impossible to work there, one day Raul and Ana and others actually went into the clinic through the door in a dugout canoe to rescue medicines and bring them to the house where I held clinic on the front porch. Some people helped dry out medicine bottles, and we hired children to help us spread out the wet patient records around our yard to dry them out. Some of the bottles brought from the clinic were caked with mud. It would be January before we could work in the clinic again. I didn't have a lot of patients, but I did see many with fungal infections of the feet and legs, the result of wading in water and mud.

Two amusing incidents occurred during this time. One day a lady came to the clinic carrying a paddle for her dugout canoe. Even though she had come from a different part of the village, she had to come through water. She was afraid someone would steal her paddle, so she brought it with her. The other incident was when a black man came to see me and said, "Do you speak English?" I had to laugh—I guess I really must have looked like a Honduran. I assured him that I could speak English!

Excitement was generated one day when we heard a helicopter overhead and then saw it go down. It had land-ed at the soccer field and had brought food supplies from Martinique, an island belonging to France. We drove our pickup over to the field and made two or three trips to the school with the food supplies they brought. We wondered how the people would get the cans of vegetables and beans open since they don't eat those kinds of foods. After think-ing about it, however, we knew they could use their trusty machetes to open the cans. The helicopter also delivered prunes; I warned the people not to eat too many at one time. One day some people came to our house with a box of some of the supplies the helicopter had brought. We told them we didn't really need the supplies, but they insisted we take them since we helped to carry the supplies from the soccer field to the school.

With the bridge out at Bajamar and the road out, it became a challenge to get into Puerto Cortes to replace gas tanks and get supplies. It took some time to repair the road. Until they did, we took a bus to Bajamar, rode a motorboat to Travesia, and took a bus into Puerto Cortes. When the road was finally repaired, we took one bus to Bajamar where we waded across the lagoon and took a bus to Puerto Cortes. One day we entertained onlookers as we waded through the lagoon, which was deeper than usual, and I fell in the water. It was nice to have something to laugh about.

During this time, John became really sick with vomiting and diarrhea. I could not get the vomiting stopped. Because he was becoming dehydrated, We knew he needed to get to San Pedro Sula so he could have an I.V. I drove him to Bajamar. We called Dean Cary and asked him to meet John in Travesia. The sea was rough that day, so the boat had to go out some distance to find a place where it was not too rough. Dean took him to the hospital where they put him on I.V.s, and he recuperated rapidly. It was funny when one day I called him and he could not get the nurses to understand that he needed a drink of water. So I called the hospital and asked them to get John some water.

We were grateful to have a cell phone by this time. Several people had relatives in the States who called us to find out how their family was doing after the floods. People also called us personally from the States. We even had a call from the American Embassy in Tegucigalpa. Our cell phone bill was high, but it was worth it to be able to be in contact with the outside world.

In spite of the difficulties, a record number attended our Christmas Eve service with 203 present. The crowd was so large that many of the children had to sit in the aisle and many adults had to stand. The highlight of the service was the 40 children who had memorized and sang eight Christmas songs. The young people and adults also presented two Bible dramas. We ran out of popcorn balls, even though I had made 193 of them. But everyone did get an apple.

## Getting Back to Normal—Whatever That Is

At the beginning of January, some from the church went to clean up the clinic and paint the inside. I finally started seeing patients in the clinic the first part of January. I was thankful for the visit of Wilda Rush and Jeri Ashley, two nurses who came on January 6 to help me get medicines sorted and replaced in the clinic. On our way to Puerto Cortes we found that the road was out again between Travesia and Bajamar. So because of a rough sea on the day they arrived, we spent two nights in San Pedro Sula and one night in Puerto Cortes. We used the time in San Pedro Sula to go to the Christian Bible Institute to help bag rice and beans and other items for the people whom Bill and Margy Hoff were helping. We drove to Travesia on January 9 and left our car with a friend, took the boat to Bajamar, and found transport to Las Brisas. The next day John had to walk four kilometers to get a bus to take him to get the pickup. Wilda was with us for two weeks, but Jeri stayed until March 31.

Wilda, Jeri, and I went to the clinic at Crique Maria. The floods had destroyed the road along the beach, so we got

342

the boat just a half kilometer from our house and rode about twenty minutes on the Chamelecon River, then out to the Caribbean Sea for twenty-five minutes, and finally rode another ten to fifteen minutes on the Ulua River. This village had been flooded after the hurricane with many homes destroyed, but an organization from the Catholic Church was building new homes in the village. These houses would be on cement poles to avoid a future disaster.

I.D.E.S. and congregations from throughout the U.S.A. provided funds that allowed us to continue to help people with food supplies. We were able to buy rice and corn seed, insecticides, and fertilizer to help those from five villages to plant their crops. We made two trips in the boat that took me to the clinics and helped people in those villages to plant . John had not been out on the sea, but he enjoyed going with me as we took supplies. It was on one of those trips that the man who took us asked me to read what was written on the life jackets we were wearing. We all had a good laugh when we read that the life jackets were for people weighing seventy pounds or less. Fortunately, we didn't really need them!

Planting rice and corn in the rural villages is hard work. First, the farmers spray the land where they will plant to dry up grass and weeds. Then they use their machetes to dig up the ground and plant the seed. As the crops grow, they again use their machetes to chop the weeds.

Our friends, Chepe and Chela, arranged for us to pick up three big bundles of clothing they had received from the States. We were able to give clothing to four hundred children in five villages.

When the people didn't need more help with planting their crops or with food, we used the funds we had received to help them build latrines, or as John liked to call them, outhouses. They were different than the old outhouses we used to have in the States. A septic tank was built and the user poured water down the toilet. Having the toilets also cut down on parasitic infections that I saw so often in the clinic. The people dug the holes for the septic tank, and John helped them lay the block and make the top for the septic tank. We bought the toilets, and the people had the responsibility of building the structures around them.

Ana took a nursing course in Puerto Cortés that she completed in March 1999. She began working full time with me in the clinic. With Ana, I was able to do more of the rural clinics. It was also good to have her in the clinic when we went on furlough later in the year.

# Furlough 1999

We arrived in the States to start our furlough on May 20. This was a traveling furlough as we shared with congregations in fourteen states. While we were on furlough, John counted the number of beds in which we had slept and kept track of how many miles we traveled. I counted how many churches we visited and how many times I spoke. By September 3, we had traveled over seven thousand miles and slept in thirty different beds!

Two special events occurred in North Carolina. We spent time with our "cupid," Floyd Clark and his wife in Creswell. The second was when we visited in Durham with people who were from Las Brisas. They invited us to their home for a meal. When we walked into the apartment where they lived, we saw a big container of meat cooking. My first thought was, "I hope they don't expect us to eat all of that." But we hadn't been there long until someone knocked on their door. A man came in and the women filled a container with meat, beans, rice and tortillas and gave it to him. These women were very enterprising. They cooked and sold food to single Latin Americans. They also cooked food at noon and took it to construction sites to sell. The men worked in construction and the minister with whom we stayed said that the Central American men had a reputation for being very good workers.

We also visited John's two sisters, some of my relatives in Maryland, and many, many friends. By September 3, I had spoken thirty-three times in twenty different congregations, at a nursing home and in homes of friends. I would share with six more congregations before we returned to Honduras. By the time we were ready to return to Honduras we had traveled ten thousand miles in seventeen states.

Raul and Ana took care of the work in Las Brisas while we were in the States. When they wrote, they assured us that things were going well. Soon after, we left for furlough. they rented a bus and took thirty-three members of the congregation to the annual Christian Church Conference. We appreciated their work—and looked forward to returning home to work with them.

# Chapter 29

# A New Millennium in Honduras

## Settling Back into Life in Las Brisas

We arrived home in Las Brisas to hear the sad news that many people had lost their rice crop when salt water got into the fields. Those who didn't lose their crop were not getting good prices, so they were holding the produce, hoping for a better price later. People were thankful for the fish and fresh water shrimp they could get in the river to supplement their diet of rice, beans and tortillas.

In December, we attended three weddings—two in San Pedro Sula and one at Las Brisas. A longtime friend and minister from a congregation in Puerto Cortes married Suyapa. Eight days later, he did the wedding ceremony for the teacher who had taken care of the girls studying in the city. Then in Las Brisas I did my first wedding ceremony. Raul was in Mexico on vacation, leaving me to do the ceremony.

The Christmas Eve service was well attended. Some of the women again helped me make popcorn balls. John couldn't make toys because our generator was broken, but we found some toys in the city to give to the boys; the girls received either dolls or dishes.

# Medical Work Always Calls

A blessing from furlough was the help we received from Leland Houser of the Blountville (TN) Christian Church. He took me to King Pharmaceuticals in Bristol, Virginia, and they donated two large boxes of medicine for use in the medical ministry. Having this medicine was a blessing, for soon after I returned, I went to Crique Maria to hold a clinic under the trees. I saw seventy-nine patients.

I continued to do a clinic at La Barra. We had started having it at the school, but later a community center was built, and we moved the clinic there. The road to the river was improved so that instead of getting the boat to cross the river a half kilometer from our house, we drove three kilometers. The boat would often be loaded with people who had come from Puerto Cortes with supplies. One lady always took a big cooler with chunks of ice to sell to people in the villages. One time there was a chest of drawers in the boat, and there were always cases of cold drinks and beer, bags of rice and beans, boxes of other food supplies, and our boxes of medicine. The boatman took the people to La Sabana first, so it took us some time to get to the community center to start our clinic.

Although I had retired from delivering babies, in March of 2000, I did deliver a baby boy to a young girl. This was her first baby. Her mother had her bag packed, thinking she needed to go to the hospital, but I was able to deliver a healthy baby without complications. The bed was low. Because of my knee problems, I could no longer get on my knees, so I had to bend over the bed. That left me with a sore back by the time the delivery was finished. Even so, it was fun being a midwife again.

# And Visitors Continue to Come

Tamara Miller and Cindy Frasure visited for two weeks in January 2000. I had worked with both of their dads who were doctors at Mashoko. At that time, both girls were only eight years old. Tamara was now a registered nurse and studying to be a nurse practitioner; Cindy was in her last year of medical school. We had a rough sea the day we planned to do a rural clinic, but we ended up having forty-three patients. They examined two hundred patients during the two weeks they were in Las Brisas. On their final day, they sutured a machete wound. After they left, I was busy with the rural clinics and saw a few over two hundred patients when I went out three consecutive Fridays.

In October, Lori Marietta, a nursing student from our supporting church in Hanoverton, Ohio, came to spend just over a week. She was doing a cultural study of another country as a part of her nursing studies. She was able to talk to the local midwife and others to learn of some of their customs concerning health in the village. She also helped in the clinic.

# The Church Moves Forward

While we were on furlough, a group from Christ in Youth from Tegucigalpa came to Las Brisas to start a building that could be used for Sunday school. We hired a builder to help John finish it and get the roof on. Then John built shutters for the windows and two outside and one inside door and put screens on the windows and around the top of the building to try to keep out the mosquitoes. After he finished that project, he built more benches with backs for the church.

The children of the congregation had a second Christmas in April 2000. A congregation in Arkansas had sent two boxes with Christmas gifts in October 1999, but the boxes didn't arrive until April. The week before Resurrection Sunday, we gave the children a gift and a bag of popcorn. As you can imagine, we had some happy children!

We started once again entertaining families from Las Brisas for Sunday dinner. When we started this project, we had only fifty families in the village, but by now there were seventy-one families.

God provided a minister for our congregation at Las Brisas. Raul and Ana felt the Lord's leading to go to Mexico, and they left in November. Thanks to some of the other Honduran ministers, we found Reyno Hernandez who had been preaching in the state of Santa Barbara. He came to Las Brisas the first part of October, giving him a month with Raul before he left.

Soon after we returned to Las Brisas from vacation late in the year, we had a special service at the church for Delci Velasquez. She had just completed her three-year primary teachers' training course and wanted to give thanks to God for allowing her to complete her studies. I baked a cake and her family provided Coke to share with the congregation. We received permission for her to teach at Las Brisas for which we would pay her salary. Later, though, she was assigned to the school at Las Brisas and received her salary from the government.

Those in the Las Brisas congregation were hard workers and loved serving the Lord. In March 2001, we had a work day at the church with many  working to make the grounds around the church building look better and to give the inside of the building a thorough cleaning. Some men cut the grass around the clinic with their machete and cut down

350

some dead trees on the property. A hole was dug to burn trash, and several of the children gathered up stones and put them at the end of the Sunday School classroom. Since the people didn't want me to do manual labor, I stayed at home and made doughnuts and a big cooler of Kool-Aid for the workers to enjoy after their hard labor.

The church had a fine group of faithful women. Many had husbands who were not Christians. These women wanted to earn money so they could contribute to the offering. Many women's groups in the States responded to this need by sending pillowcases and material and embroidery floss so the women could embroider pillowcases and make table-cloths to sell. To encourage them, on many Saturday morn-ings I made several dozen doughnuts for the women sell; that money was also put in the offering.

## The Ministry of Education

By 2000, we were helping sixteen girls to continue their education. Seven were staying in the house in San Pe-dro Sula. One was studying in Santa Barbara to become a teacher. Eight were studying at the Franklin Delano Roo-sevelt High School in Puerto Cortes. Nine were from Las Brisas, six from the mountains and one from La Barra de Chamelecon.

## Another Knee Replacement

In 2000, I had my second knee replacement. My left knee seemed to get bad very quickly. It was so bad that I could hardly walk down the hill to church. The Lord provided the funds through a life insurance policy that John had forgotten he had. I did well, but the doctor told me that this surgery had been very difficult. One day before I was discharged from the hospital, the doctor asked me to walk down the hall to encourage an older lady who also had a knee replacement. Even in the midst of surgery, I could minister to others.

We took a five-week vacation in the States. We wanted to attend the National Missionary Convention in Knoxville, and I was able to rest a bit after my knee surgery. We saw a lot of missionary friends at the convention and friends around Knoxville, visited John's sisters in South Carolina, and enjoyed a big Thanksgiving dinner in Indiana with lots of relatives at my sister's house.

# Furlough 2001

We had planned to start our furlough on June 1 to visit supporting congregations in Indiana, but my mother died on May 5. Dr. David Eubanks called to ask about a visit to us and to tell me that he had received a call from my sister to tell me I needed to call them. Mom did not have much longer to live, so we quickly arranged to leave earlier. Even so, we still didn't arrive before her death. Mom lived to be 96 and was ready to leave her earthly home.

Since our first speaking date wasn't until June 3, we had time to relax and help my sister and her husband around the house. I was also able to attend the alumni banquet that celebrated my fiftieth year of graduation from high school.

During this furlough, we shared with eighteen congregations in Indiana, and I was the missionary for Vacation Bible School at two churches. One of the highlights of our furlough was when we drove to Spencer, Indiana, to see two couples from Zimbabwe who were in the States.

We kept in contact with the people in Las Brisas via email, phone calls, and letters. They were building a new home for the minister. Amy Hill, the nurse serving in the mountains, drove to Las Brisas twice a month to see patients in the clinic.

While we were on furlough, the lady who had been helping in the clinic gave birth to a little girl and decided not to work any longer. As I prayed and thought about finding someone else, I thought of Eva Deras, one of fine Christian women. I wrote to ask if she would like to work at the clinic. She told me later that it was an answer to prayer since her husband had no work and they really needed the money. She started working before we returned from furlough.

## Back in Honduras—Late 2001

After having been gone for nearly five months, I had a busy two months in the clinic when I got back. Patients started coming in record numbers. In November, I was able to hold a clinic at Crique Maria. I first saw my boatman's son who had a fever and vomiting before we even went out to sea. Then, before we got to Crique Maria, we came upon a man in a dugout canoe. He had an infection on his foot. I examined him from the boat and gave him medicine for infection and for pain. When we finally got arrived, we held our clinic under the trees.

While we were on furlough, Samaritan's Purse had built thirty-six block houses, each with a cement floor and tin roof, for families in Las Brisas. What a blessing to the people who had been used to living in houses with bamboo walls, a dirt floor, and a palm leaf roof. No screens had been placed in the windows, but John took care of that after we got back from furlough.

Before we left for furlough, we had been in contact with our missionary friends in Mexico, Rich and Leta Atkinson, about Ulisses Solano who had read our newsletter and wanted to visit Las Brisas. We arranged for him to visit while we were in the States. He stayed in the house where Raul and Ana had lived. He was still in Honduras when we returned. It was evident how much the people, the children especially, loved him. He often shared coffee and bread with some of them before Sunday School.

Another wedding occurred on December 8, 2001. This wedding was for Fernando Velasquez and Delci Velasquez—not related, by the way. Delci was the teacher we were paying and Fernando had been a big help to us when we had been on furlough. They would live in Puerto Cortes, but continued to come to Las Brisas on Sunday morning for the services.

Instead of the people exchanging gifts at Christmas 2001, they gave an offering, a total of $60, which was sent to I.D.E.S. This was a significant offering for people who had little to share and an indication of the maturing Christian community in Las Brisas.

# Chapter 30

## Life to the Honduran Beat
## 2002-2004

## Visitors, Of Course

In January 2002, we had many visitors.  The first were David and Margaret Eubanks from Johnson Bible College where David was President.  We were without a pickup, so Mark Hoff took them to the bus station in Puerto Cortes.  We took the bus from Las Brisas to meet them and bring them back by bus to Las Brisas.  Our bus was late leaving Las Brisas.  We knew we couldn't get to the bus station in time, but we had Mark that they would be fine at the bus station, even if we weren't there.  We finally arrived to find them sitting at a table.  While they were with us, David  chopped down a dead banana tree, helped John dig a hole for the new sign in front on the church and preached on Wednesday night with me translating.

When we took David and Margaret to San Pedro Sula to the airport, we also met Vera Mushrush who had come to computerize as many patient records as possible.  She would have finished them had she not been limited in how long she could use the computer since we had only solar power.  She also went with me to the clinic at La Barra de Chamelecon and was fascinated as we waited for the boat to see a girl making milk shakes with a blender operated by a battery.  She also went with me to the clinic at Crique Maria.  Her birthday was the day she left.  Three of the Christian sisters from the congregation also had birthdays in February, so we celebrated all their birthdays at our ladies' meeting.

Two days after Vera arrived, we welcomed David and Geri-anne Griffith who were sailing the Pacific. They had disem-barked in El Salvador and made the trip to Las Brisas by bus. We had arranged for them to spend the night at a hotel before taking the Citul bus from San Pedro Sula to Puerto Cortes. That would put them in the bus station where they could get the bus to Las Brisas. Unfortunately, people at the hotel told them to go by Impala bus which took them to a different bus station. They told the people there they wanted to go to Las Brisas, but there was also another place called Las Brisas nearer to Puerto Cortes. They were taken there. They were fortunate enough to find the home of a missionary couple who brought them late at night to us. They spent four days with us. Since both are doctors, they saw all of the patients at the clinic on Monday and Tuesday and went to Omoa to the orphanage to check the girls. David also sutured a machete wound for a little boy.

July brought many more visitors. The first were Toby and Amy Hill and his sister and her two children. Then Christine Vijil came with her three children. Christine also brought Janice and Faye Rostvit, Daesha Batteiger and Holly and Heidi Brompton from Colorado. Toby and Amy and Christine and her children returned to the mountains, but the others stayed so they could go with me to the clinic at Crique Maria.

What a trip!! The sea was rougher than usual and we hit a big wave that soaked all of us. It ruined Daesha's video camera, a camera belonging to the twins, and my cell phone. Chelsea's feet flew up when the wave hit, and as her foot flew up, one of her flip flops flew into the sea. While I was seeing patients under a mango tree, the rest were lead-ing singing and telling Bible stories. It was a busy day with

356

seventy patients, but it was also an exciting day when first a green mango fell from the tree on my shoulder and later when I found a snake draped over my shoulder.

This group also spent a day visiting people in the village, leading Sunday School, and helping with Vacation Bible School. The three girls and the twins were in charge of the opening exercises for the V.B.S.

Not long after the group from Colorado left, a group of five from Billings, Montana, arrived. They went to the school and took Polaroid pictures of all of the children and helped them to make frames for their pictures. One morning the men dug holes to put in the metal poles that would carry the solar power electricity from our house to the church building. They also took two pickup loads of children to the beach and went with me across the river to the clinic where they held a one-day Vacation Bible School with the children.

In the summer of 2002, I received a letter from Helen Goff of Lincoln, Nebraska, asking if she could spend some time in Honduras. She had been making trips to Ecuador, but no trip had been planned for that year. A doctor friend in Lincoln, Mike Keralis, sug-gested Hon-duras. She and another nurse arrived in November to spend ten days. That started a yearly trip for Helen that lasted until 2009. Each

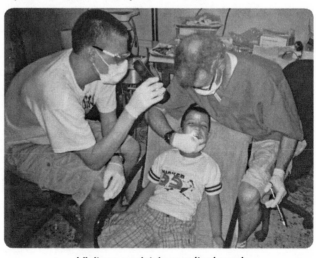

*Visitors assist in medical work*

357

time she brought at least one other person, often more. Those who came were doctors, dentists, nurses, and others with a variety of skills and interests, all of whom contributed immensely to our ministry. They always brought candy for us and the children, pie fillings, chocolate and other types of chips, pens, pencils, medicines, toothbrushes and tooth-paste, dental equipment , and most important of all, the love of God. One year they brought hymn books so that each member of the congregation could have a personal hymnal. In the eight years the groups came, the doctors examined 1,840 patients and the dentists pulled 1,803 teeth, filled 207 teeth, and cleaned the teeth of about 16 people. The young people in the groups were a blessing to the children as they taught and played with them.

We hired some of the women of the congregation to cook the noon meal for the large groups. I had to provide only breakfast and supper, and the women helped by providing refried beans and flour tortillas for supper.

Sally and Lynn Johnson, faithful contributors to our ministry for some time, came with their two daughters to see the work. Sally, a doctor, kept busy seeing patients. The day after they arrived, we went to Remolino where Sally saw fifty-two patients. In between seeing patients she showed the children

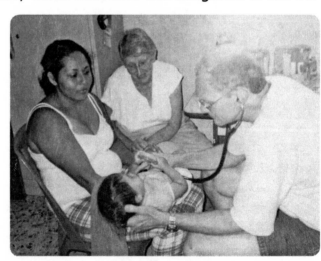

*More visitors at work*

358

how to blow the whistles she had brought. Their visit was very timely, for a young man had cut the tendon in his finger with a machete, which Sally, an emergency room doctor, could repair.

From the last of May to the last of June in 2003, three nurses from Illinois were with us. They helped in the clinic and taught English words to some of the children as they in turn learned Spanish from the children.

## Medical Work Always Calls

In May, I helped a group from Mercy Ships to have a clinic for two days at La Barra. With thirty people from the Mercy Ship, we had the clinic at the school instead of the community center in order to provide more space to work. Doctors, nurses, and nurse practitioners, even some dentists, were in the group. They saw over two hundred patients in two days and brought a lot of medicine.

The Mercy Ship was in Puerto Cortes for some time. In August some came from the ship to teach men some agricultural and carpentry skills. A couple of women also came to teach women some crafts including how to make flowers using corn husks. The second Friday in August, a Physician's Assistant, a nurse, and two others went with me to the clinic at Crique Maria. The Physician's Assistant and the nurse saw all of the patients while the other two gave out clothing. They also gave some of the children coloring books. I had to laugh at the volunteers' reactions. Only just over fifty patients came that day, but the two women were tired out. I had seen seventy by myself the month before!

In June, we helped Tom Schneller of Disciple Makers with a medical clinic in La Ceiba. John and I had taken a bus to

La Ceiba earlier to get permission from the health department for the clinic. The clinic was held in the church building. We saw 441 patients in five days. I started out translating for one of the doctors, but a Honduran nurse saw that we were moving too slowly, so I ended up seeing patients while someone else translated.

## And John Keeps On Building

I continued to find something for John to do. I didn't want him to get bored! His project in 2002 was to build ten desks for the children to use during Sunday School. They had only benches before this, and when they colored or wrote, they had to hold their books on their laps.

## The Church Continues to Minister

The congregation continued to have additions. I led a class for some of the young people to teach them what was necessary to become a Christian. After the class five girls gave their lives to Christ and were baptized. When we had returned from the States, we brought a series of flannelgraph lessons. John put up a flannel board in each of the classrooms, and I taught some of the women how to teach lessons using the flannelgraph.

The women continued their meetings. We enjoyed having the birthday party so much in February with Vera and the three women that we continued having birthday parties for the women. Two faithful members moved to Tegucigalpita, a city west of Puerto Cortes. On day several of the women and I drove there to have a meeting at their home.

Because I did so much baking, I had thought many times of putting a sign on our front porch "Spratt Bakery." I think it began when I started baking birthday cakes for the women.  In September, I baked five cakes for the children to celebrate Children's Day at the school. Every month I baked four or five or six cakes for special occasions.  I baked some at the request of others—and charged $2.75 per cake!

A special day was observed in Honduras in September 2002 with celebration of the "Day of the Bible."  Our congregation and members of the Pentecostal Church gathered in front of our church building and walked just over a kilometer to the community center with the children carrying signs with Scripture verses and all of us singing songs and choruses.  When we arrived at the community center, we were joined by women from the Catholic Church.  The children quoted Bible verses. the women from the Catholic Church read Scripture, and the minister of the Pentecostal Church gave a short message.

When Wilmer Sandoval and Gilma Avilez were married on December 13, 2003,  it was the first wedding held at the church between two young couples who had not lived together.  Amable Rivera came from San Pedro Sula to do the wedding ceremony. The wedding was followed by a meal and the traditional wedding cake. The new couple lived in Puerto Cortes where Wilmer worked and studied at night and Gilma continued her high school studies, but they came to Las Brisas for the weekend where they led the youth meeting and Wilmer taught the adult Sunday School class.

## Letting Go of One Ministry

We turned the work of the girls studying in San Pedro Sula over to Julio Corea completely in 2002. The house was turned over to Tom Schneller of Disciple Makers Mission.

Although we continued to provide some funds for the ministry, we were relieved of the responsibility for it.

# A Longer Furlough

When the group from Nebraska came in March 2004, Dr. Dave Paulus told me that I should get my left knee checked in the States. Though I had a replacement in 2000, for the last few months, at times, especially early in the morning, the knee would swell and be very painful. Since we were scheduled for a furlough to start in June 2004, I asked my sister to get an appointment.

Soon after we arrived in the States, I went to see the doctor, and he told me that the replacement I had in Honduras had slipped and another one would need to be done. Since I already had our speaking dates scheduled, I asked him if I could wait until after we visited all of the churches. He said it would be acceptable if I could take the pain. We visited congregations and friends in Indiana, Ohio, Maryland, Virginia, West Virginia, South Carolina, Tennessee, Missouri, Nebraska, Iowa, Minnesota, and Illinois.

A special treat was visiting with people from Las Brisas who were living in Virginia. The Sunday we spoke at the Tri-City Church of Christ in Hopewell, Virginia, Raphael Lezama and his wife and brother came to the Sunday School service where we had a video to share. We had not realized that the first scene in the video was of their dad driving a horse-drawn cart. As soon as they saw him in the Video, they said in unison: "Mi papa, mi papa" (My dad, my dad). After church we ate at a pizza restaurant where another Honduran made the pizzas. Later in the week we visited him at his apartment where he called his wife in Las Brisas. We also visited Hondurans who worked at a Chinese restaurant.

Another special occasion was in Lincoln, Nebraska, where we saw many of those who had come to Honduras and also the Plettners with whom I had worked in India.

Both John and I needed surgery—I the knee surgery and John cataract surgery. John has his cataract surgeries on October 20 and November 3, and I had my knee surgery on November 15. I did well and worked hard on my physio-therapy. Our longer stay allowed us to enjoy some special visits that we otherwise could not have made. One was to Ohio to visit with Dean and Karen Cary. We enjoyed a meal with Wilda Rush who had visited us many times in Honduras. And we, with my sister and her husband, went to Quincy, Illinois, to the retirement party for Henry and Betty Pratt. Betty is my first cousin, and Henry was one of my best pub-licity agents: wherever he served as a minister, he encour-aged the congregation to support my ministry.

# Chapter 31

## Slowing Down
## 2005—2007

## Back to Honduras

We returned to Honduras on January 10. We were very happy to be back in Honduras. But we were not happy to see the damage the termites had done to our home while we were gone so long. We couldn't even get our back door open. It took a week to get the house cleaned. The good news was to see the electric lines and poles all the way to Las Brisas. Our electricity was hooked up on February 3. It was wonderful to have an electric refrigerator and to be able to use the microwave. It was especially good not to have to be concerned if we had enough sunshine to have lights as we had to do when we had solar power.

## Medical Work Continues

It didn't take long to become busy in the clinic. I was also able to get to the rural clinics in February, March and April. For the first and only time, I was a bit concerned when we returned from a clinic in February. The sea had been calm when we left, but it was really rough when we returned. I knew it was bad when the boatman made me put on a life jacket. The boat tipped sideways a couple of times. Over and over in my mind, the Scripture in Psalms came to me: "What time I am afraid, I will trust in Thee." We made it safely back.

During our time in the States, I had encouraged people to send empty medicine bottles, and many had responded.

Two big stacks of boxes had arrived in Honduras by the time I got back.

Mark and Shanda Delaney Oakley and their three children lived in San Pedro Sula for some time while Mark was the head of the Chiquita Banana Company. They were active in the International Christian Fellowship led by the Hoff families. Twice Shanda made the trip on the sea with me to a rural clinic, each time bringing a different one of her children. Because of Mark's position, she had to take two bodyguards with her. We had always taken medicines in cardboard boxes, but Shanda gave me several sturdy plastic containers to use when we were on the sea.

In March 2007, one of the young women completed her training as an Auxiliary nurse, and I received permission for her to work with me for her service year. Since the clinic was open only three days a week, on Wednesday she worked at Travesia and on Thursday at Bajamar at the government health care centers. I typed out some protocols on treating patients for her to study and worked with her in examining and pre-

scribing medicine. She was a very intelligent young lady and learned quickly. At last my prayers were answered for a Honduran nurse to work full time in the clinic.

After our return to Honduras from furlough in late 2007, she saw most of the patients, though I was there if she needed to ask

*Yes, it's a live chicken*

questions. We took turns working in the afternoon. It was especially nice to have two of us when we went to Crique Maria since we have such large numbers of patients there.

## And Visitors Keep Coming

On our first Sunday back home a group that had been helping Bill Hoff with construction at the Institute visited. We were especially pleased to welcome them because long-time friends Larry and Ada Johnson were in the group. One of the group preached for our morning service.

On July 22, 2005, Tom Schneller of Disciple Makers brought a bus filled with visitors from Kentucky. We took them on two boats to the clinic at Crique Maria. The twenty people who made the trip took small gifts for the adults and children. As I examined patients, one from the group cut hair for forty people. Two nurses helped by taking blood pressures and temperatures while I saw patients. They also took Polaroid pictures and gave them to the people, a real treat for the recipients.

At the last of March in 2006, Jerry and Marietta Smith and their grandson and Alan and Karen Smith and their daughter visited. I had worked with Jerry and Marietta in the '60s at Mashoko. At that time, Alan was ten years old; now he was a pediatrician in Kentucky. Having two doctors was a special blessing. The day after they arrived, we went to Remolino for a clinic where Jerry and Alan saw seventy-three patients. On Sunday, two of them taught children in the morning and evening services. On Monday, Tuesday and Wednesday, Jerry and Alan saw a hundred more patients. The grandchildren helped in the clinic, and Marietta cooked our noon meal.

Ten people from Montana and South Dakota came in July. The bridge across the lagoon at Bajamar was not passable, so our minister and I went to Puerto Cortes where we hired a bus to take us to San Pedro Sula to pick up the group. We drove to the lagoon where we had to wade across to the place where John was waiting for us. There was not room for all of us, so John took the luggage and some of the people. The rest of us started walking. We had walked only a short distance when John returned to pick us up. The next morning we divided up into two groups to visit families in the village to invite the children to a Vacation Bible School that would be held on Thursday, Saturday and Sunday afternoon. Some of the women taught the classes while the visiting group did the crafts. On Friday they went with me to the clinic at Crique Maria. While I saw seventy-four patients, they taught the children and entertained the adults. On Saturday, one of them did some wiring for our minister.

Before the team left, Johnnie and Vicki Orr, missionary friends from near Tegucigalpa, came with their big family of seventeen children—some their own and others whom they were rearing. They set up a tent in our yard where the boys slept, and the girls slept in their big van. They brought their own food, but used our kitchen to cook. For a short time we had thirty one people with us!

We had visited Rich and Leta Atkinson in Mexico three times. Finally they were able to visit us in November 2006. With them was their grandson and Ulisses Solano who had spent time at Las Brisas in 2001. On Friday, all of us but Rich went to the clinic at Crique Maria. On Saturday, we rented a bus and they joined us and some of the congregation to go to the graduation services of the Christian Institute. A young man from Las Brisas was among the graduates.

Rich preached for the church during their stay. Since he was fluent in Spanish, I didn't have to translate.

# Life in the Church

One of the greatest blessings of living in Las Brisas was to have so many friends among the women of the congregation.   One of those that we all loved was a lady who didn't get to worship services often because she had crippling rheumatoid arthritis.  Sometimes one of her sons would carry her from her house to a path where they could push her the rest of the way in a wheelchair.  The minister had been able to get her a wheelchair so she could come to church occasionally, and we tried to have our ladies meeting at her home often.

Another project I had promoted on furlough was to encourage people to send materials and embroidery floss so the women could do handwork to sell.  One lady made a beautiful cloth for the Communion table at the church, and she was also sold some of her work to provide money for the offering.

I continued to invite the women to our home frequently.  I made cakes and Indian samosas, and we always had a good fellowship together.  We often had our meetings in homes of people we hoped would come to Christ.  One of those was a woman who had had breast cancer.  She had been a Christian, but hadn't been in church for a long time.  After our visit, she started attending church and became one of the most faithful women.  One of her daughters also gave her life to Christ and was baptized.

Each year in January, Christ in Youth conducts a conference for the churches in Central America.  In 2006, it was held in Honduras at a campground near Tegucigalpa. Eighteen youth from our congregation attended!

Trinidad Jimenez was one of the first men to live in Las Brisas.  We were all saddened when he died in 2006 from prostate cancer.  Not long before his death,   he had given his life to Christ.  The night he died, he asked our minister and some from the congregation to have a short service with him.  He left a big family—twelve children, sixty-one grand-children and forty-seven great-grandchildren!

A wedding was the highlight at Las Brisas in Febru-ary 2007. The bride wore a wedding dress that had been brought by Lynn and Sally Johnson when they had visited several years before.  The groom was the young man who had just graduated from the Christian Institute.  It was a beautiful wedding.  They had their wedding dinner at the community center which would accommodate more people than the church could.

The newly married couple received a call to minister to a congregation in the mountains between Tegucigalpa and San Pedro Sula and moved there just before we left in May for furlough.  The congregation was proud to send a Timothy to another area to minister.

The congregation continued to grow; four people gave their lives to Christ  and were baptized in April and May. Three of the four were adults.  Three of them were related to Trinidad Jimenez who had died the previous year.

# A Stateside Break

Though 2007 was furlough year, this time we  did not travel much.  Some of our congregations had increased sup-port.  Therefore, we recommended to all but two congrega-tions outside Indiana, even some in Indiana, that they sup-port Tom Schneller and his ministry instead.  This would be our last visit to one congregation in Tennessee and to some churches in Indiana.

While we were in Indiana, we again stayed with my sister and her husband. They gave us royal treatment. We spoke during this furlough to twenty congregations. We also visited some of John's nieces, his only living sister, Betty, who was living with her daughter in Charleston, South Carolina, and friends in Louisiana.

While we were in the States, we received the sad news that the husband of one of the faithful Christian women in our congregation had been shot and killed. At first no one knew who shot him nor why, but later, it was determined that it was a revenge killing instigated by someone who was upset because he and his brothers had bought several acres of property in Cerro Cardona.

# Chapter 32

## Retirement?  Never Entirely

## Medical Work Never Ends

Even though medical needs are forever present, the places where a clinic is needed changes. In December 2007, we made our last trip to Remolino. Only seventeen patients came that day, and a government doctor was also having a clinic near that village once a month, removing any pressing need for me to go there any longer.

Mike and Robin Keralis arrived for a visit in February 2010. We didn't have as many patients as I had hoped while they were with us, nor did we get to go to the clinic at Crique Maria because of the rough sea.  But we were able to visit several families in the village.

The day Mike and Robin returned to the airport,  Ziden and Helen Nutt arrived.  We wanted their visit to be a time of rest and relaxation for both them and us.  And it was. We played a lot of games, Helen and I visited some of our congregation, and Ziden made good progress on

*Our good friends Ziden and Helen Nutt when they visited us*

a book he was writing about Good News Productions. The day before they left, I invited the women to a meeting at our home and Helen shared with them about her family and they shared with her about their families.

## The Church Is Always Our Life

Each year in November, the congregation celebrates the anniversary of the start of the church at Las Brisas. In 2007, we celebrated fourteen years with a special speaker from Guatemala. The young people provided the special music, and we had a full house at all of the services.

A special event in the life of a Honduran girl is her fifteenth birthday. Some families have a special party for their daughters. In April 2008, the second daughter of our minister celebrated her fifteenth birthday, and nearly all of the congregation were invited to the minister's home to celebrate with her. One of my former Sunday School students in the mountains in the early '80s and now a graduate of the Christian Institute, came from San Pedro Sula to give a short message of encouragement. Some of the young people sang special songs, and everyone enjoyed a meal of fried chicken, rice and salad.

The whole country celebrated Children's Day on September 10 each year. In 2008, the community provided several piñatas for the children, and they had races and other contests for the children. The women served them a meal at noon. The following Sunday we had piñatas for the children at church, and the minister's wife and daughters prepared enchiladas for the them.

November 2008 brought both joy and sorrow. We rejoiced when a brother and sister gave their lives to Christ and were baptized.  At the time of their baptism, they lived in Cerro Cardona, about three-quarters of a mile away from the church.  The Thursday following their baptism, the dead body of their father was found near the entrance of our village.  We were so proud at how our congregation rallied around the family, finding the widow a place to live, helping her build a kitchen, and providing food for her and the family.

In January, two young men gave their lives to Christ and were baptized.  After their baptisms, one of them  gave a testimony telling us that it was his cousin and our minister who had led him to Christ.

In February, a double wedding occurred at the church. The grooms were brothers.  One married the daughter of our minister and the other married a woman with whom he had lived for thirty years and with whom he had seven children.  What a wedding it was!!  There were nine bridesmaids and groomsmen.  We lost count of how many younger children were in the wedding serving as flower girls and ring bearer.

For many weeks in 2009, I held a Bible study on Wednesday night for the young people we were helping to study in Puerto Cortes.  We had to discontinue the classes when I had surgery and again later because of political problems within the country.  Even though the studies were curtailed, major remodeling of the church building occurred when we needed more room.

Tragic circumstances often bring their own blessings.  It was true in December 2009, when one of the faithful Christian women was diagnosed with a brain tumor. To have the needed surgery she had to make a monetary deposit which she didn't have.  We were able to help because of a recent gift from some friends whom we knew would be  happy the money could be used for her. It was some time before surgery could be done. But it was finally successfully completed. All the congregation praised God for answered prayer. And a great blessing was that her husband returned to the Lord.

The church continues to be faithful, and God worked in the lives of people in Las Brisas during2010. Fourteen people, ranging from ten to forty-nine years of age, gave their lives to Christ and were baptized.


# A Short Vacation

After the wedding in February, John and I took a four-week vacation, leaving Honduras on February 17, allowing me to attend the fiftieth anniversary of my graduation from Johnson Bible College. It was not a good trip for John. He got chilled at the very cold Houston airport and ended up with a terrible cough and cold that made us decide that this would be the last time we would go to the States during the winter months. I did enjoy being at Johnson where we saw many friends at Homecoming. After Homecoming, we visited Floyd and Clara Clark at the nursing care facility where they lived and then drove south to Tallahassee, Florida, to visit one of John's nieces and her husband and son. While we were there, I had a joyful reunion with a friend whom I had not seen in fifty years. From Tallahassee, we drove to Charleston, S.C. where we visited with three more of John's nieces. Then we went up to Clarksville, Maryland to visit with one more niece and her husband.

We returned to Honduras with one suitcase full of toys given to us to share with children in the village.

# A Little Time for Recovery

When the group from Nebraska arrived in March 2009, Dave Paulus saw a place near my nose that he thought was a cancer. He told me that I should have it checked. We found a dermatologist and I visited her to find that I had a cancer near my nose and one on my leg. She referred me to another doctor, and he scheduled surgery to remove both cancers. The one on my leg was quite large, requiring a skin graft. He recommended a hospital that he said would not be too expensive. I had the surgery done in the morning and left the hospital about noon. The doctor was right about the cost—the entire procedure cost only $371. The nurse at our clinic changed the dressings. It took some time, but I healed completely and the pathological report showed that all of the cancer had been removed.

Just when I was nearly healed, John developed swelling and pain in his right knee. We made several visits to an orthopedic doctor. He had fluid drained from his knee, had it injected first with cortisone, which gave him a lot of relief, and then had three injections of gel into his knee. I also had to make some trips to my cardiologist to get my blood pressure under control.

# Fifty Years of Blessings

On August 1, 2010, I completed fifty years as a missionary. It was on that day in 1960 when I boarded a plane to leave for Rhodesia and Mashoko Mission. On August 28, I completed twenty-six years of service in Honduras. John and I celebrated our twenty-third wedding anniversary on October 17, 2010. God has blessed me beyond measure. Only through the guidance of His Sprit have I been able to serve Him for so many years. And I also know that through these fifty years, I have had literally hundreds of people praying for me.

John and I plan to retire, die, and be buried in Honduras. We will continue to serve as we can and encourage our Christian brothers and sisters in Las Brisas as long as God permits.

*The Colts have fans in Honduras*